FATHER POWER

FATHER POWER

Henry Biller, Ph.D.
and
Dennis Meredith

David McKay Company, Inc.
New York

To our parents,
our wives,
our children.
They cared.

FATHER POWER

Copyright © 1974 by Henry Biller and Dennis Meredith

SECOND PRINTING, MAY 1975

Library of Congress Catalog Card Number: 74-14018
ISBN 0-679-50520-2
MANUFACTURED IN THE UNITED STATES OF AMERICA

Acknowledgments

We wish to gratefully acknowledge our editors Eleanor Rawson and Sandi Gelles-Cole for their enthusiasm, high expectations, and incisive comments.

Material from *W.C. Fields by Himself*, edited by Ronald J. Fields, published by Prentice-Hall, Inc., Englewood Cliffs, New Jersey, copyright © 1973 by W.C. Fields Productions, Inc., used with permission of the publishers; from article on Maren Seidler, written by Nina McCain, originally appeared in the Boston *Globe*; March 4, 1973, used with permission of the Boston *Globe*; from "Chris Evert: Miss Cool on the Court," *Time* magazine, August 27, 1973, copyright © by Time Inc., used with permission of *Time*, The Weekly Newsmagazine; from *Wilt*, by Wilt Chamberlain and David Shaw, published by Macmillan Publishing Company, Inc., New York, copyright © 1973 by Wilt Chamberlain and David Shaw, used with permission of the publishers; from *Picasso: His Life and Work*, by Roland Penrose, published by Harper & Row, Publishers, Inc., copyright © 1958 by Roland Penrose, used with permission of the publishers; from *My Brother, Ernest Hemingway*, by Leicester Hemingway, published by World Publishing Company, copyright © 1961, 1962 by Leicester Hemingway, used with permission of Thomas Y. Crowell Company; from *Einstein: The Life and Times*, by Ronald W. Clark, published by World Publishing Company, copyright © 1971 by Ronald W. Clark, used with permission of the Thomas Y. Crowell Company and the Harold Matson Company, Inc.; from "The Human Side of Pro Football," written by Bob Ryan and Ray Richard, originally appeared in the Boston *Globe*; September 9, 1973, used with permission of the Boston *Globe*; from *The Story of a Novel*, by Thomas Wolfe,

Contents

SECTION THREE: FATHER POWER—CRISIS AND CHALLENGE

Section One

THE BASIS OF FATHER POWER

1 / *Introducing the Father*

Before we plunge into this manifesto for the father, we'd like to take a few pages to talk about ourselves, this book, and how we came to write it.

First of all, this is a somewhat lopsided book, and it's meant to be. We concentrate primarily on one member of the family—the father—and one relationship—the father-child. We believe that such a focused book is necessary, because the father has been left out in the cold by practically every book written on parenthood, on childraising, and even on the general roles of men in society. Books for parents almost always speak to the mother, or, if anything, to the father as only incidental to the family. In our chapters on father power and society you'll see why this discrimination occurs; it is enough now to realize that it does.

Even if books on childraising were balanced in their view of parenthood, they still wouldn't do what we hope this one will, because "parents" is a group composed of two basic kinds of people—fathers and mothers. Fathers are traditionally and psychologically different from mothers, and both deserve special consideration.

Though the book is addressed to fathers and fathers-to-be, we hope mothers, mothers-to-be, sons, and daughters will read it. We also hope it will be read by physicians, teachers, journalists, psychologists, psychiatrists, social workers, lawyers, judges, and other professionals who affect society. We all badly need a greater respect for the father and a realization of his vital role in the family.

We're going to offer a great number of suggestions for fathers on how to be effective with their children. Although these suggestions have worked well for many fathers, they won't work for everybody. Don't be buffaloed into using our suggestions, or anybody else's, because they come from "authorities." The first and foremost rule in using this book is that you feel comfortable with any suggestion before you accept it. It's not as important how you play with your child, discipline him, or talk to him, but that you do it with love and with confidence in yourself as a parent.

We shall be very realistic in dealing with the family today, even to the point of offending some who have idealized views of what the family should be. Of course, we're not downgrading those ideals, only saying that they are not yet realities. For instance, though a great many mothers today work outside the home, in the *majority* of families the father is the only family member who has a long-term career. Men also hold the majority of highly skilled positions in our society. Though the nature of men's and women's work should, and probably will change, these differences exist today, and realistically they make a difference in the kinds of parents mothers and fathers are. When we discuss such differences, we are not taking a stand on what should be, only on what is. We shall, however, point out where the family and childraising can be improved, and where we think they are going.

Throughout this book we shall commit what in some circles has become a journalistic no-no—we shall use *his* as a pronoun referring to both males and females. When we write, "The child should have his say," our child should be considered *either* a son or a daughter. Keep this in mind and we will be freed of charges of sex bias, and you will be freed of the old myth that fathers are important only for their sons. Fathers are every bit as vital to their daughters as to their sons.

Our Interest in Fathering. Who are we to write a book on fatherhood? First, Henry, a clinical and developmental psychologist, has written over forty scientific publications, many of them dealing with his research on fatherhood. He has written two professional books concerning the father-child relationship. (For researchers reading this book, more technical treatments of fatherhood research can be found in his books *Father, Child, and Sex Role,* and *Paternal Deprivation.*)

Throughout his professional career as a teacher and psychologist, Henry has been struck by the fact that so little research has been done on the father—that the father has been ignored by the social scientist, as well as society. Henry became determined to try and help reverse what he considers a dangerous trend in today's family. As a clinical psychologist, he has been continually confronted with the crucial influence of the father, in both the development and treatment of family problems. As a teacher in a university setting, and a community educator, he has been impressed by the lack of information but nonetheless great interest others have in the father's role.

Personally, a series of events in Henry's life greatly contributed to his interest in the father-child relationship. He was very close to both his father and grandfather, but they both died before his sixth birthday, within a span of less than two years. His own fatherhood of four young sons, Jonathan (eleven), Kenneth (ten), Cameron (six), and Michael (three), has greatly stimulated and enriched his knowledge of fatherhood. As he sees the profound effect he and his children have on one another, and as he remembers his own early years of father enrichment followed by years of father deprivation, he realizes that fathers *must* be confident of their importance to be most effective in the family.

When Dennis and his wife first began thinking about having a child, Dennis searched for information on what his role as a father would mean to his child's development. He found almost no books or articles on fatherhood, at least none that recognized that the father was as important as he knew his father had been in his own life. When he began remembering his own childhood, he realized even more that, though his father had been highly involved with him, his father probably didn't fully realize his own importance because of the way society had treated fatherhood. His mother was fully aware of her importance in the family—and she was very

important'—because everybody knows how important mothers
are. But not fathers.

As Dennis and Henry considered the nature of fatherhood
in America, first for a magazine article and later for this book,
Dennis experienced a consciousness raising equal to that
experienced by feminists realizing how unfairly women are
treated in society. For instance, Dennis remembers going to a
shelf of biographies of famous people who had made great
social and scientific contributions to the world to find out if
any of them had come from father-involved families: what he
discovered was that almost every book he picked up contained
a story of profound influence by a father. Most of the famous
people had grown up in warm, encouraging families and had
both an involved mother *and* father.

As a journalist, Dennis came to realize how the father had
been neglected by the popular media. As a science writer, he
realized how the father had been neglected by the scientific
community. Dennis's estimation of himself as a father, and of
fathers in general, continued to grow as he and Henry worked
on this book.

Fatherhood can be more challenging than any profession,
more rewarding than any hobby. *Yet thousands of books have been
written on men at work and men at play, but very few on men as fathers.*
We hope this is changing and hope this book represents a
change for the better.

Although there may be some chapters of this book that you
may feel do not apply to you, each chapter has something in it
for every father. For instance, in Chapter 2 we cover
preparation for fatherhood. Although you may already be a
father, you may find useful information there on the psychological effects of fatherhood and methods for preparing for it.
These may help you to better understand the kind of father
you already are.

WHAT IS FATHER POWER?

The principal danger to fatherhood today, and to the
American family for that matter, is that fathers do not have

the vital sense of father power that they have had in the past. Because of a host of pressures from society, the father has lost the confidence that he is naturally important to his children— that he has the power to affect children, guide them, help them grow. He isn't confident that *fatherhood is a basic part of being masculine and a legitimate focus of his life.*

By father power we do *not* mean power to be used over children, tyrannical power, or paternalistic power. Rather we mean the pervasive, profound power that is a part of your and every other father's nature as a parent. Paternalism is the use of masculine power to shape a person into something the paternalist thinks he should be, regardless of the wants of the person. Father power is the use of your profound, natural influence to help your child become what he wants to be. You not only teach your child what he will need to know to prosper in the world, but you also give him an important sense of independence from you—his *own* sense of power.

By advocating that you realize your father power we are not at all denying the existence or importance of mother power. There is not a "power see-saw" in the family. If you become more effective with your children, it doesn't mean your wife will become less so. In fact, using father power will aid your wife in becoming a more effective parent. It could relieve her of the enormous burden of childrearing she has had to assume because of the widespread noninvolvement of the father in the family.

Father power is different from mother power, and your child needs both in order to develop properly. Among the many differences in fathers and mothers we'll cover in later chapters is that they are attached to their children differently. Both you and your wife love your children because they are yours, but your wife's attachment is a more deeply physical one. She has given birth to the baby and, some scientists believe, possesses a hormonally influenced attachment to him. Mothers have been glorified as a source of security, warmth, and love from time immemorial. And, indeed, they are.

On the other hand, your love for your child is less physiological. It comes more from the knowledge that the child is yours, from your protective tendencies toward the child, and from the way the child reacts to you. But your kind of love—more judging and more challenging—is vital to the child. You dare more with the child, you help him to push himself and to use his talents to their fullest. Because you have been the parent traditionally more likely to be involved outside the family, you link the child with society. You not only give him a chance to go out into society as you introduce him to your adult world, but you also teach him about the rules of society by the way you discipline him—a way that traditionally has been different from that of the mother.

Father Neglect. It's difficult to attach numbers to as subtle a psychological problem as today's father's lack of confidence as a parent. But there are some indications that something is seriously wrong with fatherhood today.

Over 10 percent—about 8 million—of the children in this country live in fatherless homes at any one time, and three times that many are fatherless for a significant part of their childhood. In some ghettos over 50 percent of the children are fatherless. These are father-absent children.

The most widespread problem though, is the chronic neglect of children by fathers who are living with their families, that is, father-deprived children. This neglect is pervasive; it is not just present in the homes of the poor where the father has lost self-respect, or the homes of the affluent where the father is out chasing the buck. The majority of fathers in the various strata of our society have very little close, regular contact with their children.

We believe the public recognizes the problem, though it is resigned to it as part of the "natural order" of family life. For instance, a 1972 survey of 350,000 readers of *Better Homes and Gardens* revealed that an astounding 87 percent of the respondents believed that the father in most families didn't spend enough time with his children. The respondents, presumably mostly members of this country's large middle class, included fathers and mothers of various age groups and educational levels.

Father neglect is such a profound problem in this country

that a significant number of children have become "walking wounded"—victims of subtle psychological violence, a result of the void of chronic father neglect. Whether the deficits in these children's lives permanently affect them or are at some point overcome, they nevertheless affect the happiness and fulfillment of a great many people.

The enormous leap in the crime rate over the past decade, we believe, is one indication of the societal effects of father deprivation. Certainly, it would be naïve to blame the rise in crime solely on the lack of father involvement, for it is the result of many things—the increased opportunity for crime in a crowded, mobile society; the anonymity in modern society; the concentrations of wealth amid widespread need; and other such factors.

We feel, however, that most inducements to crime could be better resisted if every child had a warm, competent father. In fact, father *absence* may not even be the major cause of delinquency-related problems in youngsters; the real problem may be the present but uninvolved father.

The effects of father deprivation on criminal activity in a society have been noted by social scientists. Researchers studying large numbers of societies frequently find that those in which the father is relatively absent or uninvolved have a higher rate of theft and crimes of personal violence. In later chapters you'll come to understand why father-absent or father-deprived children are more likely to be delinquent, to have sexual problems, and to suffer emotional disorders than are well-fathered children.

A strong bond between father and child helps the child learn to accept more responsibility for his own behavior. And father-child closeness also enables the father to more profoundly teach the child what society expects of him in the way of responsible behavior.

Though until now father power has been on the wane, we see the opportunity for a new kind of father to emerge, different from any of his predecessors. We think that Women's Liberation, less rigid definitions of masculinity and femininity, a questioning of materialism, and easier work and better working conditions are all putting the father in a position to enter into family life more positively than ever before.

To some extent young men today have recognized this opportunity and are grasping it, but they still need help. A major roadblock to effective fatherhood has been the lack of information on the importance of fatherhood.

EVOLUTION OF FATHER POWER

Obviously, the human father is biologically necessary to produce children, but he is also necessary in a social sense to give his children the best chance for survival. Fatherhood evolved as a natural role for men in the human family.

Although many lower animal species show evidence of father involvement, this is more an instinctual, biologically dictated involvement, built in to assure survival of the species. In man, however, a strong cultural concept of fatherhood is added to an innate father instinct. This cultural concept of fatherhood—that a father is responsible for a certain set of offspring whom he fathered—gives the father a strong impetus to actively teach his children and help them emerge into successful adulthood.

"Fathers" with Tails. The lower primate species—our ape and monkey cousins—show evidence of the innate primate father instinct and also hints of the cultural fatherhood that is full-blown in the human species.

All monkeys and apes, though, aren't what we humans would consider "ideal" fathers. "Fatherhood" among apes and monkeys encompasses a wide range of behaviors. The male marmoset, for instance, takes over almost complete care of the young, giving up the infants only to be nursed by their mother. Baboon and other monkey males are often seen grooming infants. On the other hand, male monkeys in other species ignore the young, or even view them as tasty morsels.

An important facet of the father instinct of male monkeys and apes, however, is their role in protecting the young. While

the male howler monkey of Central America will bite off the
tail of an infant who annoys him, he has also been known to
risk his life to retrieve a fallen infant whose mother has been
shot by hunters. Male howlers have even been seen making a
bridge with their bodies from tree to tree so that infants could
cross. Even male monkeys who usually completely ignore their
offspring will protect them fiercely at other times when they
are threatened. Workers with captive rhesus monkeys find that
if they take an infant from the cage to treat it, males in nearby
cages will go wild with fury, throwing themselves against the
cage window, threatening and screaming. This seldom happens when adult monkeys are withdrawn from the cages.

Human fathers, we think, possess the same fierce protectiveness toward their children. Dennis knows that when he carries
his baby daughter through a crowd he feels much more
aggressive toward those in the crowd than when he is alone.
He feels a powerful, protective instinct toward his daughter.

The male primate is an important socializer of the young. It
is a general rule that among social primates the first exploring
an infant does is not of his environment—the trees and ground
around him—but of other animals of the group, and males
usually allow infants to find out about them, even allowing
such behavior as tugging and biting, which they would not
tolerate from other adults.

Male and female monkeys play with the young in different
ways. While mother monkeys more often enfold their offspring
or act as impassive home bases, male monkeys are much more
vigorous, chasing, play-biting, and wrestling with infants.
When Dennis holds his daughter, he often turns her around so
she can rest her back against him and watch the world around
her, secure in his arms. "I could never do that," his wife once
remarked, "I couldn't see her face that way." It was clear that
Dennis got as big a charge out of watching his daughter
learning about the world as he did from holding and cuddling
her.

Though many of the paternal actions of male monkeys exist
on the vague borderline between cultural and biological
instinct, evidence for cultural fathering, rising above instinct,

is obvious in many monkey troops. For instance, in some troops of Japanese macaques, males adopt one-year-old infants while the infants' mothers give birth to new infants.

The Human Father: A Small but Vital Step. It took the pressures of a new kind of environment to evolve the overtly cultural father, the male who was socially recognized as responsible for protecting and teaching certain children of a certain female. The new environment was the open grassland, full of opportunity for hunting food and full of danger. For man to be successful in this new area he had to develop his intellectual talents, for they were all he had. As his intelligence evolved, his brain got bigger; and as an infant, he needed more time to develop and to learn the many ways of using his superior brain. The human infant is all brain and little brawn—an incredible one-seventh of his body weight is brain. He stays in the womb longer than his ape cousins, his infancy is twice as long, and he remains a juvenile twice as long. All these developments required a new institution to allow for survival. Protection was needed for the mother and long-helpless infant, as well as a way to pass on the valuable knowledge needed for survival. A place was needed to store and divide up hunted food and to provide a central meeting shelter. The new institution was called the family; the new place was called home.

It really didn't take much of a change for the human family and fatherhood to evolve. Our simian ancestors already displayed jealousy toward rivals for their mates, a sense of kinship, a potential for year-round sex, and a social nature. And, as we said, the males also had a strong fathering instinct.

But to build on all of these primate traits other developments also had to take place. Year-round, immensely enjoyable sex evolved to bond man and woman permanently. A preference for a particular mate and a sense of belonging to that mate became a necessity. There was a division of labor; the man went out hunting, the woman guarded the child and the home.

For the helpless infant to be properly protected evolution

favored two protectors. The mammal mother had always been a protector of children because of her intimate involvement with the child's birth and feeding. In order to develop his protective tendency, the father had to acquire a sense of possession toward a few well-defined charges, and these were naturally his own and his wife's children. A man's specific "property" would be better protected than a group's.

The concept of fatherhood was also important for the child because he had much to learn. The man-woman division of labor meant that certain talents were developed better by the mother while others were better practiced by the father. The most effective teaching was on a one-to-one basis, and thus, the individual father was favored. He would know the child well and would be closely attached to him.

All this attachment to the father was clearly an advantage for the child, but what did the father get out of it? What physical mechanisms attached him to the child? He was attached to the female because of the male-female sexual bond, resulting in a protected home and what later came to be known as true love. Certainly, part of his attachment to the child resulted from the child's attachment to the mother.

But the human father also possessed the basic nurturant disposition—the "father instinct"—which the child satisfied. This nurturance was different from the strong, physical mother-child bond, but not much. The hairless father, like the mother, was very touch-sensitive. His sensitive skin heightened his enjoyment of sex but also made pleasurable the warm physical contact with a child. And, just like the mother, the father was profoundly attracted by the round-faced, big-eyed "cuteness" of his infant. Other senses also told him the child belonged to him: though his sense of smell wasn't keen, it was influential, and the child smelled not only of home but of family—an individualistic smell that became noticeable and important only after the family separated from the troop into single units.

Another attachment to the child stemmed from the father's natural curiosity—a strong trait in our species. Millions of years later curiosity would take him to the moon, but during the evolution of man, it made the father want to see what this tiny, warm, nonthreatening creature was all about.

The father also found that when he nurtured this creature, the infant, it became attached to him; it would mimic him and respond to him. To early man, as to today's man, imitation is the sincerest form of flattery, and it was flattering to see an image of himself mirrored in the behavior of his child.

There was also much to be learned from the child. The child, after all, was a young creature, exploring the environment around him and learning about it. He often made mistakes from which he had to be rescued, but he sometimes stumbled upon something new, something useful to be passed on to succeeding generations. Maybe "man" didn't discover fire after all; maybe the first burning log was brought into the cave by some child who didn't know any better.

Although there are immense cultural and subcultural variations, it is the father-mother-child triangle upon which the human family was built, each member benefiting by the other.

THE FATHER ACROSS CULTURES

We've talked about the development of the human family as if there were just one kind of family, just one kind of father. Of course, this is not true. Throughout history and across cultures there have been many kinds of peoples in many kinds of environments, each society seeking survival in its own ways and each with its own concept of fatherhood.

Scientists examining these societies have seen some in which the father is a strong figure and others in which he is almost a stranger in the household. Rather than study all the variations in past and contemporary fathers, let us examine some of the major features of the father role across cultures.

Division of Labor. Regardless of the enormous variations in climate and society throughout the world, fathers traditionally have almost always been responsible for certain kinds of tasks and mothers for others. In this division of labor, fathers almost always do the hunting, fishing, and other necessary strenuous activities to support the family. By contrast, women almost always take care of activities such as housework, cooking, and child care. Interestingly, in some nomadic tribes, which follow herds of wild or domestic animals in search of grazing ground, this division of labor is still observed, even when "women's work" is really much more physically strenuous than males': while men have only to walk along with the herd, women have to put up and take down tents, tan hides, make clothes, cook the food, and do practically all the heavy lifting.

Those who read this with a sense of superiority about our own present-day cultural "flexibility" should realize that American families often have just as absolute a division of duties. Instead of carrying stones for the fire, the male now carries out the garbage; instead of herding animals, he cares for the family car. Unfortunately, we are just as "illogical" as some nonliterate societies. Our division of labor is so strong and absolute that *the working mother often finds herself doing two full-time jobs because the father balks at the least bit of child care.*

We should also point out that the woman in most societies is every bit as vital a breadwinner as the man. She was probably the first farmer, and her job of organizing and running the household was of equal importance.

Child and Sex Role. Another relatively constant feature of most societies around the world is the way children of different sexes are raised. In most cases, girls are taught to be more nurturant and responsible than boys. Boys in turn are raised to be more self-reliant and achievement oriented than girls. The result is that males become what are called the "instrumental" leaders and the females the "expressive" leaders. In other words, the male is said to be the executive head, the person who primarily organizes activities and judges and dispenses punishment. Females are said to be the family mediators, who resolve conflicts, soothe disputes, and generally make peace. As we shall see in later chapters, these features of male and female roles describe only part of the vast complexities of sex differences.

Father Power Across Cultures. In most societies the father usually has some amount of power over his offspring. In societies from which many American fathers are descended the father was an almost unquestioned, often tyrannical ruler. Many American fathers trace their history back to three of the most socially powerful patrarchies ever to exist—the Hebrews, the Greeks, and the Romans. In other societies, such as some in the Pacific Islands, the father is less influential but still has some power over his children. But one thing is constant: Even though only about 20 percent of societies in history have formulated exclusive one-man-one-woman mating customs, *all societies recognize the responsibility of some male to be involved with a family's children*—to teach them, act as a model for them, and introduce them into society.

Environment is not the only factor that influences a society, for many kinds of societies have been found within the same kind of environment. What is more intrinsic to a culture is *the kind of family in it,* because *the family* in many ways reciprocally *influences the culture.* The family is where children usually receive their basic training for their roles in society. As we said, the father's particular role differs from society to society. He is sometimes highly available to the family, sometimes at home irregularly, in other societies constantly absent; he is sometimes dictatorial, sometimes weak, sometimes effective and involved. The mother's role, however, is generally much less variable. She is closely tied to the child in a bond that began when she carried the infant inside her. She generally nurtures it, feeds it, cares for it. Although maternal behavior does vary from society to society, it seems relatively more constant than paternal behavior.

We believe there is a strong link between the quality of fathering and the resultant quality of men and women in a society.

So, since the father's role is more variable in societies than that of the mother, the best way to improve the family, it would seem, is to educate the father, to change his behavior, teaching him how to be the best kind of father he can be.

Admittedly, this is a rather simplistic view of the socialization of the child, both because of the complexity and individuality of human beings and because of the ever changing roles of the sexes in society. But our basic contention still stands: To improve the family and society as it now exists, we must begin to influence and educate the father.

2/ *Preparing for Fatherhood*

Most books on parenthood begin by assuming that everybody wants to have children. We begin this chapter by acknowledging that this is not necessarily so. Your first duty as a parent is to decide whether or not you *really* want to be one. Parenthood requires a continuing effort over two decades or so, as well as considerable inconvenience and money. The rewards to a parent, most people feel, are enormous, but some people may wish to devote their lives to other pursuits, and this is a perfectly legitimate wish.

Why Have a Child? People vary widely in their predispositions toward, and training for, childraising. Some people may not themselves have been brought up to value childraising. An only child, for instance, when grown and married might find the presence of another, dependent human being an imposition. The child of parents who themselves didn't enjoy being parents might also not enjoy being a parent. A person who is especially fastidious or sensitive to his environment might find intolerable the disruptions and clamor children may visit upon a household. Each person, we believe, also has a natural limitation on the number of people with whom he can have a deep relationship. Any decision regarding childbearing should take these factors into account.

Thus, before your family is even begun, both you and your wife should sit down and determine whether you want children and your motives for wanting them. Neither a husband nor a wife should let pressure from the other force him into parenthood.

Though society has changed to some degree, it still exerts considerable pressure on you and your wife to become parents.

A man is still thought of as less than a man and a woman as less of a woman if they do not have children. This is absurd, and you should recognize that although involved fatherhood is legitimately masculine, choosing not to become a father does not imply a lack of masculinity. Many young marrieds have experienced the questioning, expectant silences from in-laws or other relatives when they call home or the "Well, when are you getting started?" cocktail-party chatter. As annoying as such pressures are, they are in no way valid reasons to start a family.

There is also considerable sentiment developing in this country against childbearing, especially among the younger generation, and especially against having more than two children. Parenthood should be a qualitative, not a quantitative, thing. Large numbers of children strain both the resources of the parents and also the resources of the country. However, parents who are committed and who want more than two children should not feel guilty about having them. A truly wanted and well-treated child is unlikely to be a burden on society. He is more likely to be a contributor to his society than the child who is unwanted or only halfheartedly welcomed.

Rather than advocating that each family have the requisite "2.1" children required for zero population growth, we would rather see people free to have no children or seven children, depending on their resources and commitment and not on social pressures. It only matters that the *average* number of children per couple is about two.

A desire to have someone who is completely dependent on you is another illegitimate motive for having children. Some parents also want to "get even" with the world or to create a human being who must achieve all the things they have not. To most, if not all, people children represent a link with immortality, a chance to influence society and to have a form of one's personality live on after one's death. Certainly, the reasons for parenthood are many, and it is acceptable for some of the above to be present to a degree, but they should not be obsessions.

If you look forward to learning and growing with your parenthood, have a child. If you recognize that you want to father a person who will eventually leave you to become a functioning, achieving member of society, have a child. You should also recognize that having a child should be an outgrowth of a healthy personality. You and your wife like yourselves and each other and feel that others similar to you would be a benefit to society. If these are among your basic reasons, then by all means have a child.

Family experts are constantly warning couples not to have children just to hold together a shaky marriage, but it still deserves emphasis here. Have children only if you and your wife are thoroughly committed to a life together. Otherwise, the child may either grow up in a maelstrom of ill feeling or else be subject to the trauma of divorce. Lack of security in marriage is a legitimate reason for not having children, but unfortunately it is seldom an openly discussed one. Don't be hesitant about bringing such insecurity out in the open in discussions with your wife. It is better that such instabilities and their reasons be discussed early in a marriage.

Even if you are sure of your steady relationship with your wife, a child can still strain it. Children have unique effects on marriages. By putting strains on the union, children tend to break up shaky relationships—or fuse strong ones into solid, lasting partnerships. Children also affect the indifferent marriage, one in which the partners merely tolerate each other. In such a case a child might provide a focus for the parents that allows them to neglect each other without pangs of conscience. This is, of course, not fair to the child, because he may find himself constantly in the family spotlight. Neither is it fair to the parents, who are missing out on a good marriage and merely postponing the loneliness and acrimony that will occur after the child leaves.

Financing a Child. How well your marriage can withstand the financial hardships involved in raising a child must also be included in your considerations about having a child. If you and your wife are not the type who can on occasion do without, a child could become a resented intrusion into your lives and your finances.

Because fathers have traditionally been the primary bread-winners in families, they are most often the parents who worry about financing a baby. In fact, worries about finances are often the father-to-be's major roadblock to the enjoyment of the beginning of his child's life. You should be completely confident of your ability to support a child before you advocate having one; this will remove a major source of anxiety.

To aid in working out budgets, we have included a brief rundown on the costs of having and rearing a child. In figuring the initial medical costs of having a child, consult your insurance policies to find out what medical expenses are covered. Average obstetrical and delivery costs run around $1,200.

As a very general rule it will cost between $100 and $200 *per month* to raise your child, depending on the economic level at which you live. The first year and later the teen-age years are the highest in cost. These monthly estimates include every-thing a child would need to get by: food, clothing, housing, medical expenses, transportation, education, and spending money. Some of the costs are "hidden." For instance, you would probably not think of including the cost of gasoline used in taking your child places, but it is a factor in figuring overall costs. Our estimates also do not include the possibility of the child working, getting a scholarship, or being covered by medical insurance.

The $200-per-month figure assumes that you give the child some luxuries, in addition to the basics of food, clothing, and housing. It allows for savings toward a good college education, giving her or him music lessons, vacations at summer camp, more expensive toys, etc.

The $100-per-month figure assumes you live on a stricter budget, buy secondhand baby furniture, make maternity and children's clothes at home, and receive financial aid for the child's education. But each family is different, and costs vary according to region and life-style.

One myth that we should dispel is that children are "cheaper by the dozen." Each additional child will be almost as expensive as the first one. This even assumes that you and your wife reuse baby furniture, baby and maternity clothes, and some older child's things, such as bicycles, for your second child. Expenses for food, clothing, housing, education, etc., are additive with each additional child.

The Surprise Father. Though you and your wife should have a firm understanding that having a child is a two-person decision, there are the occasional cases of "surprise" pregnancy. Both mistaken and intentional surprises could be the fault of either parent. You can "forget" your birth-control measure just as she can "forget" hers. Whether your wife's surprise pregnancy was a mistake or intentional may be a major factor in your decision of whether or not to have the child. Even if your wife became pregnant unintentionally, your advocating aborting the child against her deepest wishes could harm her self-esteem and your relationship together. If having the surprise baby only means changing your timing of children, by all means have it. If, however, the pregnancy represents having an altogether unwanted child, do not feel that a pregnancy means you must raise the child. If the child is fully unwanted, and, if it is ethically acceptable for you, consult a physician about the possibility of an abortion, or consider putting the child up for adoption.

Thoroughly examine your and your wife's motives should the pregnancy apparently be an intentional "mistake." Such a pregnancy may be an indication that there is something in your relationship that one of you feels a baby would remedy. It can be a signal that you and your wife have lost touch and that your marriage is in deep trouble. If either one of you expresses a desire not to have the child, the other should listen.

Examine Your Feelings. In any case, the best rule to follow is to examine your feelings about having children. Have quiet, thorough discussions in which you and your wife air your feelings, both positive and negative. This way, doubts and fears will be carefully discussed. Also, any fear that either of you might have about the other's attitudes or behavior can be dealt with. You might use the preceding sections or other articles on childbirth as a format. Read these sections together and discuss each point.

Unfortunately, American courtship customs usually don't include thorough discussions on how you and your partner feel about children. The process of deciding whether to have a child may give each of you greater insight into the other's attitudes. By such discussions, you will both have gone a long way toward clearing away obstacles to a complete and cooperative effort to give your new baby every advantage.

As a father-to-be, don't feel that you have to be all enthusiasm and eagerness about having a child. Expectant fathers, especially first-timers, frequently have at least some negative thoughts about having a child—including fear of responsibility, jealousy, or a "trapped" feeling. As we shall discuss later, a father-to-be who tries to repress negative thoughts about pregnancy and fatherhood will be subject to guilt and anxiety. Discussion can be most flexible between just the two of you, but if you have difficulties in opening up with each other, seek professional help. Preferably, whomever you ask to help you should have specific training in family counseling whether the professional be a psychologist, psychiatrist, social worker, or clergyman.

Mothers and fathers are usually quite different in the way they approach the decision of whether to have a child. Several women who read preliminary drafts of this section on the reasons for having children declared to us, "But what if you just love babies and want to have one? Isn't that a good enough reason?" Though many men do just "love babies," we think that most aren't really that attracted to babies in general. Perhaps it's because of a lack of some maternal instinct, but more likely it's just because men don't get that much of a chance to be around babies in the first place.

In any case, there are differences; the next time somebody brings a baby into a group of men and women, watch the differences in their reactions. While the women will generally crowd around and admire the baby and want to hold it, the men may want to see the infant but are not as enthusiastic or interested.

So, when men decide whether to become fathers, they tend to do it on a much more cerebral level than women do in deciding to become mothers. All this "objective" thinking flies out the window, however, when a man actually *becomes* a father. We liken a man and a baby to two magnets. When the magnets are far apart, there's not a strong attraction, as is the case between a man and a baby before the man is a father. But if a man is emotionally ready and is brought close to his own infant, like two magnets close together they'll probably attach to one another and may become inseparable.

Dennis had frankly never been that attracted to babies. When confronted with one, he would usually pat it on the head, say something mildly complimentary, and go on his way. That was before his daughter, Wendy, came along. She, of course, is, according to Dennis, the most incredibly beautiful, intelligent creature ever born. And he has discovered that he is more attracted to other babies as a result of having his own.

Your Own Father. Besides trying to sort out your motives for wanting to become a father, you should also prepare yourself for effective fatherhood by trying to understand what kind of father you might become and why. One good way to do this is to "live your life over." Take time, preferably when you are alone and your surroundings are quiet, to remember as much as you can about your childhood and your relationship with your own father.

Introspection about your own childhood can help you greatly to become a good father. Because you were, in effect, in the same place your child will be, you can clearly recognize mistakes to avoid and strengths to be valued. Your memories will probably be mostly of specific childhood occurrences rather than of relationships. Use these memories to gain insight into what influenced you most about your father, what kind of man he was, and what kind of man you have become.

Viewing your own father back over the years will usually

give you a good idea of some of the factors influencing the type of father you will be. You and your father have the same ethnic background, and you are probably constitutionally similar. Also, your relationship with your wife has been influenced by that of your father with your mother.

You may have rebelled against your father at one time. You should analyze why this rebellion took place. Was it a reaction to temporary or permanent differences in temperament and outlook or was it a reaction to some definite failing in your father or in you?

Try to remember other male influences in your life, such as friends, relatives, or teachers. Why were you attracted to them? Did they have qualities you would like to cultivate in yourself? Were there other men whom you wanted to avoid being like, and why?

Another important clue to your potential reaction to your new child may be how you got along with your brothers and sisters. How did the arrival of a new baby affect your relationship with your mother and father? Did you take care of baby brothers and sisters, or were you the one who was cared for? How do you remember reacting to such care, whether given or received?

In contemplating your childhood, you will probably realize a great deal about your father's feelings toward you and how he expressed them. You may also realize some of the disappointments and frustrations that accompany fatherhood and be better prepared to accept them. Both these kinds of revelations are evident in an anecdote told by a friend of ours:

It seems that when he was quite young, his father, out of work because of the Depression, could not afford an expensive bicycle the boy badly wanted for Christmas. Instead, his father gathered parts from junkyards all over the city, bought a sturdy but rusty old bicycle frame, and set to work in the basement to build a bicycle. After weeks of work he had fashioned a bicycle that was a work of love for his son. Our friend took one look at the bicycle, however, and was sorely disappointed, for it was not the bright, shiny, new one he wanted, and he felt ashamed to take it out with his friends, who had new bikes. He began treating the bike roughly, running it into trees and letting it fall over in the street. When his father found out about it, of course, he flew into a rage.

In recounting the story, our friend said that he understands now that his father's rage was primarily one of disappointment and hurt, and not of anger. "By looking back on it, I realize how hard it will be sometimes for me to be a father and also how I'll have to work hard to understand my daughter's outlook on things."

Though the intervening years may have helped you to become more objective about your relationship with your father, you may still have a great deal of ambivalence toward him. Try to recognize your emotions toward your father, and deal with them. He may, for instance, have loved you very much and been a good father, but his attitudes toward certain things may have turned you against him. On the other hand, he may have been great fun to be with but failed to provide you with the consistent emotional support that children need.

Hopefully, you did have a close, supportive father. Your readiness to give of yourself in order to become a good father is aided by a strong model from your own past.

Becoming a father may spur you to work out some problems with your own parents that have bothered you since childhood. It may enable you to understand your parents realistically, with all their strengths and weaknesses, for the first time.

For instance, one father, John, was the son of divorced parents. As a child, whenever John misbehaved or lost his temper, his mother would inevitably say, "You're going to wind up just like your father if you're not careful." Otherwise she never talked about John's father and never even told John what she meant by "just like your father." She felt it her duty to keep John away from his father, toward whom she was very bitter.

John knew he looked like his father and feared that whatever mysterious flaws his father had he would have too. Finally, with Henry's support, when John was about to become a father himself and was worried about what traits he would pass on to his own child, he decided to seek out his father, whom he had never really known. He was relieved to learn that his father was "really a pretty okay guy." He learned that his father had stayed away from him because of threats of police action by the mother. He also discovered that his father had talked to his teachers and had maintained an interest in his progress in school. After finding out about his father's efforts on his behalf, John lost his self-doubts and began to gain confidence about his own ability to be a good father.

Learning About Children. Besides preparing for fatherhood by remembering your own past and coming to understand your own parents, you can put yourself in situations where you get a chance to interact with children. Take part in a school outing with the children of a friend or relative, work with the Cub Scouts, or get to know infants in other families. An especially good way to preview how you and your wife will react to a child is to baby-sit for friends.

Both men and women, just before they become parents, seem to be quite open to relationships with young children. This is often because children are a novelty to them and also because other children aren't competing with their own children for their time. Thus, this period is an excellent one for you to learn about children in general.

Don't expect to be attracted to children much more than you were before, though. As we said earlier, many fathers really tend to be attracted only to their own children. Also, just playing with children or baby-sitting with them is not at all what it will be like to be a full-time parent. In any case, your fatherhood may be like a hot bath—easier to take if you immerse yourself a little at a time.

Another good preparation for fatherhood is to observe the fathers around you. What things have they done that you admired? Where have they had difficulties and, in your opinion, made mistakes?

For instance, when Dennis was preparing to be a father, he remembers observing two fathers with very different attitudes about their children and their work. The fathers both worked in an office near his. One father occasionally minded his children at work while the wife went shopping or attended classes she was taking at the local university. While they were with their father, the children were able to see what he did to earn a living. He showed his children, a boy and a girl, some of the equipment and techniques he used and let them tour the offices to learn what else was going on and to meet his coworkers.

The other father, however, seldom, if ever, brought his children to work. The sons would appear occasionally with their mother, or the father might bring them in if he stopped in on his day off. These children couldn't have had a clear idea of what Daddy did at the office. As we shall see in a later chapter, the actions of the first father gave his children a definite advantage in their development.

In your observations be careful not to make snap judgments about other fathers, though. Even though you may resolve to avoid such pitfalls in your own fatherhood as you observe in others, certain traps may be seductive. For instance, you may vow never to bury yourself in your work like some fathers you see but may find yourself six months later coming home with a bulging briefcase because of "unavoidable" commitments. And despite your earlier admonitions, you may lose touch with your child.

If you already have children, you yourself are the best person to observe for the successes and failures in fatherhood. By talking with your wife and reviewing your own attitudes and behavior with your previous children you can at any stage improve your parenthood skills for your whole family, not just with the new baby.

FATHER AND PREGNANCY

Just as you should be fully involved with the decision to have a child, so should you be with the progress of your wife's pregnancy. Pregnancy can be a rewarding time for growing closer to your wife, or it can be hell. A lot depends on your attitude.

You and the Obstetrician. The choice of your obstetrician should be a joint decision, with each of you contributing on the basis of your own observations. The obstetrician will probably be chosen initially because of recommendations of a friend or your family physician. At the first visit, you and your wife should determine if she or he is the kind of person to whom you can comfortably turn for help. Also observe how willing the doctor is to include you in office briefings. You should be invited to take part in all discussions on weight gain, hygiene, travel, exercise, sexual relations, hospital arrangements, etc. If the doctor does not recognize you as a viable member of the husband-wife team, look elsewhere.

An indication of the undesirable "technician" or assembly-line type of doctor is extreme rigidity regarding such variables as sexual relations. Each pregnancy is different, and your doctor should be interested enough in each one to gather sufficient data on it. The doctor's restrictions should be based on your particular case, not on a set of inflexible rules. However, don't expect your doctor to become *extremely* involved in your case, as do the doctors in television dramas; they all have many other patients to care for.

Some husbands become jealous of the obstetrician, either consciously or unconsciously. If the doctor is male, the husband may resent the fact that his wife, the woman whom he loves and who is bearing his child, is being looked after by another man. If the doctor is a woman, the father may feel particularly left out as the wife and doctor discuss pregnancy —two women conferring about a woman's role.

The visit to an obstetrician's office may stimulate such feelings very strongly as a father-to-be brings his wife in and she disappears behind a door to be examined, leaving him to read magazines. A man may also feel resentment at the restrictions the doctor may have to place on him and his wife—on activities, travel, and even on sex. But realizing that these irrational resentments may occur is usually enough to head them off.

Helping Out. Just as in most situations, in having a baby two heads are better than one, so your role should be an active one.

You can keep notes on the doctor's instructions, watch for symptoms of problems, help your wife stick to diets and sleep schedules, and help with countless other details of the pregnancy. You can help your wife obtain her information from reputable sources and not from "card-table diagnoses." Women are always eager to talk about pregnancies, especially their own, and information they may pass on to your wife could be very erroneous.

Your wife's pregnancy will be made much easier if you take part in exercise programs or childbirth training classes along with her. Strongly supporting her in eating right, quitting smoking, and relaxing can help not only her but the unborn child as well.

Her physical symptoms may include morning sickness during the early stages of pregnancy, odd food cravings, discomfort because of her enlarging abdomen, pelvic changes, heartburn, gas pains, or urinary frequency. Your doctor should fill you in on these and other possible problems. She may go through such psychological changes as an increasing dependency on you, sensitivity, sudden mood swings, fears and nightmares about the baby, and depression.

At the same time, she may withdraw emotional support from you as attention comes to focus on the baby. You must realize that this is usually just a temporary situation; you have not lost her affection and you are not in competition with the child. If, however, her withdrawal from you is very strong and you are constantly feeling ignored, this could be a danger sign. Her withdrawal or even resentment of you may become a permanent thing, either induced by pregnancy or by some problem in your marriage. It may go away temporarily but may surface again during the next crisis or strain on your marriage. Talk out these feelings and/or seek professional assistance. An understanding obstetrician could be the best source of help.

Your general attitude during pregnancy should be one of calm support. Supporting your wife will help not only her but also the actual physical well-being of the unborn child. Excessive fear and anxiety in the mother can lead to a greater number of complications in pregnancy, delivery, and the overall health of the newborn.

As the supportive parent, you should help with the job of arranging hospital and other facilities for the baby and of observing your wife for any out-of-the-ordinary symptoms. Try not to become overtly alarmed when such symptoms show up. Your wife may look to you for signs as to how she is progressing, and panic may alarm her. You can avoid alarm by thoroughly learning about the symptoms and problems of pregnancy.

You may also occasionally have to play the role of "villain." If guests or other duties are tiring your wife, you should not hesitate to suggest that the guests leave or that the activity be dropped. This "watchdog" attitude serves several purposes: (1) You are in a better position to objectively observe your wife than she is herself. She may be totally absorbed by her pregnancy or else too involved in whatever she is doing to realize how tired she is or how bad the activity might be for her. By playing the conservative, you may draw her attention to her condition and enable her to better evaluate her activities. (2) You may give your wife an out if she really doesn't want to have the guests or continue the activity. You probably know each other well enough to do a fair job of reading each other's thoughts. You can tell if you are a welcome villain and can ask her outright in private. (3) "Villainy" and all your other signs of interest in the pregnancy will reassure her that you still care about her and the baby.

Be very careful about kidding your wife about her shape or such symptoms as morning sickness. If she shows the slightest bit of discomfort with any such dialogue, drop the practice immediately.

Emphasize how attractive she looks when she does, but don't tell her she looks great when she doesn't. Your compliments should be based in truth; they will have a much greater effect.

You can help your wife a great deal, both physically and emotionally, if you make it a practice to unobtrusively help her in her daily activities. An offered arm when crossing the street or climbing stairs can be quite a lift. Special cushions for riding in the car or a comfortable, supportive chair will show your concern. Taking over some household duties is also a help, but not so many of them that you seem to cut out her importance. Emphasize that she is always of vital concern to the family's well-being.

One frequent pitfall, however, is that you may come to defer to your wife to the extent that you become resentful. Any deferment should be done with the expressed purpose of making a pregnant woman comfortable and happy, not with treating her as a sick person. Treating her as an invalid might cause her to believe that she is one.

Don't Overreact. Do not feel it necessary to curtail your normal individual activities during pregnancy. Pregnancies, especially first ones, may have a profound psychological effect on your life, and further disruption will only heighten any possible impact. Fathers-to-be, especially first-timers, may experience a feeling of being tied down or hemmed in by approaching family responsibilities, and a night out with male friends is a good way to remedy this. It may help remind you that there is still a big wide world with all its problems and that any difficulties you are experiencing may not be really as serious as you think. It is a perfectly normal practice, and neither you nor your wife should feel guilt about it. And, of course, continue to have nights out with your wife.

One source of resentment in an expectant family is a working wife's departure from her job to have the baby. A woman who is dedicated to her profession may have lost a major source of satisfaction in her life, along with feelings of independence and competence. Even if the baby is thoroughly welcomed, such a woman may come to resent her husband and, perhaps subtly, the baby. She may then make more demands for companionship and attention from her husband than usual.

If your wife is dedicated to her job, encourage her to work during pregnancy, but help her to take it easy by chauffeuring her to and from work, etc. After the baby is born, when both she and the baby are ready, she can go back to work part-time, change to a more convenient job, and/or hire a housekeeper. We shall discuss father and the working mother in a later chapter.

The husband of a working wife may come to resent the burden placed on him by the loss of his wife's earnings. If you realize the possibility of such resentments, they can usually be prevented.

If you can afford it, one possible way of easing the combined impacts of quitting a job and having a baby is for your wife to quit working a while before she becomes pregnant. This way, both she and the family have time to adjust to lowered income and new schedules and concerns.

We have discussed many problems of pregnancy thus far, so we feel a balancing statement is in order. Though there may be difficulties, the pregnant woman is usually very happy and fulfilled.

Pregnancy and Sex. Physicians all seem to be "experts" on how the expectant mother is to handle her sex life, but very little has been said about the father-to-be's sexual problems.

A survey in the late 1960s by sex researchers William Masters and Virginia Johnson on the effects of pregnancy on sex, revealed a significant flagging of interest by fathers-to-be. Of seventy-nine men questioned, thirty-one gradually ceased sexually approaching their pregnant wives at some point in pregnancy. Many of these men did not know why their interest waned. Their reasons ranged from being turned off by the wife's physical appearance to fear of harming the baby.

However, some husbands want sexual intercourse even more during pregnancy. Though many men are simply "turned on" by a pregnant woman, some husbands are only trying to get closer to their wives, because they feel threatened by the intrusion of a child into their marriage.

The majority of pregnant women interviewed by Masters and Johnson declared that they experienced a substantial increase in sex drive and appreciation during the middle months of pregnancy. Often this level was higher than before pregnancy.

A major compliment you can pay your pregnant wife is to

be sexually aroused by her. If, indeed, you are and the physician has placed no restrictions on your sex, by all means play the ardent lover.

The husband who is not sexually aroused by a pregnant woman should discuss this fact thoroughly with his wife so both can understand the reasons for lack of interest. Perhaps different coital positions, erotic clothing, or different surroundings could spur your sexual interest. Do not, however, feign headaches or pick arguments with your wife should you feel aversion to sex. Withdrawal of support for a pregnant woman can be very traumatic for her.

The reason some men aren't sexually aroused by pregnant women is that pregnancy emphasizes the mother role more than the wife role. This might cause the husband to unconsciously associate his wife with his own mother or another mother image, triggering a whole set of anxieties about sexual relationships.

The sex appeal of the father-to-be, however, is not likely to be as changed, because approaching fatherhood is not as physically obvious as approaching motherhood. Also, males in our society traditionally separate sex and parenthood, while the female has usually been taught to associate sex with family life and motherhood.

During pregnancy, there will be times when sex is not feasible or possible. You should obtain a full explanation of any restrictions from your physician, as well as full answers to any other questions about sex.

During the first three months of pregnancy nausea and fatigue might occasionally put a damper on sexual activity, but this is usually not a serious or long-term problem.

In most cases, sex can be enjoyed until quite close to delivery, but in some cases the physician may rule it out. In the Masters and Johnson survey, 77 out of 101 wives were warned to avoid intercourse during the last three months of pregnancy and for some time afterward. Clearly, this kind of strict prohibition has not been borne out by medical evidence, and more research needs to be done on the risks involved.

Physicians should base their prohibitions on firm medical data, not habit.

In any case, sexual interest on the part of the woman will tend to diminish during late pregnancy. Many women are uncomfortable during the last three months because of symptoms such as backache and fatigue. Others, however, declare they are surprised that they are quite sexually responsive when their husbands do approach them during this period.

Late in pregnancy, the uterus may undergo spasms when the woman has an orgasm. Occasionally, these may last as long as a minute after orgasm, causing an "odd" sensation for the woman. These are usually harmless and should cause no alarm.

Such contractions, the "delicate" condition of the wife, and "old husbands' tales" may cause the father not to want intercourse during the last three months to avoid harming the baby. These fears are medically unfounded.

A precaution that should be taken during the last months of pregnancy is to avoid extremely vigorous intercourse, particularly that which puts pressure on the wife's abdomen. You and your wife can find coital positions that are more comfortable for her.

Whatever your restrictions with regard to pregnancy and sex, do not feel that you are a villain because you want sex or a saint because you go without it. Six ejaculations per week is no less virtuous than two per week.

We know of one pregnant wife who saved up money from the household budget so her husband could afford a prostitute. Admittedly, this is a rare case; few women would have the outlook or temperament that would allow such a practice. Also, it would probably be hard to decide where to list the expenditure in the household budget.

Husbands are more likely to have extramarital intercourse during their wife's pregnancy than at other times because of possible sexual prohibitions or flagging sexual attraction on either partner's part. Some expectant fathers may seek extramarital sex as a form of rebellion against being forced into

adulthood and its responsibilities. Others may feel that the
seductive woman they married is becoming a traditional
hausfrau because of her pregnancy. The overdependent man
may seek out another woman to derive support from at a time
when his own pregnant wife becomes more dependent on him.

Then there is the man who seeks extramarital sex because
his pregnant wife reminds him of a mother who rejected him
when she was pregnant with a younger brother or sister.
Henry treated one such man, a young salesman named Ralph,
who began therapy because he was very anxious, was having
fights with his wife, and had started to become very sexually
interested in other women. It turned out that his wife was
pregnant. Even though her pregnancy had only just begun to
show, Ralph had become sexually turned off by her.

After several therapy sessions Ralph finally recalled, "When
I was a kid, my mother was pregnant with my younger
brother. He came along and everybody forgot about me. I
think that's really the way I feel about my wife's pregnancy."
As he probed these feelings, he began to talk about them to his
wife, and as they gained understanding together, Ralph's
whole attitude changed.

The incidence of extramarital intercourse could also be
partially the wife's fault. Some women use pregnancy as an
excuse to get back at their husbands by refusing sex. They may
also make demands for attention or service far above those
that would normally be called for by their condition. Regardless of the reason, if you do get yourself into the situation of
having extramarital sex, be aware of the possible conse-
quences. A pregnant wife learning of infidelity on the part of
her husband is much more emotionally vulnerable than the
nonpregnant woman. In addition to doubts about her ability
as a woman and recriminations against both you and herself,
she may also become convinced that her physical condition
makes her no longer attractive. Because she may be more
dependent upon you, an extramarital affair will cause her to
feel betrayed and despairingly vulnerable. Other people often
see the straying father-to-be in one of two ways: His affair may
be seen as understandable due to his frustrations, or he may be

especially damned for cheating on a mother-to-be. Try to deal with your sexual frustrations before they lead to extramarital relationships.

Because a new mother's nipples are erotic centers of pleasure, women who nurse their babies may be more interested in sex after the birth of their child. Some women even experience orgasm while suckling their babies. Your wife may feel as if she is indulging in some form of sexual perversion and resume sexual activity with you quickly to allay that feeling. On the other hand, she may use the eroticism of suckling as a partial or total replacement for sex. You both must realize that such eroticism is a natural mechanism for bonding together mother and child, for giving the mother pleasurable feelings about her baby. This sensuality may also serve to heighten the mother's and father's sexual interest in one another and to strengthen the family at a crucial time.

Deciding About Breast Feeding. One major decision that should be made before the child's birth is whether or not your wife should breast-feed your baby. It may surprise you to know that you have a role, and an important one, in this decision. The most important factor in determining the success of breast feeding is the attitude of the mother, and you definitely affect that attitude. If you are jealous of the baby or if you urge your wife to resume "normal" activities as soon as possible, she may be deterred from breast feeding, even if she wants to. Also, women must be quite comfortable and secure to breast-feed, and you contribute a great deal to this security by your encouraging, supportive attitude.

Most fathers are accepting when the decision has been made for their wives to nurse their offspring. If your wife wants to breast-feed and is of good health, breast feeding can help the baby because:

1. Human milk is the best and most natural food for the human infant. It has the best proportion of nutrients and is free of bacteria and other contaminants.
2. Breast-fed babies are less likely to develop colic, diar-

rhea, and constipation, because breast milk is so easily
digestible.

3. A yellowish fluid called colostrum, secreted from the
breast after childbirth and before milk flows, gives the
breast-fed infant resistance against infections and pro-
tects him against food allergies.

Mistakes in the preparation of a formula are avoided because
the food is ready-mixed in a very convenient container. And of
course, breast feeding can offer an enormously satisfying
emotional experience for the new mother.

You can get prepared formulas, however, and they have
proven quite adequate for the great majority of babies whose
mothers may not want to breast-feed or simply may not be
able to. For we must emphasize that the most critical factor in
the baby's early emotional development is the quality of
parent-child interactions and not the type of "container" from
which he is fed.

Psychological Effects of Pregnancy on the Father. Severe
psychological problems in prospective fathers are uncommon
or are short-lived. The great majority of men generally enjoy
becoming fathers. But men do not undergo the extensive social
preparation for fatherhood that women do for motherhood.
Fatherhood is more of an abrupt, sometimes jarring turning
point in a man's life, while motherhood to a woman is likely to
be more an expected fulfillment of a "natural" role.

You will probably go through three stages of perception of
your unborn child. During the first stage, after your wife has
missed her period or first found out about her pregnancy, your
image of the child will be vague. You will not really feel the
immediacy of becoming a father.

When the fetus quickens and begins to move, the fact that
you are going to become a father becomes a much more real
and immediate possibility. Dennis remembers this point
vividly. As his pregnant wife grew larger and larger, he
worried principally about providing for the child, buying the
right furniture and readying a nursery—all very cerebral. But
when he felt that first thump his child made against his wife's

belly, all that changed. Suddenly the child was real. It would have a real body and a real personality, and he would be its father. He would help name it, help save for it, and help it become a functioning human being. It was a profound, moving realization.

When your wife becomes very obviously pregnant, your preparations for fatherhood become much more active. You begin increasingly to notice children and to practice for fatherhood.

From our experience, there seem to be three particularly prevalent categories of fathers' attitudes toward marriage and pregnancy:

(1) There is the husband who readily and eagerly accepts the responsibilities and fulfillment of being a family man. Such a husband considers the pregnancy a gift and becomes very close to his wife.

(2) The totally career-oriented husband often regards prospective fatherhood as a burden that interferes with his job responsibilities. Such a husband tries hard to reaffirm all his old habits and denies the need for change in his way of living. For instance, he may want to take his pregnant wife on long camping trips and otherwise act "normally."

(3) The emotionally immature husband approaches fatherhood casually. Often this husband is frightened at the prospect of having to support a wife and a child, where previously he had been financially dependent on others. His main problem is making the transition from carefree adolescent to responsible adult. His wife's pregnancy is frequently accompanied by marital crisis and conflict with relatives.

One such case was that of Conrad, who was a "professional" student. He had never really held a steady job, spending his time taking various courses that never seemed to lead to a final degree because he kept changing majors. His wife, who was a teacher, supported him, as did his parents before he married.

When Conrad's wife became pregnant, Conrad became very resentful of her. They began having severe arguments, and Conrad even moved out of their apartment. After a series of therapy sessions with Henry, Conrad finally realized that he was actually afraid of the coming baby and its attendant responsibilities. When he was a child, his mother had been very sickly, and his father was himself afraid to take responsibility for Conrad, so as a boy he had been shunted from relative to relative. His wife's pregnancy brought up the extreme aversion to and fear of responsibility his own father had passed down to him.

Regardless of the type of person you are, the strain of pregnancy may surface in the form of emotional problems, though the majority of expectant fathers have a grand time waiting for the baby.

Researchers studying expectant fathers find them occasionally subject to fits of frenetic physical activity, minor psychosomatic ailments, and deviant social behavior because of these psychological adjustments.

Some fathers-to-be may feel it necessary to reassert their physical and mental prowess, because they feel fatherhood aging them. They may embrace highly physical sports or immerse themselves in demanding new hobbies.

A common reaction to pregnancy is for the husband to work extra hard, especially during the latter phase of pregnancy. Such a husband increasingly stays away from home for long periods of time. Though the apparent motive for such men is to get ahead and provide for their coming child, restlessness and anxiety might be the actual motives. Such a reaction to pregnancy should not, however, be confused with the heavy work load associated with getting started in a career.

Some men develop symptoms of pregnancy, including abdominal pains, loss of appetite, indigestion, colic, nausea, vomiting, temporary weight gains, backaches, and peptic ulcers. Insomnia and restlessness are reported by some fathers, and others become bedridden toward the end of their wife's pregnancy. This is reminiscent of the custom of couvade found in many primitive societies. In couvade, the husband takes on many of the behaviors of giving birth, taking to his bed when his wife begins labor and going through all the motions of labor himself. Moaning and thrashing about as he "gives birth," the father is attended to by family and friends, given gifts, and put on a strict diet and told to rest. This curious practice has been given all sorts of explanations. Anthropologists cite envy of the mothers' ability to bear children, assertion of paternity, warding off evil spirits, and sympathy with the mother as causes. Perhaps some of these could be used to explain modern cases of couvade.

Couvade is particularly prevalent in societies that don't have strong, involved fathers. This could indicate that the practice stems from a basic identification of the man with the woman's role, because of discomfort with his own sex role. This may also sometimes be the case with couvade in our society, when a father feels ill during his wife's pregnancy or has sympathetic "labor pains."

Psychologically healthy men can easily handle the occasional disruptions in their sex lives that pregnancy brings, but in emotionally disturbed fathers, such a disruption may lead to outbursts of sex offenses. Drs. A. Arthur Hartman and Robert C. Nicolay, two Chicago-based psychologists, found that sex offenses among first-time expectant fathers are over twice as high as for other married men who get into trouble with the law. The sexual offenses are most likely to occur during the last four months of pregnancy, when sexual deprivation was most likely. The offenses included molesting children, masturbating in public, rape, attempted rape, making obscene telephone calls, and sending obscene letters. The researchers theorized that the offenses stemmed from a combination of the men's weak impulse control and the immature adjustive reactions to the tensions brought on by the wives' pregnancies. Of course, all this doesn't mean that sex offenses are at all common among expectant fathers, just that among maladjusted expectant fathers sex becomes more of a focal point of their problems.

Training Yourself for Childbirth. Though you may have been around children all your life, not until your own first child is born will you really experience the full impact of fatherhood. It is also the first time you have been married to a mother, not just a wife. Since this is a profound time of learning for you, the more deeply involved you are with the preparations for and actual birth of your child, the better it will be for both your fatherhood and for your relationship with your wife. This involvement should be a positive, happy one.

Take full advantage of books, magazines, and your obstetrician's advice to get a thorough background for fatherhood. As we'll discuss later, however, there are serious deficiencies in many popular books and magazines in their treatment of the father. What you read should be considered in light of what you learn in this book about the importance and value of fatherhood.

Although preparative courses are not absolutely necessary, you and your wife are well-advised to undertake them. We strongly encourage you to be present in the labor and delivery rooms and to be prepared for what you will see there. For a well-prepared husband, being at his wife's side when their baby is born can be a profound and moving experience. And your presence can be a great help to your wife.

Even if your wife has taken a thorough tour of the obstetrical facilities beforehand, and many have not, you can help dispel the fear of unfamiliar surroundings by being with her when she is in labor and delivery. During labor, giving the mother-to-be back rubs, holding her hand, helping her to relax and breathe properly, wiping her brow, timing contractions, and observing her progress, can be of great help to her and to the medical team.

Just by being in the labor room you will calm your wife, make her delivery easier, and could even thereby help produce a healthier baby. One obstetrician we know of noticed that whenever he asked a father to leave the labor room so he could treat the mother-to-be, she would become more nervous and her contractions would become more painful. He tried an experiment: He simply asked fathers-to-be to step out of the room, without administering any treatment to the mother-to-be. Sure enough, the mother still became nervous and uncomfortable. Even if he didn't *do* anything, the father, by his mere calming presence, aided the delivery of his baby.

But if you have not taken a childbirth preparation course, or if you are a very sensitive person, some things you may see in the delivery room may upset you. The groaning and panting of a woman in labor and even the usually minor amount of blood visible during childbirth may upset you. You may be surprised, however, at how little this will affect you. Dennis remembers being uneasy at viewing the living-color films of childbirth shown during childbirth education classes he attended. But during the actual birth he was so excited at seeing his new daughter that he wasn't bothered in the least.

In any case, your presence is an individual preference. Neither you nor your wife should feel that you are deserting her and the child if for some reason you do not wish to be in the labor and delivery rooms. More important is the fact that you have been committed and involved with your wife throughout her pregnancy.

Resistance to Fathers. Unfortunately many hospitals and doctors still do not allow the father in the labor and delivery rooms regardless of his preparation. These hospitals and doctors also do not realize the extent to which the father is becoming "imprinted" into his role of father at childbirth. Doctors and nurses should realize that their job is to encourage proper development of the family, *not merely to be childbirth technicians*. Hospital officials who fail to provide full access— and not just waiting rooms—for fathers simply aren't doing their jobs.

The reasoning of many hospitals and doctors for not allowing fathers in labor and delivery rooms doesn't hold up in view of actual experiences with fathers, particularly when fathers have been educated about what to expect in the delivery room. For instance, they claim that the fathers in the delivery room might witness procedures, such as suction and resuscitation, that might frighten them or make them faint. This is an odd assertion when one considers that the mother is in that same delivery room, often witnessing the same procedures that are barred from the father's view. Doctors who hold such opinions either don't respect fathers as much as they do mothers, don't consider the feelings of either parent as very important, or simply haven't been exposed to our growing knowledge of a father's importance in all aspects of family life.

Some doctors also fear the possibility of the father suing them should an emergency occur during the birth process. They ignore the fact that only 5 percent of pregnancies present major problems, and the majority of these can be anticipated by a thorough early diagnosis. In any case, hospitals that allow husbands in delivery rooms find that fathers, in fact, gain a great deal of respect for doctors by watching them handle emergencies. Husbands who have seen the child born can also better accept the truth about any medical problems the child may have at birth; they do not feel that the doctor is "putting one over on them" or that the problem is necessarily the doctor's fault. Husbands who are educated in childbirth problems and who watch the child being born also seem calmer about handling medical crises at home when they occur. Invoking the medical mystique is clearly no way to launch a father on his way.

Prepared Childbirth. Prepared natural childbirth, with the father coaching, can be very gratifying for both parents. One widely used method is named after the French physician Fernand Lamaze, who made it popular. In Lamaze classes attended by the father and mother-to-be, the pregnant woman is taught to dissociate uterine contractions from the experience of pain, through repeated reinforcement of the notion that such contractions are not painful. In Lamaze classes, a mother learns to relax abdominal muscles voluntarily so she doesn't tense up when the time comes to deliver her baby. Her husband goes through childbirth exercises with her and coaches her during the actual process.

Besides the husband-wife exercise classes, informal discussion groups can be held during which husbands and wives are encouraged to ask questions together, even about such traditionally "female" topics as bottle versus breast feeding, and the important period of adjustment for both immediately after childbirth. Couples can be shown films on childbirth and given tours of hospital facilities. Husbands can be prepped on where they will change into delivery room garb for the birth of their child and what they will do in that room during the birth.

Incidentally, don't expect your baby to be "cute" at birth or immediately afterward. A baby may be wrinkled or red at birth, but will round out and become incredibly attractive after a few weeks.

If you are worried about your newborn's condition, don't be afraid to question your obstetrician closely. Question him about anything and everything you think may be wrong with the baby. If you read books on childbirth, you will realize that newborns often have disfigurements that may appear serious but actually have no permanent significance whatsoever. Temporary distortions or swellings of the head or face, eye hemorrhages, cross-eyedness, skin lesions quickly heal. The newborn also has a tendency to breathe roughly, hiccough, and snort—all usually perfectly normal.

Preparing Your Other Children. If you already have other children, you also have a unique role in preparing them for the arrival of the baby. Your other children may be jealous of the arrival of a new baby, even when your wife tries to involve them in the experience. Because the children see you as being more separated from the childbirth experience than your wife—you are not pregnant—they may accept your attitude toward the pregnancy more readily than your wife's. They also may be more willing to talk out their fears with you.

Make sure that you have quiet talks with the children as the pregnancy progresses, explaining why Mother may not be feeling well and telling them how they can volunteer to help when the baby arrives. Help your children become involved in preparations for the baby; paint the nursery and fix up toys for the baby together. Let them preview what the baby will be like by showing them pictures of other newborns and explaining what babies are like. A family shopping trip during which you, your wife, and your children help choose clothes for the baby can be another way of giving your children a sense of responsibility about the baby.

Don't launch such talks with the overt purpose of keeping your children from getting anxious, however. If they sense your purpose, this usually makes them more anxious. We know one psychologist who was so caught up in the possibility of his children's sibling rivalry with a new infant that he kept cautioning his children against being jealous of the newborn. Of course the children came to believe that they should be rivals with the new baby, and that was exactly their attitude when the mother came home from the hospital.

While, as we said, you should encourage your children to help out with the baby, don't force them into being junior parents. Many parents have the notion that an older child, especially a daughter, will be able "to take care of everything" when the baby arrives.

Also, don't push children you already have into behaving older than their years just because you have a new baby. If you have a two- or three-year-old and bring home a new baby, your child is still only two or three. He hasn't matured overnight.

One father we know named Brad had a young son, Jimmy, age five, whom he delighted in bouncing on his knee and fondling when he came home at night. When Brad and his wife had a new daughter, Cindy, things changed abruptly and harshly for the little boy. "Well, you've got a baby sister now, Jim; I guess we're going to have to skip all the cuddling at night; you're getting too big anyway," his father told him.

Needless to say, Jimmy became not only frightened and insecure at the loss, but jealous of the new baby. He began misbehaving, wetting the bed, and even hit his sister as she lay in her crib. At first Brad was quite angry and spanked his son several times. But with a little coaching he came to realize how he was forcing his son into maturity too early, and the nightly cuddling sessions resumed. Jimmy improved rapidly, and is now quite happy with his little sister.

Often a father can use this period of adjustment to help solve an older child's problem. For example, one father we know, Joe, used the period in which his wife was in the hospital having a new baby to get close to his shy, three-year-old daughter, Susan. Joe had been away a good deal in his job as an engineering consultant during the past year, and as a consequence his daughter had become extremely dependent on her mother. Susan wouldn't go anywhere unless Mommy was with her and seldom strayed far from Mommy's side in the house.

With his wife in the hospital, Joe decided to take two weeks off, not only to be with his wife, but to get to know Susan better. For the first few days Susan cried frequently because her mother was away, but with patience, Joe finally got her to enjoy several activities with him like making breakfast, going for walks, and playing with the dog. Father and daughter visited the mother often, which allayed Susan's fears. When Cindy's mother finally came home with the new baby, Susan was a much more adventurous and independent little girl.

Hospitals are making quite a thing about so-called rooming-in programs in which the newborn is allowed to stay with the mother. We would go much further; hospitals should have rooming-in for the whole family. The birth of the baby should be a gala occasion, with husband and children spending the postpartum days with the mother in the hospital. Such rooming-in would not interfere with either the baby's care or the mother's if rooming-in suites were designed properly. For instance, husband and children could be placed in a suite adjoining the mother's but arranged so it would not enter upon any hospital corridors. Families could use separate entrances from the outside so they would not intrude on hospital routine. A preparation room between the suite and the mother's room could be used to don masks or hospital gowns, if necessary. A heavy door could be closed should the mother wish rest or need special treatment. Such adjoining suites for the father and children should cost no more than a motel suite, because the special care used in maintaining hospital rooms would not have to be taken.

This arrangement could greatly benefit a family's adjustment to a new baby. The father and mother would have access to the newborn, and the children might relish the exciting occasion of going to the hospital to have a baby. Furthermore, mothers would not be cut off from families at a time of emotional stress—probably a factor in the period of depression many women go through after childbirth.

3 / Father and the Newborn

You may think that once your baby is born, you are a full-fledged father, but that is not entirely correct. During the first year of your daughter's or son's life, your wife is learning to be an accomplished mother just as you are learning to be an accomplished father and your offspring is learning to be an accomplished baby.

Father and the Baby's Sex. Often the most difficult initial adjustment many new fathers must make is to the sex of the new child. Expectant fathers overwhelmingly want a boy as their first child and often don't want to stop having children until they have a son. To a lesser degree they will advocate continuing to have children until they have a daughter, but this is more often "for my wife's sake."

Expectant fathers often joke about wanting a boy, saying they will "send it back if it's a girl," or about buying the fetus a football.

This preference for a male child also applies to women, the majority of whom, in most societies, want a male as their first, or at least as one of their children.

There probably will always be a basic preference of fathers-to-be for at least one male child, because a fundamental reason for having children is to perpetuate one's self. Fathers want to have someone like them whom they can teach and who will be a male like themselves. This may be a basic kind of preference in primates, since other male primates, such as baboons, appear to take more interest in male infants than in female infants. Throughout history, initiation rites, religion, and customs have emphasized the role of the male child carrying on for his father.

Besides this legitimate reason for wanting a male child, however, is a devaluation of females in our society. Both males and females have been taught to value more highly male thinking styles and potentials. True, in our society men do achieve more than women, but this should be changed, and one way to change it is for fathers to begin valuing baby girls as much as baby boys. Don't view your child as being restricted because of its sex. Its sex is only a part of the total personality, all of which you will play a major role in shaping.

Disappointment in the child's sex can lead to strains on the family at childbirth. New fathers tend to get more angry and irritated with female infants. Such prejudice surely has profound effects on the husband-wife relationship and on the future of the father-daughter relationship. Don't work yourself into a psychological corner before the birth by emphasizing the importance of the baby being a boy or a girl. Sex is not so important as the fact that the baby grows up to be a successful, happy human being.

As might be expected, baby girls and baby boys are treated differently from birth. Part of this differential treatment may come from basic differences in the two sexes at infancy, besides obvious genital differences.

For instance, baby girls often seem to respond more to sounds and sights around them. Boys seem to be more vigorous physically and to cry more than girls. Parents, who are very sensitive to a newborn's personality, react to these differences by talking to their girls more and handling their boys more vigorously.

Because fathers tend to be the parents who are the most vigorous and physical in handling their infants, their different attitude toward boys and girls can considerably affect physical development. Everybody has seen a father roughhousing with his baby son, but treating his daughter like porcelain, declaring "But she's a girl!" In reality there is no real difference between the fragility of male and female infants.

The results of such parental attitudes, with a nudge from innate sex differences, show up very definitely by the end of the first year. Girls learn to talk earlier and better than boys. Boys venture farther from their parents, stay away from them longer, and look at them less than girls. Boys tend to be more aggressive, trying to push around a barrier placed between them and their parent. Girls are more likely to stand and cry in frustration.

We doubt that all these differences in the way boys and girls are raised will ever disappear from our society; perhaps they shouldn't. To the extent that sex differences correspond to what an infant really tends toward, differential treatment is valid. The happiest child is one who is comfortable with what he has become because it fits his abilities.

But you should realize that to be well-rounded, a person, male or female, must possess assertiveness, physical ability, verbal ability, tenderness, and an ability to relate to others. Don't plunk your infant into a rigid category—be it football player or mommy—because of your own preconceptions. Let the baby develop along his own best lines, in many directions. We shall talk more about sex differences in later chapters.

Bringing Baby Home. The addition of a new baby to a family creates a whole new series of relationships, which may take a while to sort themselves out. We have developed a diagram to illustrate how complex the changes make the family. B.B. (Before Baby), the relationships are relatively straightforward—the husband and wife interact directly. A.B. (After Baby), family relationships are greatly complicated. Not only do the father, mother, and child affect one another, but each is affecting and affected by the relationship between the other two. How the mother relates to the child may affect the father, producing perhaps jealousy if the father has a history of childhood rivalry with his brothers and sisters. The father will also affect the mother-child relationship by his attitude toward it. In the same way, the relationship between the father and mother affects the child, and the child affects the relationship between the father and mother.

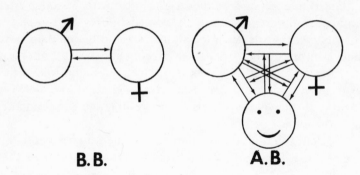

B.B.   **A.B.**

If you already have other children, the relationships get even more complicated, but we shall spare you another geometry lesson. Just imagine our figure with more circles and a great many more arrows.

Women who have had an uncomplicated birth usually leave the hospital after about three days. Sometime during the first ten days after giving birth about two-thirds of all women experience episodes of sadness and crying, known as post-partum depression. Though hormonal changes in the mother's body contribute to this depression and the fatigue that accompanies it, much of it may be psychological. The pressures of being a new mother, the trauma of childbirth, and, significantly, a feeling of neglect or rejection by the husband may play significant roles in postpartum depression in some mothers. For others the depression may not be severe at all, representing only a return to normalcy after the exhilaration of giving birth.

The new mother may also feel subtle resentment toward the baby. She may feel that she needs care and attention and that the newborn is getting the lion's share. She may feel keenly that she is losing her attractiveness, her career, or her effectiveness in the family.

Obviously, you can do a great deal to alleviate these feelings. If you are careful to show your dedication to your wife as well as your new child, she should not feel neglected. Help her keep busy with activities she enjoys. As soon as she has recovered from childbirth, take her out on a "date." Generally make sure she knows how important she is as a mother, wife, and person.

There are a number of specific things you can do to help your wife recover psychologically from childbirth:

In the hospital, she has probably learned many practical tips on baby care that you don't know about. Having her coach you in the techniques will give her confidence that she can still be an effective, active person.

Don't be shy about being physically affectionate toward the new mother. Make it clear that she still turns you on sexually, even though you can't have sexual intercourse immediately after childbirth.

You will probably have to run the household and care for your other children while she is recovering, but don't feel that you have to become a total expert. Consult her frequently so she will realize that she is still vital to the family's operation.

If you usually talk out problems about your job with her, don't stop simply because she has just had a baby. Involving her in your problems will show her that she is still very important to you.

It is ironic that women, especially those in the upper middle class, sometimes hire a nanny or a nurse to take care of their children while they take over running the house when they return home. Thus, they give the complicated, delicate job of childraising away and retain for themselves the everyday chores of keeping house. If you are going to hire help, hire a maid.

We have known cases where the father may take on extra work to pay for help, instead of pitching in himself. He may feel that this is the only way he can respond to the new demands of fatherhood. It obviously isn't.

The Father's New Social Position. Your first child will cause changes not only in how you view yourself, but also in how others view you. These changes may be a bit rougher on the father, because his role, unlike the mother's, has seldom traditionally been thought of as being a major one. Thus, while the mother may have been brought up to feel fulfilled by her new role, the father may feel tied down by the infant.

Because new mothers concentrate so many of their energies on the new child, you may have to manage many social duties. Just as when your wife was pregnant, you should now not hesitate to ask friends or relatives to leave if you feel mother or child (or you) are being imposed upon. The mother, who with her child is the center of attention, may feel it impolite or ungracious to ask for privacy. We stress again that all couples are different. Your wife may resent any "management" on your part, and you should never treat her as anything less than she is—a competent adult.

If you have unmarried friends or couples without children, they may feel uncomfortable or ambivalent relating to you in your new role. In fact, one of Henry's friends felt so uncomfortable about the birth of the Billers' first child that he subtly tried to intervene in the relationship. He tried to bait Henry into confronting his wife with the question "Who do you love most, me or the baby?"

Close personal friends may resent the intrusion of a child, or be uninterested in your ubiquitous string of pictures of the new baby. Such jealousy or disinterest may be especially noticeable in male friends' attitudes toward a new son. For instance, Henry had one close friend who reacted very possessively when Henry wanted to include his son Jonathan in their activities. "I would really like to go with you, but please don't bring your kid," he would say when inviting him places. His friend was so jealous of Jonathan that he would ignore him when visiting, not even looking at him.

On the other hand, your friends' reactions could be very surprising. People who have never evinced interest in children may react very warmly to yours.

Your friends may also feel that your personality has changed drastically and that you are no longer interested in the get-togethers or hobbies that you once shared. Be careful that you don't allow yourself to get so wrapped up in your new duties that you forget your friends. Give friends and friendships time to adjust to your fatherhood; don't rule out another person or couple because they may be cool to your new role at first.

After the baby is born, if you notice signs of such changes in your relationships, make sure that you welcome your old friends into your new family life. Make it clear to them that you want to maintain your relationship with them. However, don't feel that you have to have a certain number of friends or go to a certain number of parties in order to keep your social standing. If you have to restrict your social contacts after the birth of the baby, make it clear to your friends why you cannot go out. If your friends are good ones, they will understand.

One source of resentment, especially on the part of fathers, is the loss of freedom because of new family responsibilities. Before you and your wife can go out you may have to first find a baby-sitter and prepare everything for the baby, which makes the whole affair somewhat of a chore.

One good remedy to this problem of preparation, especially in the wife's case, is for you to stay home and mind the baby when she wants to go out. Encourage her to become involved in night courses or other activities, which will give her time to herself. Also take occasional nights out yourself. Don't feel that a baby requires that you give up your interests. He just adds a new dimension to them.

Sometimes Take Your Baby with You. The best way to get out occasionally and also to give your baby valuable learning experiences is to take him with you. An infant is a remarkable creature, for he is soaking up knowledge of the world around him like a sponge. The more experiences, sights, sounds, smells, and tastes you expose him to the more he will learn. In most cases, you don't have to change your activities in order to bring your baby with you. An infant can learn a great deal by going golfing, watching tennis, going boating, or experiencing almost any other activity you take part in.

You can even take your baby to parties if you know your hosts well and are sure they do not mind. Your child might enjoy being played with by the hosts' children and when he is tired will learn to go right off to sleep. This will also help your child to be adaptable, and you will have much less of a

problem with him when you visit relatives, have parties
yourself, or take vacations.

Of course, the extent to which you can take your child with
you depends on your temperament and the child's. A difficult
baby or parents who run out of patience do not make for
happy outings. Neither do parents who do not carefully
control their child in other people's homes. Adjust your
schedule and activities until both you and your child are
comfortable.

FATHER AND THE FIRST YEAR

> There's a time at night, when we bring her into bed with
> us, just before we go to sleep, that's the most beautiful
> you can imagine. We're all close together and she's so soft
> and warm.
>
> —A machinist about his baby daughter

One major myth about fatherhood is that the father doesn't
have much effect on his child during the first years of life. It is
generally thought that the mother is the primary parent
during this time and that the father is nice to have around but
is not badly needed. "Just wait till he/she is old enough. We
can really have fun together" is a common feeling expressed
by fathers.

The Myth of Mothering. One of the reasons that many
fathers feel unnecessary is that they see an impenetrable
emotional wall around the mother-child relationship. Since
our society has always tended to view things in terms of
opposites, the fact that the mother is deeply involved with the
child subtly means to many that the father is to be excluded.

The mother-child bond is, no doubt, a unique one. The
human mother, like other mammals, probably undergoes
hormonal changes that make her biologically disposed toward
mothering behavior. She has also a very strong attachment to
the infant because she has carried it within her for nine

months. The pleasure of nursing and the responsibility of providing the infant with a food source can also strengthen this bond. Also the socially approved pleasures of cuddling and protecting a warm, helpless infant increase the mother's feeling of nurturance toward the infant.

But we stress that initially this bond is but a one-way attachment. The newborn has no innate preference for one parent or another, or for the natural parent rather than a foster parent. Newborns just like to be held and stimulated, and the identity of the holder isn't really important to them. Mothers are attracted to newborns—not newborns particularly to mothers. And the need for food is not the only reason infants attach themselves to other people.

Experiments done with infant monkeys illustrate the relationship of physical dependence to psychological dependence on the mother. Animal behaviorist Harry Harlow, of the University of Wisconsin, and his colleagues placed two groups of newborn rhesus monkeys in separate cages, each with two kinds of substitute "mothers"—one constructed of welded wire and one covered with soft terry cloth. In past experiments the baby monkeys had immediately attached themselves to the soft terry-cloth mother. In this experiment Harlow attached bottles of milk with nipples to the cloth mother in one cage, and to the wire mother in the other. He found that no matter where the food was, both groups of monkeys spent the largest amount of time with their cloth mothers. The monkeys with the food supply in their wire mothers would leave the cloth mothers only long enough to feed, and then return. This shows that the infant monkeys needed the comfort of the terry "mother" as well as the food.

Though infants do usually attach to their mothers first, this attachment doesn't remain exclusive long. Other attachments are added as the baby branches out into the new world. In fact, a significant number of infants make just as strong, or stronger, initial attachments to their fathers as they do to their mothers.

Though the mother is usually the first attachment the baby makes, by age three months many infants react to the father almost as much as to the mother, cooing and smiling and becoming excited at his approach. In fact, by their second year infants who are well fathered show approximately equal attachment to both parents.

We are not really sure attachment to a person is even possible until most infants are three or four months old. It is not until that time that the infant really begins to comprehend that different people exist. Before that the baby may not even know who is whom—only that food is available, that it has to burp, or that it is uncomfortable. It will attach to a "source" of food or comfort and not to mother as a person. If both parents are involved, an infant will show joint attachment to the mother and father as soon as it is able to discriminate among people.

However, men in our society have been brought up in an atmosphere that is "antifathering." They have been taught to feel that spending time with infants is unmanly. Men have learned that the feeling of a baby snuggling and bending his body and grasping at hair or clothing should be uncomfortable for them. They have been taught that physical contact between people should elicit aggressiveness or sexuality. Just as females have been required to stifle competitive impulses, so males have been taught to stifle nurturant ones.

Men in America, especially lower-class men, may be brought up almost entirely by women. Since the only people they see dealing with children are females, they get the idea that it is a definitely nonmasculine responsibility. Wanting to be thoroughly male, they then avoid child care like a plague. They deeply fear that caring for children will cause a loss of masculinity.

Later we shall discuss in more detail the problems of preconceived notions of masculinity and feminity. A good example of how these notions affect thinking about early childhood is Freud's theory of identification, still accepted in many circles. In the early 1900s, Freud theorized that all children first identify with their mother, and boys must later switch their identification to the father for normal masculine development. Since Freud's theory was conceived in a society in which women did almost all of the early childrearing, it's only natural that he would postulate a basic, exclusive psychological identification with the mother for both boys and girls.

In fact, fathers have always been capable of nurturing newborns and there is no reason children cannot identify initially with the father as well as with the mother. However, in our society many fathers have been taught to stifle their expression of physical nurturance and to show affection only indirectly by providing the infant with material things.

Father Noninvolvement. Most fathers spend far too little time with their infants. In 1971, psychologists Peggy Ban and Michael Lewis, at the Educational Testing Service in Princeton, New Jersey, studying one-year-old infants from middle-class families, found that their fathers spent only about fifteen to twenty minutes per day playing with them. In another study of forty-five fathers, the time spent with the baby averaged out to about eight hours per week. We suspect that this time might have been composed of the twenty minutes or so per weekday as reported in the first study, plus a few hours on the weekends. Compare this with the enormous amount of time mothers spend with their children.

Talking does affect a baby, yet most fathers spend very little time in such communication. Perhaps talking to a baby seems undignified, or embarrassing, but communication is an extremely important talent for an infant to develop, and if he receives encouragement from both his mother and his father, he will develop much better. Talk about everything under the sun to your infant. Don't be embarrassed at singing, crooning, or making funny noises at him. Even the newborn responds by movement and attention to human speech.

The Advantages of Father. But what other advantages does interaction with a father offer a baby? One major advantage comes in the contrast to the mother that you offer the child. You are usually larger than your wife, your voice is deeper, your clothes are different, and you move and react differently. Thus, you offer the child a different kind of person to learn about. By contrasting you and the mother, the infant learns that different people can be looked to for different needs and different expectations. For example, your infant may prefer your wife when he is hungry and you when he wants to be rocked to sleep.

You also handle the child differently than the mother, you are more physical, throwing the child into the air and playing with him more vigorously. This seems to be not only because of your lesser concern with protecting the child but also because of your more physically vigorous nature as a male. For instance, in front of Dennis's house runs a dead-end street that the neighbors use to air their babies in their strollers. Dennis had become used to seeing the young mother of one infant pushing her charge sedately up and down the avenue as the child ogled the world around him. One day, however, he looked out the window to see the stroller come whizzing up the street at breakneck speed, the infant sitting exhilarated in the seat. Behind the carriage loped the child's father. It was obviously his turn to air the baby, and he was giving it a ride much different from the leisurely stroll of the mother.

Because of your upbringing, if you are involved with your infant, you are more likely to stimulate him to explore and push himself to new achievements and to investigate new objects. On the other hand, fathers, because of their achievement orientation, may also find it harder to accept a child's imperfections. In later chapters we shall talk more about these pitfalls.

The difference in your daily schedule from that of your wife also affects the baby. While most mothers of very young children are usually around all day, only leaving the baby for short periods, you usually leave for much longer periods. Your comings and goings can be great affairs to him, composed of elaborate preparations and good-byes and hellos—there are more peaks and valleys in your relationship with him than your wife's. You thus begin to teach the baby that you go away and come back at certain times, even though those times seem to him impossibly far apart. You also teach him emphatically about structure and predictability, that certain things are done for certain purposes. For instance, he may connect your preparations for leaving with those that are made for him when he goes out. He then may realize that these preparations are generally made before going somewhere. If he is attached to you, he is much more likely to benefit from such stimulation because he is more interested in your actions.

Incidentally, your wife can help the baby realize the regularity of your comings and goings and your importance in the family by excitedly declaring to the baby, "Daddy's home!" or "Daddy's coming home in just a few minutes!" And, of course, you should do the same about her comings and goings. Your high valuation of each other will affect very much how the baby reacts to you both.

Infants' shortened time sense can cause your relationship with your child to suffer badly should you be away from home for a long time. If it is possible, try to hold off long trips away from your family until after the baby is about two years old, until he understands clearly that you are a permanent fixture in his life and that you will return.

Your close fathering of your infant will also make it much easier for him to accept periods of separation from his parents, to be less afraid of strangers, and to be more exploratory. In 1973 a group of Harvard University psychologists discovered this in a study they made of thirty-six one-year-olds. The team of psychologists interviewed the fathers in order to separate them into groups of high, medium, or low father interaction.

The psychologists then studied how the infants reacted when various combinations of the mother, the father, and a stranger entered and left a room in which the child was placed. They noted, for instance, when the infant cried, played with his toys, or looked at the people or at the door.

The psychologists found that the children cried mainly when left alone with the stranger and usually not at the departure of one or the other parent. This meant that the child was afraid of the stranger, rather than necessarily missing its mother or father. Significantly, the researchers found that the children with highly involved fathers showed little crying, fretting, or disruption of play when left with the stranger. Children of less-involved fathers on the other hand were very disturbed when left with the stranger.

All this seemed to indicate that children with involved fathers had been exposed to more experiences and are more intellectually advanced. Thus, such infants could cope better with being alone with strangers. Another possibility was that the well-fathered infant was used to having more caretakers. In any case, fathers made a difference.

Other differences in your schedule of activities can also be used to teach the infant about the world. If you and your wife split the chores and usually go to different kinds of places on errands and if you each take your child along, he can learn about a greater variety of situations. The machinery at a service station, the objects in a supermarket, or the activities at a sports event can make for a great learning experience for the infant. The child may not even understand what is going on, but experiencing new things with someone he loves and trusts will nevertheless be thrilling for him. By watching, he may, in fact, learn many things that he will not use until much later.

For example, Dennis spent much time during his formative years in a south Texas neighborhood bar. His father would take him when he went on Saturday or after work to get a cold beer and talk with his cronies. Dennis really didn't know what the place was about, but he remembers having a ball climbing on the beer cases in the back room, venturing into the icy, walk-in cooler, and meeting the people coming into the bar. The experiences in that bar were among the most vivid of his youth.

Some of Henry's earliest memories are of being allowed to watch his father's weekly poker game. Even before the age of two he vividly remembers standing on his tiptoes to watch his father deal the cards. The rattle of chips, the clink of coins, even the smoke were all exciting. Being allowed to sit on his father's lap for a while before bed was a special treat when a card game was in progress. One of Henry's favorite pastimes today is playing cards.

Fathers, Mothers, Infants. Other advantages a father may confer upon the child come in the way he affects the mother. The mother-infant bond is considered a sacred and profound thing in our society. The intensity of this bond, especially for the first-time mother, may create the feeling of an enormous burden of responsibility and intense emotion. By assuming your proper role in sharing responsibility for the child, you are relieving her of part of this psychological burden, and it may make her much happier about her motherhood.

You can also head off the possibility of too-close mothering. A mother may feel threatened with her baby's independence. She has been taught that the child is a main character in her life, and when the child goes out on his own, she may feel a loss of her importance.

Some mothers may create a sort of symbiotic relationship between themselves and their child, discouraging the child from being independent. Such a mother is constantly with and responding to the baby. She teaches him for hours, often interfering with the baby's own attempts at trying things out. Such treatment may easily result in a child's being unable to be independent and, thus, satisfying the mother's desire for a child needing close mothering. Because you may not have the intense, physical nurturant feeling about the baby that your wife does, and because fathers tend to get a greater reward out of the child's achievements and independence, you can offset sMother-love should it be a problem.

Father's Time. Finally we come to the question of how much time you should spend with the infant or with your older child. About an hour or more every weekday of person-to-person interaction with your child seems reasonable. This doesn't mean just being in the same room with the child; it means such one-to-one activities as wrestling with him, reading to him, showing him toys, taking him places, and letting him watch you at chores. Rolling on the floor or playing with babies' toys is not undignified, especially considering the importance of what you are teaching your child. As one father put it, "If people saw what I did with my little daughter, they'd think I have something loose upstairs. All my pants are worn at the knees from getting down on all fours and playing peekaboo with her." Perhaps worn knees could be used as one sign of an involved father.

Such weekday activity can easily be divided into periods for your convenience. This might include a little time in the morning playing with the baby or talking with your older child, a period at noon if you come home for lunch, and a longer period in the evening. If you work late or at odd hours, there is no reason your offspring's schedule can't be adjusted to accommodate yours. As long as he gets enough total sleep, a baby or preschooler can stay up as late as necessary for you to get a chance to play with him. School children may be able to take naps after school in order to be with their father at night. In a later chapter, we'll make suggestions about how to blend work and fatherhood.

On weekends you can spend even more time with your daughter or son by taking them on family outings or on errands. You will find that even tedious household chores take on a whole new aura as you watch your child make new discoveries. As you mow the lawn, he is discovering the wondrous qualities of grass blades. As you paint walls, he is learning how liquids cover surfaces. A baby could even be compared to a psychedelic experience—he can give you a whole new, more sensitive outlook on things. Watch him discover his hands and how they work or figure out the reflections in a mirror.

If you have more than one child, your overall time with the children must increase, but not directly according to the number of children. You don't have to spend twice as much time with two children, three times as much with three, etc. What you do have to do, however, is divide the greater amount of time you spend with them so that each child has some special time with you besides participating in your general play with all the children. For instance, if you have three children, you might spend a period each day talking to your children and playing with them but save a little time so that each child gets a little personal time with Daddy every few days and each child gets a special outing with Daddy every few weeks.

We don't mean these guidelines to be at all rigid. Don't go around with a stopwatch and a clipboard marking off your time with each child. And we don't mean that you shouldn't save time to do things by yourself, with your friends, and with your wife.

In families with more than two or three children, particularly if they are close in age, fathers may feel overwhelmed by the time requirements of effective fathering. Make sure that you can really be committed to each child before you and your wife enlarge your family.

It is enough to simply keep in mind our general suggestion that you spend a significant amount of time with your children in general but also a significant amount of time with each child individually.

To our assertion of this some fathers have answered, "Well, at least I am home some of the time. It's not as if he were fatherless." But in some ways, it might be better if a son or daughter with such a phantom father *were* fatherless. If all a child sees of his father is a glimpse in passing, the child may come to develop a very negative view of adult males. A boy in such a situation might reject male endeavors as proper goals, and a girl might come to feel that men are generally not creatures to be valued as human beings.

If a child were truly fatherless, however, he would be more likely to seek out a male model—an older brother or teacher—and might wind up in better shape than the father-neglected child. Thus, you could very well be effectively short-circuiting your child's search for a father figure.

In advocating that you spend time with your child we don't mean that your commitment should be open-ended. Sometimes the more time a father spends with his children the more they will expect. Your children should realize that while you love them and want to be with them, you have just so much time to divide among your wife, your work, your play, and them. Talk to them about the problem if they begin demanding too much. By showing them that you need some independence they will be able to better develop their own independence, and independence is an important quality for a happy life.

With the Baby. Exercise your imagination when taking your child places. As we mentioned previously, there is really no reason both of you can't enjoy an outing on the golf links, with him riding along in your golf cart. The balls, clubs, tees, bags, and carts will be new experiences for him, new toys to learn about. So will your shots and your reactions to them.

One good practice is to keep the baby positioned so he can watch what you're doing, whether it is preparing lunch or typing a letter. In Russia, children's playpens are kept high off the ground when the infant is young and lowered as he begins to stand. An infancy spent looking at feet is not as interesting as one spent watching faces and hands.

Taking care of your child—bathing him (or taking a bath with him), feeding him, and dressing him—can also be a good way to teach him about yourself. The more you can assume these duties, the more the pressure on your wife will be relieved, and the closer you and the baby will become. Though we do advocate your caring for the child when you can, we also realize that we must be realistic about fathers' caring for infants. Child care has never been as major a part of males' experience, as it has been for females. Thus, you may not be as patient, enthusiastic, or as adept at it as your wife, and for this reason and others you may feel uncomfortable about it. Because of your upbringing, you may be more put out by the demands of the baby for nighttime feedings and diaper changes.

Wives can help overcome such discomfort by being encouraging to fathers and being willing to instruct them about child care. Many fathers have never even held a baby and may treat it like a hair-trigger bomb.

One father we know, Sam P., was deathly afraid to touch his new infant daughter, and seemingly ignored her. What his wife didn't know was that when he was young, he had hurt his baby sister and hadn't told his mother about it. He hadn't had any experience with babies since then, and it wasn't until he finally told of the episode that his wife could assure him that his daughter was not going to crumble at his touch.

Barring such traumas, and with patience, mothers can help husbands to be very adept at child care, so that daily care can be a meaningful way for father and infant to learn about each other. But if your wife doesn't feel a burden in caring for the child, and you really are uncomfortable, don't feel guilty about skipping it. Some wives, we might add, may be jealous of their child-care prerogatives. Try not to encroach upon your wife's territory if she is sensitive about it. Better still, try to help her understand the importance of your involvement, perhaps showing her some of the misconceptions mothers have about fathers that we mention in our next chapter, "Father Power, Mother Power."

As with all the other guidelines in this book, we mean these to be only very general—to be modified according to your personality. If you enjoy spending more time with your infant, so much the better for him. But be careful about cutting down your time with the baby. Fathers usually underestimate their child's needs for interaction.

You should also modify how you treat the baby according to his own personality. For instance, one baby may be relatively insensitive to the world around him, showing little reaction to sounds or handling. Another may be very alert to what is going on or to being moved around. If you handled the first baby gently and left him alone when he cried, he would not have enough stimulation to develop to his full potential. If, on the other hand, you handled the sensitive baby often, spoke to him frequently and loudly, he might end up hyperaroused and nervous.

The father-child relationship is a 50-50 proposition. You are getting just as much from your infant in learning about fathering, as he is getting from you in learning about the world. Besides learning the basics of how to care for a baby, you are also discovering what babies are all about—how they learn, how they make mistakes, and how to live with them.

You are learning, perhaps for the first time, that strength

can be mixed with gentleness. All your socializing before fatherhood may have been in being vigorous or aggressive; now you are also learning about nurturance and protectiveness. Hopefully, you will be secure enough in your masculinity not to equate handling a baby gently with being feminine.

Your child will also give you a much greater feeling of the importance of your own life. You are now responsible for the development of another human being, and not just for yourself. Statistics show that married men live longer than single men. While this is certainly due to a raft of complex reasons, the feeling of being needed that fatherhood brings must be one of them.

Fathers' feelings of responsibility and dedication to their children have in some instances determined the very survival of the father. In World War II, letters written by soldiers repeatedly told how fantasizing about their children helped them to overcome hardships and deprivations and increased their resourcefulness in actual danger. Casualty statistics, indeed, showed that single men were more apt to be killed or injured than married ones.

Unfortunately, for fathers today most learning about fatherhood is usually emergency on-the-job training. We hope this book will help you prepare your own children for fatherhood so that they won't need a crash course.

4/ *Father Power,*
Mother Power

So far we have concentrated on your sense of father power—where it stems from and why it is important. But your sense of this must be seen in relation to your wife's sense of mother power. Before we examine how your wife affects your father power, and vice versa, let us take a look at the differences and similarities in your parenthoods.

For instance, your wife's feeling of power as a parent stems in large part from the role she played in carrying the baby within her for nine months, in giving birth to the baby, and in feeding it. A result is that she finds much of her power in her ability to nurture the child and give him a secure environment.

On the other hand, your sense of power as a parent is based less on a physiological connection with the child and more on your sensory awareness of him. Besides being profoundly attracted to the child because you know that he is yours, you perceive him as being like you in many ways, you observe him imitating you, and you sense the effect your attitudes have on him. Your sense of power as a parent is focused on what your child does. You feel more fulfilled by seeing him in action and you know that your power as a father lies in how you affect those actions. Just as you find power in the outside world from what you have built and achieved, so your power in the family comes in your role of "building" the child (or rather, of helping the child "build" himself).

There are also other more seemingly transient differences in mother and father power, differences fostered by our society, which are subject to change.

An obvious difference is the overemphasis in women's lives on the mother's role and the underemphasis in men's lives on the father's role. Little Suzy has had the importance of motherhood practically pounded into her head. On the other hand, little Johnny hears almost nothing about his upcoming role as a father. In fact, he is discouraged from associating with younger children. If Suzy plays with infants, it is seen as "mothering," yet if Johnny does the same, he runs the risk of being called a baby or a sissy.

The upshot is that little Suzy, for whom motherhood will be an intense physiological experience, also has a very intense intellectual preparation for motherhood. In contrast, Johnny, who has no direct physiological attachment to the child, also has no social and intellectual training for the role. And, of course, Johnny may also have seen very little of his own father in a parenting role.

The power today's father does feel in the family is based primarily on his ability to exert general physical control over the child's environment. While Mother tells Johnny what time to eat lunch, it is Father who may make it possible for Johnny to have a lunch in the first place. Today's father feels his power is less an everyday one than an overall one and less a personal one than an economic one.

Obviously, we advocate change in this social component of mother and father power. Mothers should be weaned from the sometimes overintense, day-to-day relationships with their children, and some of these responsibilities should be assumed by fathers. Father power must stem more from the perception of the profound personal impact of fatherhood, rather than the impact of the father's wallet.

THE MYTH OF DOMINANCE

The supposed battle of the sexes has been the preoccupation of many social thinkers in one form or another from time immemorial. Such thinkers are obsessed with the notion that the father-mother relationship is necessarily a question of who dominates whom; this is a huge mistake in today's society. The whole concept of an inevitable "dominance see-saw" in which the dominant parent reduces the power of the other parent is absurd. Although we emphasize the power of the father in this book, we have by no means denied *the power of the mother,* both as a mother and as a woman. Neither do we ignore *the power of the child* to be respected as a human being.

Many social scientists have been preoccupied with a simplistic view of dominance, implying that if one parent is dominant in one area, that means he is dominant in all areas, and conversely the other parent is weak in all areas. Besides defining dominance as an all-or-nothing trait, many social scientists have also defined it in male terms—as an overt, physical trait. While they worry over who wins arguments in the family or who influences whom in family decisions, they miss the more subtle, complex expressions of dominance.

If the father wins arguments, he is thus labeled dominant by the observing researcher, who goes off to tote up his results, missing the fact that often the supposedly submissive mother goes ahead and does what she wants anyway, ignoring the noise of the supposedly dominant male.

Social scientists often ignore the fact that each parent views his marriage relationship differently. As sociologist Jessie Bernard, professor emerita at Penn State University, puts it, each marriage is actually composed of two marriages—the "husband's marriage" and the "wife's marriage." Each of these marriages is a somewhat different reality. Not fully realizing this, the social scientist, asking one parent or another about dominance, may be subjected to an unrealistic view perpetrated on him by the parent looking at his "own" marriage. Indeed, in one study in which parents were asked to answer a questionnaire about their family life, fathers consistently overestimated their dominance, and mothers consistently underestimated theirs. With all these mistakes in concept and interpretation, it is no wonder that some researchers have handed us misleading information about the nature of dominance in the family.

Many social scientists assert that in families in which the father is dominant, the children are happy and secure. And conversely, they say that in families in which the father is not dominant, the children will likely have emotional problems. Their traditional male-oriented definitions of dominance do not allow them to see that what they take to be male-dominated families are actually more of a healthy blend of mother and father power. They also miss the fact that what they perceive as mother dominance generally means father neglect. And their male orientation may cause them to miss signs of maladjustment that crop up in male-overdominated families, leading them to dub male dominance the happiest lot of all families. Actually, a careful look at the research done indicates that both excessive mother or father domination inhibits the child's development. Is it a happy family where the sons are channeled into a stifling, traditional masculinity and the daughters into a straitjacket femininity? Many social scientists apparently think so.

These same social scientists, seeing a shift in the nature of power in the family over the past few decades, declare there has been a shift in the amount of power, because to them the traditional concept of dominance is all there is. For instance, Father's opinions no longer hold sway over a daughter's decision to marry. Traditionalists may see this as a threat to father power, not realizing that the complex, subtle ways a father influences his daughter over her entire lifetime do immensely more to determine whom she marries than a one-shot decision on the father's part.

We know one couple, Bill and Susan P., who got quite caught up in the struggle of who would dominate whom in the family. As it happened, they both had been reading one of those magazine articles about the "battle of the sexes" and got to talking about who was dominant over whom in their family, adopting the simplistic theory of dominance set forth in the article. They began quarreling constantly about even the smallest detail in their lives, each trying to prove he was not the other's slave. Deciding where to go on vacation became a major brawl. Even deciding where to eat was cause for argument. One day they realized what this contest of wills had cost them, when their five-year-old daughter, Suzy, came through the living room with her suitcase during an argument. She declared that she was leaving home because "Nobody loves anybody here anymore." Bill and Susan were horrified and after several long talks began to understand that dominance was a much more complex concept than they had been led to believe.

How should you, the father, view the question of dominance in the family? First of all, unlike Bill and Susan, you should not see your relationship with your wife as a struggle for dominance by one or the other. Rather, you should recognize that each of you will be dominant in a particular set of areas in which you are competent and you will carry relatively equal influence in areas in which neither of you is more competent. There will exist some areas in which you will lead the family and others in which your wife will lead. Because one of you is dominant, though, the other is not necessarily "submissive"; you are merely deferring to the other's greater competence, while maintaining a right to have your own opinions heard. It is merely a question of division of labor along the most advantageous lines. Each of you has power.

Many of these areas of father and mother competence are relatively constant in all marriages. For instance, you will probably always have a sense of physical dominance, because you probably are more muscular. On the other hand, your wife might be the better diplomat, able to stem neighborhood conflicts, perhaps because females seem to respond more sensitively to other people.

Both you and your wife should realize where areas of dominance lie, and the dominant parent should not only take care to see that the child gets the advantage of his power in that area, but also help the parent who is not as proficient in a particular area.

Each marriage is composed of two people who have a

unique fingerprint of abilities. Don't let your fatherhood be
hemmed in by popular concepts of masculinity or femininity
or by what other parents do. If you don't like to fish and your
wife does, let her take your child fishing. If you like art and
your wife doesn't, you be the one to take your child to art
galleries.

MOTHER, THE FATHER-DEFINER

Your wife usually has a greater role in defining you to your
children than you have in defining her. Unless your wife is a
career woman and away as much as you, your children may
have to depend considerably on how she describes you to
them. Hopefully, as you realize the importance of father
power, this will change. You will increase your time with your
children, and they will not be forced to accept a secondhand
interpretation of you.

One basis for your wife's high valuation of you as a father
can be her high esteem for you as a husband. The happier the
marriage, the better the father's relationship with his children
is likely to be. This is partly because the mother lets the kids
know directly and indirectly that "Dad's okay." Boys feel that
they have their mother's blessing to identify with Dad and use
him as a model for masculinity. Girls feel that it's all right to
value Dad as the kind of man they would like to have a deep
relationship with when they grow up. Daughter also feels that
she is not a rival for Mom's affections with Dad and can safely
have that innocent flirtation with him that daughters have
with their fathers.

There is also the possibility that a mother's evaluation of a
father may become a self-fulfilling prophecy. For instance, if
she says to the children essentially, "Dad's a rat," the children
may come to believe her and begin to withdraw their affection
from him. Because he probably is not home as much, Dad
doesn't have as much chance to defend himself against the
charge and comes to feel that he has irretrievably lost his
children. He decides all is lost and that there is nothing he can

do except immerse himself in his work or spend his time with his cronies or even other women. Voila! Dad has fulfilled his wife's evaluation of him and become a "rat."

Of course, the dangers of your wife blatantly devaluing you to the child are obvious. "Well, our father isn't really that successful," or, "He doesn't come home because he doesn't care about you as much as I do" are some of the comments we have heard mothers make. Certainly, your wife should avoid this pitfall.

But the way our society is set up, your wife may fall prey to many traps she doesn't recognize simply because of how she was taught to view fatherhood. Because most mothers were once daughters in homes where father power was not appreci-ated, your wife may be the victim of several kinds of misconceptions about you, all of which cause her to devalue you unconsciously and subtly to your children. The miscon-ceptions we have detected we shall call "My Husband Only," "My Hero," "My Father," "My Mechanic," and "My Checkbook."

"My Husband Only." Your wife has been subject to the same lack of information about the nature and importance of fatherhood that you have. The lack of information about fatherhood in our society has likely discouraged her from thinking of fatherhood as an important role for you. The traditional women's media especially extol the virtues of motherhood and homemaking, which is fine, but pointedly exclude the father from the family circle. The result is that many wives simply do not think of their husbands as also being fathers. When considering a man as a prospective husband, his role as father usually does not even enter her mind, except for a brief "You want to have children, don't you?" during courtship.

"My Hero." To some wives, their husbands are the slayers of societal dragons, the protectors of the household. Thus the wife must assume her place as squire to the knight when the father comes home from a hard day's work. "Leave Daddy alone, he's tired from work," or, "Stay out of the basement while Daddy's working" is their admonishment to their children.

They appear with a martini in hand, shooing the children out to ease their husband's mind, not realizing that children are a proud obligation to which husbands as well as wives must adjust.

"My Father." Many women entering marriageable age today may have been brought up among remnants of the patriarchal fatherhood of the past. They may have been taught a concept of femininity that casts them in the role of being dependent upon men. It is only natural, then, that when such women marry, they take husbands on whom they can lean and who will protect them from the buffeting winds of society. Along come children, and the woman becomes a mother; but the man does not become a father to her children in her eyes. Rather, he remains *her* father, and she becomes extremely jealous of her children when he relates to them.

The problem of the pathologically dependent woman is rare, but the more subtly dependent woman is much more common, and so is the subtle resentment of fatherhood. You should support such a wife in becoming capable of independence, but you should not let such demands interfere with your duty to interact with your children.

By helping your own daughter to develop her independence and self-confidence, as we have described, you can thus indirectly help the next generation of fathers.

Among married couples at present men tend to be older, more intelligent, and more highly educated than their wives. As Dr. Judith Bardwick in her provocative book *The Psychology of Women* points out, this is the generally accepted standard of both men and women. So inured are we to these "required" differences that the man who is shorter, younger, or less educated than his wife is often looked on with subtle and not-so-subtle disdain by others. This is just another indication of the extent to which women look for "fathers" to marry. To some extent such an attitude will never change, just as some men will always tend to look for women like their mothers, but it is clearly overdone in our society.

"My Mechanic." The fact that men in our society tend to be thought of as the members of the family who are the fixers, the

builders, and the planners leads many wives to ignore or downplay the male interpersonal role. After the industrial revolution in this country, the male was increasingly the creature of the factory and the female the creature of the home, as father went from being a farmer to being a factory worker. And just as women came to be thought of totally as the experts on family relations, men came to be thought of totally as the experts on dealing with machines and analytical concepts. Your wife is quite likely influenced by this prejudice. "Dad is great for showing Freddy or Mary Jane about motors but doesn't really know how to understand their moods," she may say. Thus, Mother takes over these functions, cutting off a valuable source of emotional satisfaction for Dad.

"My Checkbook." As a national survey of high school girls revealed not long ago, most women still choose their mates principally on the basis of how well they will do in the world of careers and bank accounts. When asked to rate the qualities they look for in a husband, the girls tended to put ambition at the top of the list, followed by honesty and physical attractiveness.

According to Dr. Bardwick, when asked what they look for in husbands, young women usually list a whole raft of achievement-oriented traits—getting ahead, being ambitious, enjoying work, being energetic, and having a high-status profession. Women obviously put such a high premium on outside success and such a low one on being a good father that when fatherhood rolls around, the wives may be little concerned whether the father is involved. They may even be a little apprehensive if a man "lowers" himself to making father power a focus of his life.

One extreme case of such emphasis on the father-as-moneybags was that of Phyllis W., who often met her daughter's request for money with, "Ask your father; he's the one who makes the money in this family." Phyllis also consistently complained that her husband didn't make enough money. Henry learned about this case because it was Phyllis's daughter who came in for help after experiencing three broken marriages. She said, "My mother always told me that it was important that a man keep you well supported, but I guess she was wrong."

Father's Misconceptions. Ironically, misconceptions that you, the father, have about motherhood can injure your father power as well. If you see your wife as your mother, "your second-in-command," or "the chief childraiser," you will hinder yourself from being an effective father.

If she is "your mother," you may feel that she should take care of both you and the children and that you don't have a responsibility to your children. If she is "your second-in-command," you may believe that you don't need to have a direct relationship with your children, but can raise them through her. If she is "the chief childraiser," you may think you don't need to have any role to play with your children, direct *or* indirect.

Mothers "Defending" Motherhood. Mothers can also see themselves as the chief childraiser in the family, which of course hinders the expression of father power. Because of our mother-oriented tradition, mothers have come to believe that motherhood is their life, their crowning glory. The raising of children is a mission above all others. It's only natural, then, that when somebody comes along to interfere with the precious mother-child dyad, they resent it.

Women who define themselves exclusively in terms of motherhood frequently become quite defensive when confronted with the fact of a father power that equals their own in importance. Such mothers can often be recognized by their extreme hesitance in allowing their children to be independent. They often resist fiercely their son's or daughter's going out into the world, because they are mothers first and foremost and often because they don't have much of a relationship with their husbands.

Two recent major developments have helped to change this child-centeredness of women and have made more room for the father in the family. These developments are the advent of the working mother and the rise of the Women's Liberation movement.

THE WORKING MOTHER

In 1960 about 19 percent of mothers with preschool children worked, according to the U.S. Bureau of Labor Statistics. By 1972 this had risen to over 45 percent. In 1960 about 39 percent of mothers with school-aged children worked. By 1972 this had risen to over 57 percent.

This increase in the percentage of working mothers can have a definite positive impact on the family. It diffuses the intense mother-child relationship, allowing the mother to define herself in terms other than motherhood. Also important, the working mother can give the father an opportunity for a close one-to-one relationship with his children that was not as easy to come by before. Before the advent of the working mother, the father was less likely to be with the child when the mother wasn't there. She was almost ubiquitous—home when he arrived from work and always with the family on outings. Only irregularly, during trips to the hardware store or father-child camping trips, for instance, did the father get to be alone with the child. And these instances weren't especially promoting of a deep father-child understanding because of the distractions of all that hardware or of a weekend in the woods.

If Mother works, however, and it falls to Father to care for the children, he gets a chance to be alone with the child for considerable periods in the familiar home setting. One study found that one-fifth of all child-care arrangements made to aid working mothers are fathers, a promising development if fathers realize their father power.

There's always the chance, too, that the child might get to spend the time between the end of the school day and the end of the work day in Dad's or Mom's place of work, learning that mothers and fathers are competent creatures outside the home. And fathers might get to show their children that they can be competent within the home, fixing meals and cleaning house, helping to share the burden with the working mother.

Some husbands have balked at giving their blessing to their

wives' careers, fearing that it would endanger the child's development in some way. Actually, working wives can much better balance their work and their motherhood than husbands can balance their work and fatherhood. Unlike fathers, they are more likely to be confident in their parent power. Working doesn't in itself harm a woman's motherhood. In fact, the increased happiness of the mother who wants to work and enjoys her job may increase her effectiveness as a mother.

Children with working mothers are as a group similar to children of nonworking mothers in terms of emotional, intellectual, and physical development. Such children show as much attachment to their mothers as children of mothers who are housewives. This is mainly because the mother who goes off to work everyday is likely to realize that her children definitely need a period of playing with her and being with her when she gets home, and she allows for this. In fact, the child may get even more out of the working Mom than out of the housewife Mom, who may not really feel the need to interact as positively with her child. After all, she may feel, she is always at home anyway.

The fact that the working mother can be a very effective parent while still spending time away from home supports our contention that fathers can combine father power and career power.

How Fathers Can Help Working Mothers. The working mother, immediately after she has had a baby, may be in a state of indecision about her career, and you can help her to make the happiest choice.

For instance, if she looks strictly at the economic aspects of work, things may seem bleak. The income she earns may get absorbed by the new expenses of child care. But her career may be more than a source of money; it may be a source of pride for her as an effective person. Tell her she should value her career for how good it makes her feel and not just for the money she earns.

Both of you should be involved in looking for day care for the baby. Make sure you both visit the setting and talk to other parents who have children there before making a decision. Try to find a setting close to where one or both of you work so you can visit during your work day. Don't feel you have to settle for an institutional day-care center, where babies and children may be treated as little more than parts on an assembly line. You might want to form a small baby-care cooperative with a few other families—fathers as well as mothers—so that your child will be cared for with more attention and personal commitment.

Generally, it is best for you to take primary responsibility for the care of your baby, and for the care to be given in your own home. Neither you nor your wife should be reticent about presenting your special needs to your employer; you should explain to her or him that you may need special time off or will want to work unconventional hours or even bring the child to work with you occasionally. Most essential, realize that your fatherhood is as important as your career.

FATHER AND WOMEN'S LIBERATION

In calling for the liberation of women from the discrimination against them in society and for liberation from an unfair portion of the childraising burden, women are in effect calling for greater father involvement. The relationship between the Women's Liberation movement and what we hope will be a father-power movement is clear. Because the father has such an important role in socializing his children, he can affect how daughters can take advantage of greater opportunities in society and how sons react to such social changes. And, obviously, by assuming his responsibility in childraising, the father can help today's woman take advantage of greater opportunities without creating problems for the family.

The nature of Women's Liberation has been discussed thoroughly in other books, so we shall not go over the same ground. But we shall discuss what we think are the pitfalls and advantages it offers the father and the father-mother relationship.

One of the effects of women's greater involvement in society is a lessening of the emphasis on woman-as-mother. This is good in that it will relieve some of the enormous pressure on women to become mothers and to define themselves solely in terms of childraising.

But this redefinition could be dangerous if fathers see it as creating a vacuum in childraising into which they will be sucked against their will. Your and your wife's attitude toward her role outside the family can head off this danger.

Your Attitude. If your wife wants to work, to continue her education, or to become more involved in society, don't see it as an increased burden on you. Rather, realizing the enormous need for fathering in our society, you should see it as an opportunity for you as a father as well as for her as a woman. While she is gaining an opportunity to be more flexible in her choice of life-style, you are gaining an opportunity for close interaction with your child in a one-to-one relationship. The danger of your wife's subtly resenting your father involvement is lessened because she is gaining a greater confidence in herself as a well-rounded person and not just as a mother. As we said in the section on the working mother, there is a very low probability that your child will be harmed by spending time away from his mother. In fact, the child could be greatly helped by periods in which each parent has the child to himself.

Her Attitude. The mother's attitude toward branching out from the family should also take your feelings about fatherhood into account. Although we have seen heartening signs that more men are taking increasing pride in their fatherhood and becoming voluntarily involved with their children, this is not always the case. Your wife needs to recognize that your upbringing may not have prepared you for instant involvement as a father. She should not allow the rhetoric of Women's Liberation to cloud the fact that there may be human obstacles to be dealt with on both your parts.

The major danger to fatherhood from Women's Liberation lies in the gulf between rhetoric and human reality. Women's Liberationists state that the equality of men and women is their goal, but equality is too often seen in mathematical terms and not in human ones. Women's liberation also means men's liberation.

Men and women should be given a great deal of leeway to define what they want to be. Unfortunately, some feminists are trying to put women into a straitjacket of expectations just as restrictive as the one women are trying to escape from now.

This straitjacket attitude may mean, for instance, that the father is expected to treat sons and daughters alike. For reasons we will discuss later, sons and daughters may mean different things to a father, and demanding strictly "equal" treatment may be unrealistic.

Fathers may also be unrealistically expected to become involved with their children in the same way as mothers. Whether because of the way they are socialized or, more profoundly, the kinds of creatures they are, fathers will remain somewhat different parents from mothers.

Father's Effect on Mother

Though this book is primarily about the father and his effects on his children, we should touch on the effects that you have on your wife's mother power. We do this mainly to illustrate the complex web of family relationships. You not only affect your children directly, but also indirectly in the way you affect their mother. Good fathering also means good husbanding.

Father as Supporter. Just as your wife should show your children that she values you, to aid your father power as a model, so you should show that you value her. If she is to be an effective model of femininity to your daughter and a general model for your son, she must have dignity and value in their eyes. When your children see that you listen to your wife's opinions and value her counsel, they will be more likely to value her themselves.

This does not mean that you and your wife have to present a united front to the child. Too many men come home from work ready for an evening with the children only to find themselves drawn into a mother-child squabble, in which the father is expected to side with the mother. Disagreeing with your wife because of legitimate differences will not hurt her mother power and will conversely aid your child's sense of power.

Father as Liberator. A close father-child relationship is one of the principal liberators of the mother. Because of the incredible importance that has been attached to motherhood in our society and the lack of importance attached to fatherhood, too many mothers fear to strike out into new fields, feeling that their children will be harmed. In talking about the working mother we stressed the value to you, as a father, of having a working wife, because it may give you more opportunities to have special times with your child. But having confidence in her husband as a father can also do a great deal for the wife seeking liberation. It can allow her to pursue goals outside the home guiltlessly. And if you also truly encourage her activities outside the home, she will be much happier knowing her activities are valued by someone she loves.

Father as Separator. In the paragraph above, we were talking about women who wanted to achieve outside the home. But there are those who do not need outside achievement, and of these there are many who become too close, too mothering, to their children. This is not their fault but more likely the result of having had parents who channeled them into a narrow view of femininity or the result of reacting to the popular view of society that women are only mothers. You can help bring this kind of sMothering into balance by being conscious of your father power. You may have to overcome some of the misconceptions we just cited that mothers have about fatherhood, but helping your wife to realize that you have a legitimate and necessary role with the child could diffuse an overbearing mother-child relationship.

FATHER-MOTHER SEXUALITY AND THE CHILD

The marital sexual relationship is principally a husband-wife matter. However, it actually has a profound effect on your father power, just as do most other parts of the marital relationship.

If, for instance, you suffer from impotence, it can affect not only your relationship with your wife but also your relationship with your child. Some fathers with sexual problems become defensively hostile toward their children or avoid them because of a sense of shame about their problem.

Realizing the effects sexual problems may have on your fatherhood should give you and your wife even greater impetus to seek professional help. More than two lives can be ruined if these problems are neglected.

You and your wife's more indirect expressions of sexual attraction also affect your child. Your complimenting (or insulting) of each other's physical appearance and the way you hug, kiss, and express affection for one another will make an impression on your child. Your child can gain a sense of security and develop a positive model of male-female affection living in a family where there is a close, warm marital relationship.

Occasionally, what you do not even perceive as a sexual *problem* may affect your child. We know one couple, Carl and Judy E., who prided themselves on having an open, honest sexual relationship. They abhorred inhibitions and often approached one another sexually in front of their daughter, who was four. The child was confused by this sexuality and not sure about how she was supposed to react to it. She knew her parents were "different" from those of her friends because she never saw any of them engaging in sexual play.

Though sexuality is, of course, nothing to be ashamed of and ought to be accepted comfortably, these "liberated" parents created just as much anxiety in their child by flaunting their sexuality. In wanting to bring their child up "right," the parents were as rigid as the prudes they rejected. In a later chapter, we shall discuss the fostering of healthy sexual development in children in much more detail.

BATTLE OF THE GIANTS

Arguing with your child, if done correctly, can help him intellectually and emotionally. Arguing with your wife, if used properly, can also be a way to teach your child about human relationships. Hopefully, both your and your wife's arguments take into account a basic equality in your relationship.

To be constructive, your arguments should aim at resolving some solvable dispute—who should take out the garbage or whether the latest congressional environmental bill is a good one. As has been said many times before, your arguments should not be aimed at reducing the other person's power—denigrating him or trying to make him admit a basic inadequacy.

If your arguments are useful ones, don't hide them from your child. If little Jimmy gets sent out to buy an ice-cream cone every time there is a family storm brewing, he may grow up thinking that married life consists completely of sweetness, light, and lots of ice cream for the children. He will not know that arguing and resolving issues is a normal part of a marriage between two respecting, power-confident people.

Parents who try to hide arguments may not be successful, despite the lure of ice-cream parlors. Their children grow up believing argument is dangerous, to be feared, to be hidden behind closed doors—not a very good way to give a child a secure upbringing.

But exposing your child to your arguments also has its pitfalls. Younger children have much more difficulty understanding what the raised voices of an argument signify. They may not grasp that you and your wife are not irreparably damaging your relationship by arguing. So be more circumspect in your arguments in front of your younger children than, say, in front of your teen-agers. Explain to your youngsters, "Daddy and Mommy are just disagreeing. Grownups sometimes get mad at each other, just like kids do." Hug and kiss them so they will have concrete evidence of their security.

A more subtle danger in arguing is that the child may sense that mother and father disagree, not just on the topic on hand, but on the basic attitude toward their children and child-raising. As we've said, you and your wife don't have to present a Maginot line of agreement to your children. Just agree basically on your philosophy toward them. Thus, your child will feel secure in knowing that he has a firm basis, though not a rock-hard one, on which to deal with his parents.

Fathers should be particularly aware of the image they present to their children during arguments. Your wife is perhaps more intimately familiar to your child. She is the one who is around more often to bandage knees and chase away scary dogs and cuddle more. While you are exciting and interesting to your child, you are also more capable of producing anxiety in him. Children generally picture their fathers as larger, darker, stronger, more punitive, and more dangerous than their mothers.

Imagine how you would feel if someone twice your height and four times your weight became angry in front of you. You would feel quite anxious. Thus, during arguments, take a moment with the child to reassure him, "Daddy's angry, but don't be afraid." Realize your father power.

Although this is not a marriage manual, we do offer a few specific guidelines on arguing:

Think of your argument as a debate in which each person presents his side without interruption from the other. But unlike a debate, always explore the possibility of compromise, so that nobody loses.

If the argument is not about a personal matter between you and your wife, let the kids join in and listen to their side of the argument. In fact, many arguments, such as those involving whether little Johnny can go to a movie or whether the family spends too much money, should by all rights involve the children.

Also, when you argue, keep in mind that your children will probably grow up to argue in the same manner. Remembering this could be the best help of all to your argument and to your marriage.

FATHER POWER AND THE CHILD'S DEVELOPMENT

5 / Father, Masculinity, and Femininity

In aiding your child's emotional development, you should have two goals in mind above all others. These goals will help your child to develop into a successful adult and should be your aim regardless of whether your child is male or female, slim or muscular, intellectually brilliant or below average, sensitive and quiet or an earth-shaker.

Competence. The first goal is that of competence—which means that *your child has learned to use his abilities to their fullest, to be proud of what he can do, and not to be crushed by what he cannot do.*

Father is usually the parent most concerned with having his offspring fare well in the outside world, since this has traditionally been his own arena for displaying competence. But many times Father has limited aid or encouragement to his children because of their sex, economic class or race. We've all too often heard a father say, "I wish my kid could make it, but after all (she's a girl, we're too poor, he's black)."

To use your father power to help your child thrive in society you will have to rid yourself of stereotypes and take a hard look at what your child really is and what society really is.

Let's take the cases of two high school boys, Ralph and Jimmy, to illustrate how fathers sometimes fail to help their children aim at true competence:

Ralph had a ball in high school. He was popular at parties, an accomplished football player, and a sought-after friend by the other boys. When asked whether he was happy, Ralph answered with a resounding yes. Jimmy, however, was not a very popular boy in high school. He also enjoyed a close circle of friends but was more interested in debating and in the math club than in athletics. He acted in the class play and was a member of the band; his instrument was the flute.

Ralph and Jimmy both had about the same grades in high school and had fathers who were very successful and respected. However, a major difference between them was in their relationships with their fathers. Ralph's father was proud of his son and often rooted for him at football games but didn't see much of him otherwise. He taught his son that men were strong and aggressive but left it at that. Jimmy's father spent time learning about Jimmy's activities, going places with him, and simply talking with him about subjects as diverse as "shoes and ships and sealing wax, and cabbages and kings," as he would say. He taught his son that masculinity was a complex thing to be worked out by each person individually and that Jimmy should have confidence in what he felt was masculine.

Though Ralph was more successful socially in high school than Jimmy, when these two boys went out into the world, there was an abrupt reversal. Ralph took a few semesters of college work and dropped out. After basking in the glories of high school, he felt ignored in the larger world of college and work. Because he thought that being a man meant being tough and nonintellectual, he "didn't give a damn about all those sissy professors." He became a sour man, believing that the world was out of step with what he thought it should be.

Jimmy, however, blossomed. After four years of hard work at college, during which he also went out for the soccer team, Jimmy went on to law school and ended up as a public-interest lawyer.

Our point is that there was little difference in these two boys' intellectual abilities. The difference was in how their fathers had taught them to think about being competent men. Ralph learned to believe that only football playing and partying were masculine, and as a masculine, popular boy, the world owed him something. Jimmy learned that masculinity meant mainly confidence in himself and that it didn't rule out being a thinking, sensitive person.

We're not saying that football players will be unhappy in later life or that members of math clubs will be happy. What we are saying is that regardless of how outwardly successful a boy or girl may be, if he isn't taught what competence as a male or female really means, he is likely to end up very unhappy. Ralph was a failure in his own eyes because he adopted a crude, narrow caricature of masculinity. His father did not give him a close model of masculinity. His simplified version of masculinity became rapidly outmoded in the adult world.

It's extremely important in aiding your child's competence that you help him value and express his individuality. Ralph, for instance, liked to draw, but after a comment by his father that he was afraid Ralph was liable to become one of those "faggy artsy types," Ralph lost interest in art.

Another example of keeping a child from expressing his individuality is the woman who feels she *has* to become a mother because her parents teach her that motherhood is the crowning and sole glory of a woman.

Fathers particularly make the prevalent mistake of not aiming their child toward the expression of his own individual competence because of the sex of the child. Never tell your child "little boys always . . ." or "little girls don't . . ." Define your statements to your child in terms of the child as a unique person and not simply in terms of boy or girl.

Encouraging your child to be competent means using your sense of father power in even the most minor ways and not just in profound heart-to-heart talks or in helping the child make major decisions about his life.

For instance, Dennis remembers, one day while riding the bus to work, seeing a father board with his two small daughters. The father set his large briefcase beside him for the ride into work, and when he got up, one of his daughters, a tiny child of five, grabbed it to carry it for him. Even though it was quite large, he allowed her to carry it, watching her solicitously as she conscientiously lugged her Daddy's briefcase down the steps of the bus. Only when she had proudly accomplished this favor to her father and handed him the briefcase did the father accept it, thanking his daughter.

This father could have taken the briefcase from his daughter, as most fathers might have, and thought little of it. But he realized that this would have robbed his daughter of a chance to show her Daddy, a highly accomplished person in her eyes, that she too could *do* things.

Security. Helping your child toward competence is closely related to the other major goal of your father power—that of security. You should keep in mind that children tend to perceive fathers as more frightening than mothers. You are bigger and more imposing than your wife, and you can inspire more fear in your youngster. So, you have the potential of damaging your child's security more.

But, by the same token, you also have the potential to help your child's security a great deal. If your child understands that his imposing, competent father is on his side, protecting him—and especially, physically comforting and loving him— he will derive a great deal of security.

Besides feeling that he has a secure place in the world from which to explore, your child also needs to feel secure about himself. He must have a high valuation of himself as a person, a valuation that you can help him develop. You are a very awe-inspiring parent, and if you show that you think your child is a great fellow, he will come to think so too. And conversely, you can show your child that you think any misbehaviors, failures, or cases of lack of confidence are temporary lapses and not the result of a basic flaw in his personality. He will come to have pride in what he is, not shame in what he is not.

Helping your child to feel secure in his place in the world and in how he defines himself is no easy task. Some people struggle all their lives with threats to their security, both physical and mental. Obesity, lack of attractiveness, inferiority complexes, and timidity are some of the unscalable mountains in many persons' lives. Try not to do anything that would harm your child's security about himself; don't create such mountains. For example, don't criticize your child for being clumsy; rather play games with him that help develop his coordination.

SEX ROLE, BASIC TO PERSONALITY DEVELOPMENT

Fathers today—and mothers as well—are having particular problems sorting out their feelings about relationships between the sexes.

Sex role—one's masculinity or femininity—seems a very simple thing to most people. To determine your masculinity or femininity, simply look down when you're in the shower, they say. From that determination, they believe, one knows everything needed to get along in society as a man or a woman.

But sex role goes beyond the mere presence of male or female genitals. Sex role determines many of the ways a person feels about himself, builds a life-style, and gets along with others. This triangle of sex-typed feeling, preference, and acting combines to serve as a basic force in a person's life, often being a major determinant of whom he marries, what job he takes, what hobbies he likes, what movies he sees. Obviously, if he is happy in this basic aspect of his life, the other pieces will more likely fall into place.

Incidentally, possessing a secure masculinity or femininity means being happily male or female—*maleness and femaleness are biological; masculinity and femininity are psychological* and are culturally determined.

Unfortunately, we have been so preoccupied by the appearance of the two sexes that we have not really understood what masculinity or femininity actually is. We have become hung up on the obvious differences in physique, genitals, and hormones and have not really thought deeply about the real relationship between the sexes.

The extent of our fixation on sex differences shows in our use of the term "the opposite sex." Males and females are in no way opposites. In using this term, we automatically assume differences that are by no means clear-cut.

You, as a parent, need a realistic idea of the meaning of sex roles in society if your child is to be a functioning, happy adult. You, as a father, should be particularly sensitive to the impact of sex roles, for, as we shall discuss later, you traditionally have been the parent most concerned about masculinity or femininity in your offspring.

The popular stereotypes of sex roles are largely if not completely defined by cultural expectations. However, such expectations are very rigid and if taken literally can greatly inhibit the full development of the individual. On a psychological level, masculinity and femininity are not the simple contrasts we popularly picture them to be—aggressive-timid, independent-dependent, demanding-nurturant. Unmasculinity is not the same as femininity, and vice versa. An unmasculine man or unfeminine woman is a person who is basically insecure with his or her body, insecure in his or her sex role. Thus, an unmasculine man can appear quite masculine, but he may be overcompensating for this feeling of inferiority. On the other hand, a very securely masculine man may appear outwardly effeminate.

The relationship between masculinity and femininity can be thought of as two overlapping bubbles. In the large, shared portion of the bubbles are the many traits that both sexes need to be happy, fulfilled individuals. Assertiveness, sensitivity, independence, and nurturance are all in this middle portion. The traits that are uniquely male or female, which we will talk about later, are in the unshared volumes of the bubbles. Unshared traits include the more obvious facets of masculinity and femininity. Males, with their larger muscles, more often involve themselves in strenuous sports and enjoy competitive physical contact. Females, with their profound hormonal changes during pregnancy, may experience an enormous wave of love at the sight of their newborn. However, a person is much more than these simple body-defined traits. We are a whole complex of interconnected traits within the sphere of our sex.

The truly happy person is one whose array of traits can fill out his sphere of masculinity or femininity in a relatively complete way, including the shared portion of the bubbles. The unhappy person may be one who restricts himself mainly to the small portion of the sphere allotted to his sex alone—the locker-room fellow or the compulsive "sMother."

As in our bubble model, in real life you cannot neatly separate masculinity from femininity. They are not mutually exclusive compartments but are merely two facets of humanity, closely intertwined.

Sex and Society. Besides helping your child to have good feelings about being male or female, in helping him deal with his sex role you must also inform him about society's somewhat rigid expectations of behavior of males and females—what we term "sexual signposts." For instance, you might tell your son that most people in society consider it unmasculine for a boy to take ballet lessons or to baby-sit. You might tell your daughter that most people consider it unfeminine for a girl to go out for football, to fight, or to go hunting.

But at the same time, you can support both your sons and daughters, helping them to be confident to undertake an activity that doesn't fit popular sex-typed notions. You act as a realistic reflection of attitudes they may meet in society, but also as a giver of confidence to enable them to cope with these attitudes and maintain a basic security in their masculinity or femininity.

Unfortunately, many in our society take such sexual signposts as important bastions, to be defended unto the death. They may associate the length of a person's hair with the functioning of his genitals and rail against long hair on men, fearing it as some contagious, castrating disease. Fathers are especially prone to a sort of sexual panic, prevalent nowadays. They are frequently among those who issue ominous warnings about the danger of sexual neutralization in our society because of new life-styles of young men and women. This is absurd. Today's changes in the definition of masculinity and femininity are occurring principally because many people are becoming more sophisticated—they are realizing the depths of personality beyond physical differences. They are also reacting to the unhappiness that the definitions of the Tarzan-male and Jane-female have caused. Much to the horror of some traditionalists, many people, young and old, are realizing that their masculinity or femininity need not be defined outside their own bodies—that what they think and feel can act as a good guide to what masculinity and femininity should be.

Throughout this book we stress that you should treat your child as an individual, regardless of his sex, etc. You should always aim for competence and security. But this doesn't mean you should not be conscious of what your child may tend toward because of his sex or other traits. We want to prepare you to deal with what seem to be average variations among people, not to give you preconceived notions of what your particular child will be like.

Keep in mind that male-female distinctions are usually no more nor less important to a child's psychology than individual differences, independent of sex. The chubby child is different from the slim child, just as the male child is from the female child.

Though many psychologists are strongly convinced that there are basic biological sex differences in male and female personalities, they are not at all sure how much these basic contrasts contribute to overall sex differences in our society and how much is caused by the divergence in how males and females are treated. But even if there were almost no differences in basic male and female personalities, the distinction between the physiques of males and females could contribute to differences in personality.

And to further complicate it all, sex differences may become greater with age. A baby boy or girl may not contrast nearly so much with each other as a grown man and woman do. After all, the grown-ups have gone through puberty, and the woman may undergo certain additional basic physical and psychological changes upon becoming a mother that may affect her personality. (Though fathers, of course, undergo no physical changes due to childbirth, they too may be changed by becoming fathers, as we have seen.)

So with all these complications, let's plunge into the murky world of sex differences.

Sex and Hormones. We shall start at one of the bases of sex differences—the biochemical variations between men and women. Much of maleness and of femaleness is determined by delicate balances of two kinds of sex hormones, androgens and estrogens.

Though androgens are often called the "male" hormones and estrogens the "female" hormones, both sexes produce both kinds. It is the *predominance* of one or the other that creates male or female sex characteristics—genitals, body hair, voice characteristics, or breast development.

Those who contend that these hormones irrefutably determine the personalities of men or women are wrong. This includes those who contend that the hormones that tend to make men more naturally aggressive than women also make them more fit to "make it" in the world; just as wrong is the assertion that because changes in female estrogen levels during the monthly menstrual cycle make women more subject to mood swings, this makes them unreliable in the business, political, or social world. Actually, levels of male and female hormones are very much influenced by one's surroundings. Both men and women may perform completely differently from what is popularly believed their hormones "dictate," depending on the circumstances.

Male monkeys placed in a cage full of females experience a sharp rise in androgen levels as they "see their duty and do it." When these same monkeys are placed in cages of other males where they have to compete with other monkeys and often lose their positions as king of the cage, their male-hormone levels plummet.

Among females, hormones are also very much influenced by outside circumstances. For instance, sexually interested women taking birth control pills, which are basically synthetic female hormones, normally experience a swelling of breasts and shorter and more regular menstrual cycles. However, women who are passive sexually, and possibly resentful about sex, often report much different symptoms when taking the pill: their breasts might shrink, their menstrual periods become less regular.

Fear of pregnancy often causes women to have delayed menstrual periods, and women under extreme pressure, such as inmates in World War II prison camps, many times completely cease menstruating. Menstruation is dependent on the regular cycle of changes in estrogen levels in women's bodies.

These are just a few examples. What they all mean is that one's anatomy is not one's destiny. A man's or woman's hormone level is not fixed and immutable, but constantly reflecting what is happening to that man or woman. So, although male and female hormones do appear to affect behavior and physical development, it is a mistake to picture hormones as chemical straitjackets for men or women.

Though there are many physical similarities in men and women, the average male and the average female have definitely distinct physiques, other than the basic genital differences, largely because of divergences in sex-hormone balance. Adult men usually have more well-developed muscles, larger bones, lungs, and heart, and more red blood corpuscles per unit of blood. They are *on the average* taller and heavier than women. Women usually have larger pelvises, to allow the head of the baby to pass through the birth canal. Their layer of fatty tissue beneath the skin allows for thermal protection of the fetus, and their fuller breasts aid in feeding the newborn baby.

Though, as we said, the average adult male is bigger and stronger than the average adult female, in the case of children this is not necessarily true. Boys lag behind girls in many areas of development, including physical development—although boys are more active than girls even when young. Boys continue to grow, however, after girls stop, and they reach their larger mature size three to five years later.

Differences Before and Shortly After Birth. Besides being responsible for sex differences after birth, sex hormones also appear to act on the human brain before birth to produce sex-typed predispositions. These hormones appear to produce actual physical differences in the hypothalamuses of male and female brains before birth. This region in the base of the brain controls a major part of the human hormonal system—the delicate surges of chemicals that do everything from building strong bones to maintaining a supply of sugar in the blood adequate for the body's energy needs. Since there is evidence that men and women differ in the function of their hypothalamuses, there is reason to suppose that their brains may differ in other ways.

Experiments with some animal fetuses have shown that the mere presence or absence of male sex hormones in the early stages of prenatal development is enough to produce male or female animals. For instance, when one scientist injected pregnant rhesus monkeys with male hormones, the female offspring were either masculinized or a freakish male-female combination. Significantly, these female offspring were much more rough-and-tumble than other normal females, even to the point of threatening other monkeys and mounting them sexually like males.

Though monkeys are subject to social and parental pressures too, we can look upon them to some extent as "natural" illustrators of early male-female differences. Within a month after birth, male rhesus monkeys are vigorously pushing, biting, and tugging at their fellows. Females, however, avoid such confrontations, turning their heads away when challenged to fight by a young male. Male monkeys achieve independence from their mothers more quickly than females and are generally more active. The females are more likely to caress, while males are more likely to initiate rough-and-tumble play.

Similar differences have been observed in male and female human infants by the second year of life. Certainly, in both monkeys and human infants, parents can influence the degree of sex-typed behavior. However, we have to recognize that the infants' biologically predisposed behavior can also very much influence the reactions of their parents.

The point we want to make in this discussion is that biology gives maleness or femaleness a definite nudge. It is up to the parents to prepare the child to cope with those nudges and to accept what they bring.

It is not the duty of the parents to try to funnel the child into what *they* think masculinity or femininity *should* be.

THE FATHER'S MASCULINITY AND HIS CHILDREN

Before you can do a proper job of fostering your children's development as successful human beings, you must first sort out your own feelings about your masculinity and its relationship to children and your father power. If, as we suggested earlier, you have thoughtfully reflected upon your childhood, including your relationship with your own father, you should have more insight into what kind of man you have become.

There is much pressure on today's man to define his masculinity in terms of his job or economic value to his family. For the best development of your fatherhood, you should resist these pressures to narrowly define your role. Regardless of whether your job pays $6,000 or $600,000 per year, whether you are the bottom man in a company or the top, you should never be satisfied to define yourself solely in terms of your job. Always think of yourself as a multifaceted person—a father, a husband, a career man, a citizen, and an individual with varied talents and interests. Keep in mind that your masculinity plays a legitimate part in all of these roles and particularly in your power as a father. With this attitude you will find it easier to assume the many roles of the male. With a sense of the masculine nature of fatherhood, you will be more likely to devote a significant amount of your time to showing your children what masculinity is like and providing them with a positive model of manhood.

We have seen many men who are dynamic and active on

the job and in the community but are duds as fathers, because they feel that being a father or family man is not a proper masculine role. They leave all family decisions to their wives, spend their time at home satisfying their own needs and leave their children almost totally bereft of a masculine model. You should not, of course, devote your life completely to your children, but be sure that you afford them enough of your time so that they will know all the different people you are, and vice versa.

Masculine Power and Fatherhood. The feeling of personal *power* in being a male, which men are taught from birth, is an important facet of masculinity. To some men this power means manipulating people insensitively to gain one's own ends. To many of these men such power has become an obsession and a central focus of their lives. This is not, however, a healthy kind of power. A mature man's or woman's power is a feeling that he has the ability to influence his own environment, rather than be subjected to it. This kind of power in the proper perspective is useful in a person's life.

In terms of fatherhood, it is important for you to realize that your search for personal power has a legitimate outlet in fatherhood but should be used carefully. For instance, because of your strength, you convey the image of physical power even more than the mother, whom the child certainly sees as powerful but not as powerful as you. If you realize the effect that this physical power produces on your child, you are much less likely to become the fearsome creature that many men represent to their children. The father who doesn't think fatherhood is masculine may be the same one who doesn't realize the power he has in his children's lives. He is what we call the sleeping giant—napping on the couch and roaring in rage when awakened.

Use your physical power as a source of support and protection for your child rather than as a threat to him. Let him physically feel your strength by hugging and cuddling him. Don't hesitate to pick him up and carry him around. This closeness will help your son or daughter share your power. You can probably remember at least one instance during your childhood when you felt secure in the fact that your father was very strong, perhaps when he rescued you from a big dog or held you on his lap during a lion-taming act at a circus.

In addition to purely physical power, of course, fatherhood represents a great deal of psychological power in a child's life. Because your child sees you as a successful, dynamic member in the world he wants to enter, you have the power to shape significantly what your child will become. By using the power to educate, to set limits, to make decisions, you will influence much about your child's personality.

Father Nurturance. Unlike personal power, nurturance, the ability to protect and comfort a child, has been an under-valued facet of masculinity in our society. Many men believe they may express nurturance toward their children only by protecting them from outside dangers or by economically providing for the family and not through a personal, tender relationship with the child. They don't see it as masculine and thus don't see it as a natural part of their father power.

Children, male and female, possess a natural tendency to give and respond to tenderness—from both parents. If you allow nurturance to be a totally feminine domain in your family, you can hurt both your sons and your daughters. Rigid, strict, punitive fathers compel their sons to stifle tender feelings and become harsh and unloving themselves. Such fathers make their daughters feel that men are not tender creatures, that only harsh men are masculine.

To associate nurturance with femininity is a common mistake in American society. Indeed, usually we call it "mothering" instead of "parenting." Many a father holding a young son or daughter has felt slight twinges of embarrassment because he feels activities such as minding the child portray him as weak or effeminate. The father crooning to his infant may not feel himself quite the masculine male. Rather than seeing it as weakness, you should adopt the attitude that you are showing *nurturance-from-strength*. You should realize that you are actually evidencing power and competence by showing your child how to throw a ball or by cuddling him—because you are fully capable of displaying your abilities to someone who needs to be exposed to them. Thus, it is all part of your father power. Because a nurturant father helps produce a nurturant child, we've saved the more practical side of this discussion for our section on encouraging your child's nurturance.

Father, the Sex Differentiator. The father is the parent most likely to differentiate his children according to sex. Mothers are usually less concerned with distinct roles for boys and girls, while fathers tend to be quite concerned about their children growing up to be masculine or feminine. Fathers especially fear that their sons might grow up to be "sissies," and generally react very strongly against such behavior.

As we shall discuss later, you, the father, differentiate between the sexes because as the traditional breadwinner and socializing family member, you are usually more anxious about your children getting ahead in the world than the mother. You are likely to feel that functioning as a respected male or female in the outside world is vital, because this has been your primary area of competence.

Your differentiation between the sexes can have both positive and negative effects upon a child. While it certainly prepares your child for what he will meet in the world, it may also force him into a mold that he doesn't fit. Since fathers today do not usually know their children as well as mothers do, they are more likely to foist ill-fitting concepts of masculinity or femininity upon their offspring. As we discussed earlier, temper your traditional sex-role concern with concern for your child's competence, security, and individuality.

Father and His Daughter's Femininity. That fathers are particularly unnecessary in their daughters' lives is one corollary of the myth that fathers have little to do with their children's development. The traditional father-son emphasis at least gives the father some credit with his male offspring, but the corresponding mother-daughter dyad excludes the father altogether.

Fathers are important to *daughters* and *sons* in much the same way that mothers are important to *sons* and *daughters*. Just as your wife is the first woman in your son's life, you are the first man in your daughter's life. We shall see the depth and breadth of the specific effects you have on your daughter when we begin to discuss how you influence particular qualities in your child's behavior.

You act as a proving ground for your daughter's feminine behavior, a person psychologically removed from your daughter's striving for femininity whom she can use to gain an outside perspective, one from a member of the other sex. In both boys and girls this search for masculinity or femininity begins even in the second year of life, much earlier than most people think. This is the period during which boys and girls first realize they are male or female and that this means something in terms of their individuality.

You tend not to be as punitive toward your daughter as toward your son. One reason is that you see your daughter as an image of your wife and thus feel a corresponding tenderness toward her as a transference from your wife. Another reason is that she is a member of the female sex, whom your upbringing tells you must be treated with a certain permissiveness. You were probably taught never to hit girls and to defer to them socially, opening doors for them and carrying heavy loads for them.

While some of this permissiveness by fathers represents warm, nurturant involvement, it may also represent a rather uncritical, overly permissive approach to raising girls. As we shall see, being too undemanding may damage your daughter's motivation for achievement.

Because your daughter is of the other sex, you don't see your daughter as another version of yourself, as you do your son. You don't feel it as necessary to mold your daughter as you do your son. If your son turns out badly, you may see it as a bad reflection on you, but any failures of your daughter may be somewhat more removed from your own sense of worth. Don't fall into the trap of downplaying your daughter's achievements. Again, fathers are just as vital to their daughters' development as to their sons'.

The relationship among parents and children in which each

parent is more restrictive with the child of the same sex was vividly dramatized in a 1966 study at Stanford University by Michael Rothbart and Eleanor Maccoby. They taped the voice of a four-year-old who made such statements as "Daddy help me," or, "I don't like this game. . . . I'm gonna break it." Then they played the tapes to mothers and fathers, some of whom were told the voice was that of a little girl, and some, that of a little boy. The researchers found that while fathers were permissive and positive toward the "girls'" voices, mothers were more restrictive and negative. The attitudes were reversed when parents were told the voice was that of a boy; the mother was then more permissive.

Daughters identify very much with their fathers as people and not just as men. Your sons and daughters observe both of their parents to learn such relatively non-sexed-typed traits as moral development and self-confidence. Often you, the father, are in a unique position to offer an example of such qualities. You are the one who traditionally deals with authority figures, frequently oversees major family projects, and tends to have the most varied duties. This isn't the ideal way to run a family, of course. Both you and your wife should decide about buying a new car, taking a vacation, and repairing the furnace, with each contributing according to his particular abilities. We must, however, deal with the realities of many present-day families.

In any case, the daughter who is developing into a happy, feminine woman learns to understand and empathize with her father. Her close relationship with him enables her to have not only close romantic relationships with other men later, but other kinds of close relationships with both sexes.

Closeness between a father and a daughter may be psychologically dangerous when the mother is cold and rejecting. The daughter might then reject her mother, and without a positive female model she might try to pattern herself rigidly after her father, denying her femininity as a desired goal.

By having both an involved father and mother, your daughter thus learns about a broader range of traits than if she only associated closely with her mother. She will find she can get along in many situations, using many kinds of behavior, and still feel comfortably feminine. If you show your daughter, for instance, that you feel that women can be assertive and still feminine, you, very often the more physically assertive member of the family, are giving your daughter a valuable trait to use in her life.

Father and His Son's Masculinity. The father-son relationship can be much more stormy than the father-daughter relationship. A father, seeing his son as a young counterpart of himself, may try to impress his own ambitions on his son. This can bring obvious difficulties. The son may adopt goals he really doesn't want or may rebel and reject his father.

You generally put greater pressure on your sons than on your daughters to assume a "proper" sex role. There is usually considerable stress for sons to behave properly and to assume a male role. Girls who are tomboys are not nearly so frowned upon as boys who are sissies. Fathers often use such words as "horrified," "terrifically disturbed," and "furious" when asked what they would think about their sons playing with dolls, wearing dresses, or doing other traditionally feminine things.

Most studies show that there is a definite relationship between the extent to which you, the father, make decisions in your household and the masculinity of your sons. There is a catch in this finding, though. Though your son's masculinity will be encouraged if he sees Dad making decisions, the son's masculine development will actually be hindered if you are the family tyrant. Some boys who are not secure in their masculinity have fathers who punish their sons for disagreeing with them or being independent. This punishment need not be the overt physical kind to hurt the boy. Even the subtle sarcasm by the father toward a son's attempts at throwing a football or riding a horse, for instance, can harm a boy's self-concept. This does not exclude, however, *healthy* criticism *tempered with love.*

A son often has a rougher time of it than a daughter because, while his father and society are pressuring him to be masculine, a "good" child is defined to him in terms of such traditional feminine qualities as cooperativeness and restraint.

After trying to be "good" all his life, the boy has to change his outlook considerably in adulthood. He grows up and finds he is expected to be aggressive, independent, and a go-getter in order to be successful. Both Henry and Dennis still vividly remember their grade school report cards in which, though they usually did well in other areas, they consistently received poor grades in deportment because of rambunctiousness; they weren't "good" boys then, but this same trait now defines them as "good," success-oriented men.

Even if a boy does reconcile masculinity and being "good," he still may have only a vague idea of what true masculinity is. A boy with a frequently absent father must learn masculinity by trial and error. To find out what a real man is a boy may end up by consulting his friends, who may have as vague an idea as he has.

Fathers who are anxious about sex and homosexuality can also indirectly injure their son's masculinity. Such fathers, uneasy about body contact and the "dirty" job of caring for youngsters, tend to avoid their sons altogether. Such fathers become cold and formal, which their sons may sense as meaning that something is wrong with themselves. Such fathers may feel corresponding anxiety about caring for their daughters, but not nearly as much as with their sons.

6/ *Father, Self-Confidence, and Achievement*

Helping your sons and daughters to feel that they have power over their lives involves encouraging qualities of confidence, independence, achievement orientation, and assertiveness.

SELF-CONFIDENCE

You may think it ironic, but we shall begin talking about confidence building—the first "power" quality—by talking about weaknesses and limitations, both yours and your child's.

It's obvious that you can bolster your child's confidence by complimenting him on his strengths, but not as obvious that you can build up his confidence by helping him to be realistic about his weaknesses. And, as with many other areas of fatherhood, the process begins with your own feelings about yourself. You may be a great golfer but a poor swimmer, an excellent idea man but abysmal at carrying an idea to its conclusion. You may feel right at home with machines or concepts but be unable to relate closely to people. Whatever your failings—we all have them—don't hide them or refuse to admit them to your child. A principal mistake parents—and especially fathers—make is to try and appear to be a moral and physical superman to their children. The key point you should impress upon your child is that a normal person has weaknesses and faults but that these do not have to affect his overall happiness or competence as a human being. Men have a much more difficult time than women in talking about their mistakes and weaknesses, for males have been socialized to emphasize achievement and to fear and deprecate failure and weakness of any kind. Thus, we have often seen the businessman justly boast to his son or daughter of his prowess in making a deal or developing a product but be unable to admit that he has failed at other times in making some part of his business go.

On the other hand, the father who constantly belittles himself may also harm his child's confidence. Imagine how afraid a little boy or girl would become of the world if he saw the father he considered so powerful and capable, constantly admitting defeat. If you are this kind of person, it may be time for you to work toward developing confidence in yourself, for it will surely affect the confidence your son or daughter has in himself.

Then there is the father who is supercritical of his son or daughter, never satisfied with any of the child's developments. One such father we knew, Julius G., was a successful businessman who realized the importance of teaching his child but went about it in the wrong way. His son, Sammy, ten, had a knack for writing and was a very sensitive child. Though Julius was happy to read Sammy's stories about camping trips and spacemen, he never told Sammy they were good but concentrated on spelling and punctuation mistakes.

"I don't want him to get a swelled head," he told a friend. "And besides, the only way he's going to do anything in this world is if he strives for perfection and never lets up. That's how I did it."

Julius's attitude extended to all of Sammy's activities. If Sammy made something in his father's basement workshop, Julius would criticize the boy if all the nails weren't exactly straight.

When he entered high school, Sammy consistently got low marks in his subjects. He went out for the school band, the wrestling team, and the football team at one time or another but dropped each after only a few weeks. When he finally quit school, Julius took him to see Henry. Only after many family sessions did Julius painfully realize what he had done to his son and did Sammy begin to develop the ability to stick with an activity.

Superfather. Because of a strong myth that males must be physically invincible, fathers have a difficult time admitting physical weakness, which sometimes causes them to miss out on an opportunity to aid their offspring's confidence. For instance, one son we know, twenty-five years old, would invariably get seasick when he went fishing in a boat in even slightly choppy water. He was always quite self-conscious about it, feeling it was totally against the venerated man-against-the-sea tradition. After one particularly horrid bout with the surging ocean, he told his father about it on a visit back to the family home. His father admitted, after having never mentioned it for the twenty-five years of the son's life, that he too got deathly ill in boats.

"Why do you think that we never went fishing much, even when we lived only ten miles from the ocean?" he asked. Needless to say, the son felt a measure of relief, knowing that not only he but his revered father also lacked sea legs.

"When I Was a Lad." Admitting your present weaknesses might be difficult for you. Perhaps not so difficult is to tell your child, when appropriate, about the trials and troubles you experienced when you were a child. Though your exact experiences may be more useful to boys than to girls, the fact that you tell about problems you had growing up will help your children of both sexes. For instance, if your child has trouble with a subject in school, tell him about the subjects you had trouble with when you were in school. It is always an amazement to a child to hear that the imposing, supercompetent person that is his father had trouble with algebra or spelling. It also gives him confidence that he too may grow up to be competent in the world. Henry remembers vividly when his children found some of his old school report cards in the attic. "Gee, daddy got a C in English," or, "Look, he got a B in math" were the exclamations heard. Certainly, his children gained confidence that they could grow up to achieve what their father did and even do better.

Similarly, if you tell your child about the long, difficult road you traversed in gaining some skill, be it bowling or calculus, he may gain confidence that he can do it too. You may be surprised to find your children fascinated by your tales as long as you don't couch your stories in terms of, "Look how hard I had it; you've got it easy."

The fact that fathers have traditionally been the jousters with the outside world has in the past made their stories more exotic than those of mothers who may have lived in a world more familiar to the child.

This difference is changing as more and more women go out into the workaday world, but fathers and mothers are still creatures of different upbringings and concerns, and still have unique impacts in how they instill confidence in their children.

Self-Knowledge. Besides giving your child an idea of your past successes and failures, you also should help him sort out his own abilities and deficits. We have heard many parents talk about how "Judy has always had trouble with math" or how "Johnny will never do well in athletics." Such realism in parents can be a good quality, but you must be able to help your child understand not only that he may have these difficulties, but that he should not let them stand in the way of his happiness and confidence. This is a delicate proposition. You must be able to communicate to the child that he should recognize his failings but at the same time not do it in a way that will injure his self-esteem. Never tell him about a shortcoming without also emphasizing his strengths.

Also, *don't mistake temporary problems for permanent ones.* Judy may turn out to be another Einstein and Johnny another Babe Ruth after overcoming initial difficulties. (Incidentally, Einstein did have initial problems with schoolwork, so much so that his teacher told his father, "The boy probably won't be successful, no matter what he does.")

Your criticisms may also become self-fulfilling prophecies if not handled carefully. If you assert that Judy will never be good in math, she may come to believe it and may give up. Properly done, such realization of weaknesses will bolster the child's confidence and let him take better stock of himself.

Get Interested. The best way to build self-esteem in your son or daughter is to be genuinely interested in what he is attempting and accomplishing. This is a much more difficult and rare feat than most fathers realize. You are a grown man, making your living at an adult occupation and involved in adult affairs. Thus, consciously or unconsciously, you may feel that showing interest in mere "child's play" is beneath you, and you may feel slightly embarrassed at it. Because mothers more often have confidence as childraisers, they tend to feel less uncomfortable at being enthusiastic about a child's accomplishments and view them more as rewards to themselves for parenting.

This is a very odd state of affairs when you consider that fathers have traditionally been the more judging parent, valuing their child for what he does rather than what he is. The result many times of combining the "child's play" attitude with the judging attitude has been the overly demanding father. Such a father might become very interested in son Arthur's woodworking project, but declare, "Can't you do better, son? It looks easy to me!"

On the other hand, one involved father of six said, "I spend a good portion of my time when I come in from work going around and seeing what all the kids accomplished today. I go out in the backyard and watch one climb a tree, see another's drawing, and listen to another recite. I applaud each of them for what their accomplishment means to him." Whether the accomplishment is tying a shoelace, writing a term paper, or saying his first words, you should encourage each of your child's accomplishments in terms of his stage of development and not in terms of how easy it looks to you.

In criticizing your child for some act of misbehavior, take care to criticize only the behavior and not the child himself. A child should not be told that he is bad, dishonest, vicious, and the like. Coming from you, a judging, competent, high-impact parent, such criticism may make him inevitably be bad, dishonest, or vicious. Indeed, we have known children who take a sort of perverse pleasure in being miscreants.

If, however, you assure your child that you believe his pulling the cat's tail, stealing the candy, or taking the family car without permission was only a temporary failing on his part, the child will try not to do it again. It represents a threat to your high estimation of him and to his own self-esteem and not a shameful performance you had "expected."

Involving Your Child. Another good way to help your child develop confidence and self-esteem is to involve him in your own activities. Even with men's and women's roles becoming less distinct, fathers are still usually expected to take on home duties that the child simply cannot experience with the mother.

Because of modern technology and changing life-styles, fathers' home chores are becoming fewer and less time-consuming, so you should involve your child in a greater percentage of them than ever before. Unfortunately, most fathers have not really been sensitized to the problem of how little their child gets to watch them *doing* things. They miss many opportunities to involve their child in what they are doing.

While children cannot be expected to accomplish tasks on a par with adults, you can certainly find some aspect of any of your chores or hobbies to involve your child in. For instance, you couldn't expect your young child to help you paint your house. But with a little imagination, you can find many child-sized painting-related tasks that he can do to help you, ranging from handing you brushes to fetching refreshments. He can also do grown-up jobs scaled down to his abilities. Instead of scraping the whole side of the house, he could do one small section. Similarly, if you mow the grass, let him gather the clippings. If you have office work to do at home, let him sort papers or sharpen pencils.

As your child grows, give him more and more responsibility. When he is capable of doing arithmetic, let him check your figuring on your tax return. When he learns about cooking, let him help prepare a barbecue. Even if he tires easily and loses interest, he still has had the prestigious opportunity of "helping Daddy." The key is that he is working closely with you, observing you and achieving with you.

You may be surprised, even flabbergasted, at what your youngster can accomplish given the chance. Once, Henry gave his then ten-year-old son, Jonathan, a scientific paper for him to read while he sat with his father at his desk. Much to his happy surprise, Jonathan not only read and understood the paper fairly well but did an excellent job of editing, discovering several errors in grammar, punctuation, and spelling. He also asked some provocative questions about the material discussed in the paper.

Again, don't restrict your encouragements to participate to your sons. Daughters, perhaps even more than sons, need the confidence acquired from accomplishing tasks outside what society dictates as little girls' jobs.

INDEPENDENCE

Every child has a natural tendency toward independence. After he can move about on his own, his curiosity propels him away from his parents to learn about the world—but not too far away. Unfortunately, parents, grown-ups that they are, have been through years of social conditioning, and their balance between allowing a child independence and protecting him from danger may be way out of whack.

As an adult male, you have probably been an independent achiever for many years and are likely to encourage independence in your children. On the other hand you may not realize how important it is that your child have a warm, secure base from which to operate. The balance you strike between encouraging your child's exploration and protecting him is extremely important. Your child will need different mixes of independence and dependence as he grows and even at different times during the same growth stage. Take your cue from him. If he wants to be apart from you, let him be; if he needs help and cuddling, help him and cuddle him.

If you keep your child at home and are forever worried about him getting hurt, you will develop an overdependent person, always counting on others for support, rewards, and refuge. But a child who is pushed out on his own too fast may become so detached from others that he cannot ask for aid when he needs it or is unable to have a close, healthy, mutual dependence on another. A child in such circumstances may, on the other hand, retain extreme dependence on others, always searching for the love and support he never received.

The Spartan Father. Trying to mold themselves and their children into the popular stereotype of the male as the "lone warrior," fathers are more likely to push their children toward independence too quickly, especially their sons. We know one such case of George G. and his son, Rex, who was seven. George had always prided himself on being an independent outdoorsman and had tried to instill the same toughness into his son. When he and his wife would go out, they would leave Rex at home. "It'll be good for him; he can fix his own food and really learn what it is to be his own man," George would say forcefully to his wife. Whenever Rex would cry, George would admonish him, "Now just cut that out; you're acting just like a little sissy. Dry up those tears and face it like a man. You shouldn't have to cry to anybody."

The effects of this attitude on Rex finally showed up one Saturday when the boy fell out of a tree while playing. He was very quiet and stayed in his room the rest of the day, and it wasn't until his mother happened to pass by and heard him crying that she realized something was wrong. She examined her son and found that he had a broken arm and hadn't told anyone for fear he would be branded a crybaby. He was rushed to the hospital where an operation was required to save the arm because of the damage caused by the broken ends of the bones.

Rex's mother finally told her husband in no uncertain terms what she thought he had been doing to the boy. The next day

George went into his son's room for a private chat, and when his mother came in, she found them both crying and hugging each other. Both George and Rex, it seemed, had been hiding behind a falsely "tough" exterior because they feared intimacy with other people. George still had a tough time nurturing his son after that, but it took only a knowing look from his wife to remind him when he was being too rough on Rex.

Unfortunately, George's concept of masculinity is all too prevalent in our society, and all too many children like Rex have grown up to be fathers who push their own ideas of fierce, unreasoning independence onto their sons and daughters, much to the children's detriment.

Such fathers usually have such a chauvinistic view of men and women that they leave their daughters out of their admonishments to keep a stiff upper lip. But we have seen fathers so concerned with being strong and suffering in silence that their daughters are also commanded to keep their problems completely to themselves.

The Supervising Father. Then there is the father who is so used to controlling things—his office, his home, his social life—that he tries to control his child when he plays with him. If such a father took his son or daughter on a fishing trip, he would direct how to untie the boat, rig the child's line everytime it was needed, show the child where to fish, and even haul in the fish for the child.

We remember one boy named Frankie who had such a father, Phil R. Every time Frankie and his father did something together, it was always Phil, the captain, and Frankie, the first mate. Phil instructed Frankie on how to arrange his homework papers, what knot to use in tying the dog up outside, and even how to say his prayers at night. Finally, Frankie went off to Boy Scout camp one summer, and Phil discovered how dependent he had made his son. Upon visiting Frankie, Phil found out that he had driven the camp counselors almost berserk, constantly following them around asking the exact way to do everything. Without precise instruction and encouragement, Frankie was afraid to even make his bed.

Try to strike a careful balance between allowing independence and preventing frustration for the child. Give your child plenty of leeway to make mistakes but don't allow him to flounder until he loses all confidence in himself. Fathers exist in a world where mistakes can mean loss of a job and of the means to provide for their families; thus, you may be reluctant to allow your child to make mistakes. Do not be. What counts is that the child is making successive approximations toward his goal. In learning to tie his shoes, he may succeed in tying some incredibly unravelable knots, but with a little help will eventually tie beautiful bows in his shoelaces. When he's old enough to drive, he may run the family car over curbs a few times, but he will eventually learn to park it properly.

Independence offers us a good example of the need for having two parents involved in a child's development. By helping encourage your child's independence, you can help offset any tendency your wife might have toward maternal overprotection. Psychological studies indicate that middle-class children without men in their lives are much less likely to be allowed exploratory freedom.

Women themselves have often been reared as fragile and delicate creatures. Such a mother would be overly fearful of injury and would likely stifle her child, keeping him from active play and exploration. By the same token, the mother can offset your tendency to overdirect the child or to push him into things for which he is not ready.

Boys, Girls, Independence. As we indicated earlier when discussing sex differences, there do seem to be basic differences in the relationships boys and girls have with their parents. Girls tend to be closer to their parents and feel less pressure to become independent. Boys tend to be thrust away from the family to find approval in the outside world. Boys do look to their family for approval, but this approval becomes increasingly likely to be given for accomplishments away from the family circle.

This difference in how much boys and girls are encouraged to strike out on their own may be due to a complex mix of biology and socialization. For instance, because girls may be innately more intellectually advanced and sensitive than boys of their age, they may simply be easier for parents to have around than the less sensitive, more physically active boys.

Compared to the way they treat their sons, parents may not encourage independence in their daughters as much, because they see them as more vulnerable to harm by the outside world.

Finally, you the father may not encourage independence in your daughter as much, because she is a female, whom you may tend to be more nurturant and protective toward.

We frankly don't know whether our society will learn to encourage our daughters to be as independent as our sons. But we do know that you as a father should do everything you can not to hold your daughter back from exploring due to your fears. Although you may still feel more protective toward your daughter than your son, don't let your protectiveness prevent her from becoming her own woman. For example, don't automatically forbid her going on a trip into the city or going on a hike. Consider how mature she is, whether the activity is really dangerous, or whether you are being overly protective just because she is a girl.

As a matter of fact, having a healthy sense of independence enables a boy or girl to have a healthy dependent relationship with another person as well. A girl who has been taught by her father to be independent from him and at the same time know she can depend on him for return of her love will have an equally healthy relationship with other men in her life. Such a girl will neither hang desperately on to the men in her life nor resent them because she needs them. She will be able to love and be loved in return but will have the strength to walk away from relationships that are harmful.

This is also true for boys' relationships with their mothers, though boys usually have independence drummed into them from an early age. The principal problem of boys is usually the opposite of that of girls—they are propagandized to be so aloof and independent that they are psychologically unable to accept dependence on a woman for love.

Thus, many women have been made overdependent by

their fathers, and many men have been made overly independent. Each person needs a healthy blend of dependence and independence.

ACHIEVEMENT MOTIVATION

He has called on the best that was in us. There was no such thing as half trying. Whether it was running a race or catching a football, competing in school—we were to try. And we were to try harder than anyone else. . . . "After you have done the best you can," he used to say, "to hell with it."

—*Robert F. Kennedy on his father, Joseph P. Kennedy*

If your child has a strong sense of self-esteem and independence, he is already on the way to possessing a high degree of achievement motivation. As we will see, such motivation means a lot in your child's intellectual development. No matter how intellectually gifted a child is, he will never achieve to his full capacity if he does not possess a love of and expectation of achievement.

You and Achievement. A child's motivation is often closely linked to the attitudes the father has about himself. If you possess an expectation of success in your own endeavors and value high standards, you are very likely to pass this on to your offspring. At the same time, as we said in the section on independence, you should not be so obsessed with achievement that you are overly critical of your child, or so impatient as to not allow your child the luxury of failure.

You should also have enough confidence in yourself so that you can comfortably take a back seat when necessary and let your child reap the glory of his achievements. There are many fathers who throw their arms around their child after some success and say, "Boy, I sure taught you how to do that well!" Your child may well have learned a skill from you, but it was *his* achievement. Let him enjoy it. This doesn't mean that you can't joyously share in the reflected glory.

Your attitudes toward the roles of duty and money in achievement will also affect your child. Encourage your child to take a job so that he will learn that achievement has tangible rewards. But also refrain from rewarding him for everything he does. Some things, such as helping with brothers and sisters or performing chores or doing homework should be seen as a duty, both to others and to oneself.

As you might expect, psychologists have discovered that fathers of low-achieving children are likely to be just the opposite of those of achieving children. Such fathers are frequently rejecting, critical, don't think much of themselves, and aren't really emotionally involved in their children's lives.

The typical father of a low-achiever is what we call the "report-card father." He doesn't really have much to do with his children, except when it comes time to sign their report cards. Then, if the child got low grades, all hell breaks loose. The report-card father then goes into a round of bribing, cajoling, and demanding that his Johnny or Suzy get good grades, sometimes even helping them with their homework for a few nights. (The report-card father usually does the whole assignment for his child, because he "doesn't have time" to really sit down and explain things.) But after a while, it's back to the hobby shop or a night with the boys until the next report-card time rolls around.

Father deprivation doesn't necessarily lead to a lack of achievement, however. There are cases of men who achieve a great deal without an emotionally involved father, mainly because all they have ever seen of their father was his drive for achievement.

We know one man, a self-made millionaire, who was such a person. His father had been a grocer and had taken his son with him to help load produce to be delivered to the store. "I used to watch him dicker and bargain for vegetables, and it made a deep impression on me. He always impressed upon me that we were poor and that you had to hustle to make it in this world. Otherwise he had little to do with me." Though this man became quite rich as a real-estate promoter, he had problems with his marriage and his children because he knew little about how to be a whole man. He had learned from his father only the methods of making money.

Such father-neglected people as this one become obsessed with achieving, continually seeking approval for their actions in the form of money, fame, or power, yet underneath their material success, often are not happy with their lives. Be close enough to your child so that he has a whole man for a father.

Meaningful Achievement. In these days of a counterculture that seeks fulfillment through personal relationships and self-awareness, many good fathers have become defensive about being achievement oriented. Don't be. Today's fad of "dropping out" does represent a reaction against parents, especially fathers, who have overstressed financial or material success at the expense of friendship or inner peace. While such movements are meaningful in that respect, many of them have gone too far toward total rejection of achievement.

We've encountered some of these people who, without a love of achievement, have ended up trapped in meaningless, boring lives. They wander from job to job because they are frustrated and are frustrated because they have nothing to do but wander. We all need something that we are accomplished at to give us self-esteem.

On the other hand, while you encourage your child to accomplish useful things, don't fail to teach him to take other values besides economic success into account in charting his course. This guideline isn't as evanescent as you might think—a person can be just as unhappy from lack of personal commitment as from a low salary. Encourage your child to strive for happy friendships *and a sense of purpose about his life* in addition to getting a good education and a good-paying job.

Many fathers fail in teaching their children to acquire a sense of duty, which can have disastrous effects. One college student we know, Jean K., was never required to manage her own money or to account for her expenditures as she grew up. Her parents did all of that for her, not realizing they were preparing her poorly for being on her own someday. The consequence of this duty-bereft upbringing was that when Jean went off to college, she was not equipped to handle her new freedom. When classes became difficult, she simply quit attending, not even notifying the university of her withdrawal. Jean bought expensive clothes and ate steak every night; she had never learned about her budgetary duty. After one aimless and expensive semester, she left school, not because of lack of aptitude, but because she had never been taught the duty to become responsible.

So, while you should help your child with his tasks, give hints rather than solving the problems for him. While you may reward him for good grades, make it clear that you expect them of him because *he* is capable of achieving them. While you should involve him in your activities frequently, you should not control every detail of his participation.

Teaching your child to get a bang out of getting things done may include things you've never thought of. Henry remembers an incident with his son, Kenneth, when he was able to teach him the love of meeting a challenge. The issue was a small one—Kenneth had wanted to try a new brand of cereal that had been advertised on television. Father and son went down to the neighborhood market to buy a box, only to find that they had not yet stocked it. They went to another market and then another, still not finding the cereal. To both father and child the Great Cereal Hunt had become a challenge, a test of their ability to stick to a problem and to have confidence that they would eventually prevail. After more than four hours of hunting, the cereal was found, and no victory tasted sweeter. As they both sat eating a bowlful, the son had learned a valuable lesson—that you don't necessarily succeed at something the first time or even the eighth time, but you will eventually succeed if you have faith in yourself.

Fathers, Daughters, Achievement. One major problem in our society has been that up until now women have not been encouraged to achieve in the outside world. While men traditionally have been taught to be concerned with achievement in business, industry, education, or science, women have been taught to assume the home as their chief sphere of interest. Certainly, the home can be a challenging arena for some women, but many women have been thrust into the role of homemaker reluctantly because of what society and their parents taught them rather than what they really wanted.

As we mentioned earlier, the socially (and perhaps biologically) influenced closeness of a daughter to her parents encourages her to define her achievement more according to relationships with others. Sons, on the other hand, have more "internalized" achievement motivation. They tend to take pride more in self-motivated achievement, rather than in relationship-oriented achievement.

But, the actual reasons why women so seldom reach the upper echelons of business, science, and industry are less biological than social. Though basic psychological differences between men and women might make for differences in achievement motivation, more important, women have been subjected to stereotypes, which result in discrimination against them in the job market.

Even if your daughter has been very much influenced by her femaleness, you, as a father, have a particularly vital role in encouraging achievement motivation in her. You should exercise that role fully.

First, you should make achievement orientation a natural part of your concept of femininity. Make it clear to your daughter that you think she is feminine, whether she wants to be a housewife or an engineer. Be just as excited and encouraging of her when she makes an A on that math test as when she bakes you cookies. By giving your daughter a solid confidence in her femininity, regardless of her activities, you are giving her a wider entrance into society. Many psychologists point out that women actually seem to fear success. They are afraid that if they achieve, they will be considered aggressive, dominant, and masculine, and consequently will be rejected by friends and lovers.

In a 1968 study at the University of Michigan, psychologist Matina Horner found this fear vividly illustrated in an experiment she did with a group of college students. Giving female students the sentence "After first-term finals, Anne finds herself at the top of her medical school class," Dr. Horner asked each girl in the group to write a story about what followed. She asked boys to do the same with the same sentence about a boy named John. The stories written by the males usually ran something like this:

> John is a conscientious young man who worked hard. He is pleased with himself. John has always wanted to go into medicine and is very dedicated. His hard work has paid off. He is thinking that he must not let up now, but must work even harder than he did before. His marks have encouraged him. . . .

In sharp contrast many of the girls wrote stories something like this:

> Anne has a boyfriend Carl in the same class, and they are quite serious. Anne met Carl at college and they started dating around their soph years in undergraduate school. Anne is rather upset and so is Carl. She wants him to be higher scholastically than she is. Anne will deliberately lower her academic standing next term, while she does all she subtly can to help Carl. His grades come up, and Anne soon drops out of med school. They marry, and he goes on in school, while she raises their family.

Your job is to show your daughter that she need not fear success. If she is ridiculed by her classmates for being too smart or too aggressive, help her to understand that it is not she who is at fault but her classmates. If she goes out for baseball or another traditionally male sport, go to the games with her. Hug her when she wins and console her when she loses. When she suggests some improvement in one of your home chores, such as fixing a window, don't get defensive about it being "man's work." Accept her suggestion and talk about it with her.

By approving her achievement motivation, you are acting as a forerunner of men she will be attracted to later in her life, men who will also approve of her achievement orientation and with whom she can have a healthy, equal relationship.

You should make her aware that she will also encounter men who equate femininity with noncompetence and non-achievement, but encourage her to be confident enough not to be inhibited by their attitudes.

Even as you show your approval of your child's achievement, it is important for you to show that you respect your wife as a fully competent person—another example of the complementary roles that two involved parents play in a child's life.

Many women today, such as some who blossom into achievers after marriage and a family, seem to have to establish their femininity with a husband and children before they can become motivated to achieve. If your daughter feels feminine without this need to establish it through a family, she will not have to use husband and children as props to establish her own place. She can have a much more rewarding and egalitarian relationship with her husband and present her own children with a better model of feminine competence.

Because of reasons we have already discussed, fathers are more likely to accept a greater amount of dependency and passivity from their daughters than from their sons. If your wife is similarly nurturant and noncritical, the girl may have no one to show her that achievement and independence are things she should strive for.

You play much the same achievement-encouraging role toward your daughter as is played by mothers toward their sons—a role of support and affirmation from the parent of the other sex. As an involved father, your role with your daughter is unique, however, because at this point in time you are helping to turn the tide against society's tradition to resist socializing females for achievement.

ASSERTIVENESS, AGGRESSIVENESS

From birth onward males (and, thus also, fathers) are the more physically aggressive of the two sexes. Boys play rougher, get into more trouble, and court danger more than girls. This difference is partly biological predisposition and partly because physical aggressiveness is encouraged more in boys. Every father has admired his son at one time or another for being a "little tough guy."

Boys are also the object of more physical punishment than girls are, because both fathers and mothers have been brought up to be less inhibited about being aggressive toward boys. Boys' physical aggressiveness also gives parents more reason to react to them aggressively in the first place.

Thus, boys are more often punished physically by both fathers and mothers, whereas daughters are more likely to be protected and supported by their fathers, rather than punished.

Girls, generally more sensitive and mature for their age than boys, are able to find more subtle, parentally acceptable outlets for their aggression. They are more talented at using words as tools for aggression, whereas the frustrated little boy, being less advanced verbally, more often resorts to his fists.

Girls are discouraged from being aggressive not only by their fathers but also by their mothers. Mothers, being former little girls themselves, have been taught not to value aggressiveness, and they thus neither encourage it nor act as a model of it for their daughters.

All this is not to say that boys can't be effective name-callers or that girls can't throw an effective uppercut. Again, we emphasize that these sex differences occur in the context of an enormous overlapping range of individual differences among people. The boy-girl variations in aggressive behavior represent just another example of how biology and social expectations intermix.

In this discussion we shall define assertiveness as the ability to selectively and advantageously demand one's rights. Aggressiveness is one expression of assertiveness, and it becomes pathological only if it is used to hurt others.

Both an assertive and a pathologically aggressive child have the power to punch someone in the nose, but the assertive child does it only when absolutely necessary—in self-defense or when defending others. The overly aggressive child, however, feels an inner need to be constantly imposing himself on others, even by nose-punching.

By distinguishing between aggressiveness and assertiveness, we are emphasizing that assertiveness has a definite place in a child's life and is not a trait to be smothered in either boys or girls. Achievement motivation, confidence, and even nurturance all have elements of assertiveness in them, because they all require the child to extend himself outward to others and to his physical environment.

Being assertive doesn't just mean occasionally being physically aggressive. It also means making oneself heard, standing up for one's rights, and having confidence to do something one thinks is right when others say it is wrong or unpopular.

The Assertive Father. You, the father, are the parent most influential upon both your sons' and daughters' assertiveness. You are usually stronger, representing to those around you more of a potential for aggression than does the mother. You also offer a more overt, easily discernible model for aggressiveness and its proper control, because you are likely to be naturally more aggressive and also because you are more often in situations where you have to assert yourself. In most families you are the parent who deals most with outsiders. As one father put it, you are the one who has to refuse to "take all the crap." You are also the parent who engages more often in sports and other hobbies featuring an aggressive display. Ideally, however, both males and females in the family could participate comfortably in such activities. An example that comes readily to mind is the famed touch-football games of the Kennedys, which included mothers, fathers, sons, and daughters.

The negatively aggressive child is often very much the product of his father's attitude toward him. Ironically, fathers who punish their children for being aggressive may thereby cause their child to become even more aggressive. The typical hostile, overly aggressive child has a father who punishes him physically, restricts his activities, and refuses to allow him to express anger or frustration. Such a child becomes negatively aggressive because he is frustrated by his father's punitiveness but cannot retaliate against him. The child also becomes aggressive because he tends to imitate what his father does, not what he says. Such a father typically calls his child back after the child has stalked off in anger and shouts angrily at him, "Don't you ever get mad at me like that again. Apologize and don't you ever raise your voice at me." Not a very good model of democracy and restraint. If the father resorts to frequent physical violence toward his child or other people, the child comes to see force as a preferred form of action to use in dealing with others. In the section on the child's relationship with authority figures, we shall discuss the father and discipline.

Highly punitive fathers may in fact produce very different children according to how they nurture their child. If a father is *cold* and punishing, the child may become aggressive; a father who is warm and loving but highly punitive may produce an uptight, conforming child, because the child feels guilty about feeling aggressive toward such a "loving" father.

In reacting to your child's aggression, take into account the reasons for the aggression. If you teach the child that in some cases such behavior is not proper, and in others it is, then your child will be comfortably assertive, able to control his aggressiveness. For instance, if your child has a right to be angry with you, let him be. As long as his anger does not extend to unreasonable physical and verbal abuse of you, it is a healthy expression of his feelings.

Expressing anger is an important feature of healthy emotional development. A child should learn effective ways to express anger while he is very young. His anger will, thus, be a constructive force for him and not destructive. Many parents feel that a child's anger represents either a threat to them or a sign of ungratefulness. This should not be the case. You should, rather, see your child's anger as a sign of his natural reaction to an affront. A forthright sense of indignation, based on a sound set of values, is a trait to be treasured in a child as well as in an adult.

The Assertive Son. There are special problems for both sons and daughters in encouraging assertiveness. Your sons' principal problem will be learning to be assertive in the face of the traditional definition of "good" children. Children are "good" if they adopt such traditionally feminine traits as cooperation and restraint. On the other hand, aggressiveness is valued as part of traditional masculinity. Conflict over this dilemma can cause a boy to become quite confused.

So you should teach your son to use intelligent, selective control over assertiveness rather than conditioning him to stifle it. He should realize that you are not telling him that he should never argue with grown-ups but that he should argue only when he truly feels that the grown-up is in the wrong. On the other hand, don't pressure your son to "get out there and get 'em" if he is a relatively nonassertive child. Rather, help his confidence and teach him more how to assert himself in the way that comes most naturally to him.

The most prevalent mistake fathers make in terms of assertiveness is in teaching their sons to be aggressive, but not teaching them how to control it.

One little boy we knew, Charlie F., was sent to the school counselor because he was continually getting into fights and seemed to have no friends in school. If a child bumped into him in the lunch line or Charlie thought someone made a face at him, he would immediately lash out at the child and start a fight.

When Charlie's father was asked to visit the school, he asserted, "There's no problem with my son; he's just all boy. Boys are just physical, that's all." Charlie's father told the counselor that Charlie would come home occasionally and tell him he'd been in a fight, and the father would laugh and say, "That's my boy! Just don't let them push you around."

The problem was dramatized for the father when he was given a chance to watch his son on the playground from the schoolroom window. Though Charlie had never been a discipline problem at home, his father watched him beat up a boy for not throwing a ball to him, take a jump rope away from a girl, and kick another child on the merry-go-round. Charlie's father began to realize that merely encouraging aggressiveness without any other consideration is not enough.

The Assertive Daughter. Boys often develop a strong sense of confidence during childhood because their natural physical aggressiveness is effective in getting them what they want. Girls, on the other hand, are usually not allowed such latitude—they are restrained from exhibiting obvious aggressiveness of any kind. "Little ladies," they are told, "do not fight or quarrel regardless of the circumstances." Fathers must recognize and value their daughters' verbal and physical aggressiveness as a legitimate basis for an abiding confidence and assertiveness in them.

While you should recognize the possibility of innate differences in your sons and daughters, you should avoid forcing stereotypes on your daughter. While females are told that nobody likes a "pushy" or "bossy" woman, their male counterparts are admired as being "dynamic," "aggressive," and a "natural leader." You should give your daughter the confidence to see through this hypocrisy and be her own person.

Arguing. How you argue with your child will have a great deal to do with how assertive he is able to be. Most fathers do not know constructive ways to argue with a child. They may come home tired from a day of controversy with their fellows at work and refuse to argue at all. Or, they may make argument with their child a contest of wills, refusing to allow the child his viewpoint because it threatens their ego. True, fathers are often right in arguments; they have the benefit of experience. But this doesn't mean that your child should not be listened to and his viewpoint considered.

Intelligent argument is vital to your child's emotional development because it teaches him that the governing force behind your decisions is reason and that reason is his pathway to obtain what he wants. The parent who refuses to argue may find that he is the parent of a child who has decided that tantrums and threats are the only way to realize one's wishes. When you allow argument, you also teach your child to use assertiveness in pressing home logic rather than physical aggression in pressing home dominance.

We remember one ironic example of a father who brought

his son into a clinic for help with a discipline problem. "He just never listens. I tell him to stop something and he just doesn't seem to hear me." At this point the son started to say something, and he was interrupted immediately by his father's "Now, be quiet while I'm talking, son."

On a more positive side is the case of one father who got into an argument with his four-year-old son over the trade name of some cookies. The father insisted they were called Nabiscoes, and the young son said that they were Biscoes. The son abruptly got up from the table, pulled out the box of cookies from a cupboard, and showed his father that he was right. "See, Dad—Biscoes!" he exclaimed proudly. "Well, I guess you sure are right," said the father, admitting his mistake openly. Had this father been like some, he would have made his son sit still and would have called the argument to a halt, or possibly he would have muttered something about "ridiculous names." Instead, he allowed the son to assert himself and gather evidence for his case, giving the boy his due when it turned out that he was right. A rather minor incident, to be sure, but a child's most vivid experiences may be just that to an adult.

Argument also gives the child a firm foundation on which to build his conscience and his view of the world. If you bring up appropriate examples from your experience to show where he is right or wrong in arguing, you are giving him a head start on his own philosophy. Incidentally, arguing with your child may help you to examine your own logic and motives. You may discover areas in which you react very illogically and inappropriately.

The best general climate for fostering a child's intellectual growth, independence, and assertiveness is one of moderate conflict. Because of your extensive experience in the workaday world—more than likely a hard-headed, dollars-and-cents place—you provide a very useful source of conflict based on logical argument.

"Moderate conflict" may mean different things to different children. A sensitive child may be cowed at a mere tone of voice; a less sensitive child may be little affected by very intimidating words. Base your actions on your child's emotional reactivity. But this does not mean either always letting your child have his way in arguments or tyrannically overruling him on everything.

As we shall see in the next chapter, arguing with your child does not mean that you do not nurture him.

7/ Father, Nurturance, Morals, and Discipline

Until now we have discussed the parental attitudes that will allow a child to develop his own feeling of power. Fathers traditionally value highly such qualities as confidence, achievement motivation, independence, and assertiveness—both in themselves and in their children. These traits, however, are founded on something that is usually not highly valued by men—nurturance.

In the section on the father's masculinity we discussed what the attitude of nurturance usually means to you as a male; now we shall talk about how important it is to your children. Your nurturance is related to many aspects of their development, and its quality influences their moral development as much as your effectiveness as a disciplinarian.

THE NURTURANT FATHER

To many fathers, nurturance may consist solely of protecting a child from intruders and of providing for him economically. This is actually much too narrow a view of it.

We do not equate nurturance with permissiveness or passivity. A father who is nurturant still asserts his own identity, authority, and personality; he does not allow the child's personality to determine the total relationship. Neither do we equate it with overprotectiveness. Nurturance means being emotionally close to the child, accepting him and helping him, but it does not mean keeping him from exploration. Nurturance helps to build the child's confidence and competence.

Ideally, father nurturance, as well as mother nurturance should feature a whole host of physical and nonphysical demonstrations of love and regard for the child. A father should be able to comfortably hug and kiss the child, take him to a wide range of places, patiently demonstrate things to the child, verbally communicate to the child that he is loved, and give him credit for his achievements.

Many fathers believe that such demonstrations somehow weaken the child, make him dependent, make the father an ineffective disciplinarian, or, especially in the case of boys, encourage homosexuality. Nothing could be further from the truth.

Independent children are actually likely to have fathers who, in addition to encouraging independence, are nurturant as well. Fathers who are overly stern with their offspring in an attempt to produce hardy, self-reliant children may have just the opposite effect.

Nurturance fosters independence because it gives the child a solid base upon which to build. As we stressed earlier, providing security is an all-important overall function for you, the father, and nurturance is a vital part of this security.

The fear that such caring will make a father less effective as a disciplinarian is also groundless. In fact, if you have a warm relationship with a child, it will be much easier, on both of you, to maintain discipline. The child will be much more likely to accept your explanations of why you are disciplining him and will be more concerned about your opinion of him.

Nurturance also promotes sex-role security in children. Children who are secure in their masculinity or femininity are likely to have fathers who are nurturant as well as masculine, for it allows them to identify closely with the father. Thus, the son of a nurturant father will strive to be like him and come to value his maleness highly. Of particular importance, the boy will also value his own nurturant capacity. And a girl with a close, nurturant father will be more likely to feel accepted as a female. If a father has a warm relationship with his children, they will also, of course, be more likely to adopt his non-sex-typed traits, such as his moral tenets, his patterns of relating with others, and the degree of his achievement motivation.

Such children will also be more likely to be generous and altruistic, as illustrated by an interesting study made by psychologists Paul Mussen and Eldred Rutherford at the University of California at Berkeley in 1968. In their study, the researchers gave candy to each member of a group of four-year-old boys, along with two bags in which each was to place his candy to give to two other boys he liked best. The boys who were the most generous with their candy, the psychologists found, were the boys who consistently perceived their fathers as warm, affectionate, and comforting.

The fact that you are nurturant with your child—that you talk with him, hug him, kiss him, and take him places—means that you will have to be with him for significant amounts of your time. You cannot be home one night a week and make it up to your child by being especially loving toward him.

Henry and a fellow psychologist, Mark Reuter, now at the Children's Psychiatric Center in Eatontown, New Jersey, did a study that vividly pointed up the dangers of father nurturance without father availability, and vice versa. They gave personality tests to a group of 172 college men, along with a detailed questionnaire to determine how much their fathers were at home and how nurturant their fathers had been when the students were children.

Well-adjusted students were likely to see themselves as dependable, trusting, practical, and friendly. Poorly adjusted students were more likely to label themselves as aloof, anxious, inhibited, and unfriendly. Significantly, Henry and Mark found that the most poorly adjusted students had fathers who were home very little and were very nurturant, *or* were home a lot and were aloof and non-nurturant. The most well-adjusted students had fathers who were at least moderate in both nurturance and availability.

If you are not home much and are really affectionate and play with your child when you are home, he may feel very frustrated that you are frequently absent, and it may affect his personal adjustment. He may wonder why, if you appear to love him so much, you do not spend more time with him.

Conversely, if you are home a lot but are cold and distant, your child may feel that he is inadequate in your eyes, and he will feel very insecure. It would probably be better for a child with a cold, distant father to have him be home very little. At least the child would not be exposed to such consistently negative experience with a male.

Fathers often experience particular difficulty showing their emotions. Americans seem to admire the image of the emotionless, stone-faced male; at least, that is the kind of traditional hero seen in most movie or television dramas. Some fathers are particularly averse to showing emotions in front of their children because they feel it will damage their authority image. For instance, many men have trouble telling their children "I love you" or sometimes even "I am proud of you." They often effect distance by "Your mother and I love you." Even worse, the mother often finds herself carrying the whole load, saying, "Your father and I love you."

In reality, expressing your emotions both verbally and through your actions improves your authority and impact on your children. Children themselves are emotional beings. When they are happy, they laugh; when they are unhappy, they cry. If they see you as capable of emotions too, it will forge a stronger bond between you. In the section on independence, you will remember, we told the story of Rex who had been taught by his father that men don't show emotion. Rex obviously felt very isolated from his father because he could not hope to equal the father's staunch, Spartan impassivity.

So the next time the family car won't start, don't bite your lip and smile. Express yourself. At least the child will get a vocabulary lesson. The next time you are moved or sad, don't go into the den and hide. Show your feelings. The child will be impressed that his respected, competent father is capable of showing strong emotion. He won't be fearful that you are hiding some dark, dangerous secret that would hurt him if he knew.

The next time your child does something that you admire, *tell him.* The next time you feel especially loving toward the child, tell him you love him; demonstrate it by hugging and kissing.

Be as expressive as this loving father was in his letters to his son when the father was away plying his trade:

My Dear Son:

Your letter received. I am more than pleased to know you love Papa so and always want to see him. And I assure you Papa feels the same about his son. I am very proud of my little boy . . . will see you tomorrow afternoon late for a while and hope to see considerable of you during the week.

I hope you are well. All love from

Papa

This nurturant, involved father was W. C. Fields.

Though such vocal, physical, and written demonstrations of caring may be difficult for you at first, they will become easier, especially when you see the glow that a loving father puts on your child's face.

The Gift-Giving Father. A common way for fathers to express nurturance is by the giving of material things to their sons and daughters. Because up until now you usually have been the principal economic provider for the family, you usually have been the parent "from whom all blessings flow." The child of a family in which the father is the chief breadwinner realizes early on in life that his father is the person his mother goes to for money, and his father is ultimately the source of his own allowance.

Fathers are sometimes tempted to shower their children with material goods, such as toys and games. This overgenerosity is not limited to the type of father who prizes material things, either. While the materialist may see gifts as the highest form of love he can bestow, the father who doesn't care much about material goods may have a what-the-hell-it's-only-money attitude. He may see money as a nice, painless way of providing for his child's happiness.

Thus, both the miser and the spendthrift father may try to define their relationships with their children in terms of gifts. Such fathers are easily spotted by the attitude with which they give gifts. If it's a question of "See how much I love you," the gift is not properly made. If the gift is given with the spirit of "Enjoy! Enjoy!" the gift is proper and not meant as a substitute for father involvement. Attempts at bribery do not escape the child; he knows when he is being bought, when material things are being used in place of true nurturance.

The father may also give gifts to his children to gain a feeling of control, of adequacy, or of being needed in the family. He may feel that he is an outsider, a walking wallet. Thus, he may use the only power he feels he has, the power of money, to ingratiate himself into his child's life.

Another reason fathers may give is to satisfy some need in their own lives. Everyone has seen a father buy something for his child that he himself would have liked to have owned when he was young. There is nothing really wrong with this practice. In fact, it is one of the many benefits of having children: you can indulge the child and yourself at the same time. Actually, such gifts are a good way to encourage father-child interaction. If you are down on the floor playing with your child's electric train, he is likely to get to play with you. Such a habit might be harmful only when you are really pushing something on the child that he doesn't want.

Appropriate giving, and appropriate overall nurturance for that matter, depend on clearly understanding the child's values. Buy him things that he can really have fun with and that are suited to his specific personality and needs. Buy gifts that will allow him to express his imagination and competence. Don't choose a gift because it is the latest thing on the market.

A really excellent way of getting to know your child is for both of you to discuss choosing a present for him. By talking about the various possibilities, you will learn about his ambitions and talents. If you set limits on the cost of a gift or show the child the good and bad features of a toy or game, you are fostering his intellectual development. If you encourage him to earn money to pay for part of the gift, you are fostering his feeling of control over his destiny. If you promise him something for later and then actually follow through, you are teaching him to be able to wait for his rewards. As we'll see later, this is important in your son's or daughter's moral development.

Except where the gift is to be used in a joint father-child venture, let the child control it after you give it to him. Don't continually suggest how to use it.

Then there are the "What did you bring me, Daddy?" presents—*don't* make them permanent fixtures in your daily homecoming ceremony. Tell the child you will bring him something next time or that he will have to wait until another time for a present. Thus, he will learn that future rewards are worth waiting for. The confident expectation of such rewards will be a valuable trait when he goes to college, gets a job, or even writes a book on fatherhood!

It is also very valuable for your child to realize exactly what effort went into earning the money for his gift. Certainly, no father wants to be accused of reciting his fiscal troubles to his child, but telling him you cannot afford a certain item is not in this realm. Also don't be afraid to make it clear to your child that you don't want to buy him a certain item because you simply don't want to make the sacrifice. He must realize that while you do love him, it will not be to the extent of unwarranted self-sacrifice on your part. Also, don't underestimate the importance of being able to receive gifts from your child. If he hands you a mudpie, comment on the fine texture or firm body, and show that you value it for the effort it required for him to make it.

Thus, the key to gift-giving and nurturance is to understand the child's values but also to help him to understand yours.

MORAL DEVELOPMENT

But this [minor theft] became more than I could bear. I resolved never to steal again. I also made up my mind to confess it to my father. But I did not dare to speak. Not that I was afraid of my father's beating me. No. I do not recall his ever beating any of us. I was afraid of the pain that I should cause him. . . .

I decided at last to write out the confession, to submit it to my father and ask his forgiveness. I wrote it on a slip of paper and handed it to him myself. . . .

He read it through, and pearl-drops trickled down his cheeks, wetting the paper. For a moment he closed his eyes in thought and then tore up the note. . . . Those pearl-drops of love cleansed my heart and washed my sin away.

This sort of sublime forgiveness was not natural to my father. I had thought that he would be angry, say hard things, and strike his forehead. But he was so wonderfully peaceful, and I believe this was due to my clean confession. . . . I know that my confession made my father feel absolutely safe about me, and increased his affection for me beyond measure.

from *Gandhi's Autobiography*
by Mohandas K. Gandhi

All the traits we have discussed—self-esteem, achievement motivation, independence, assertiveness, and nurturance—operate within the framework of a standard of morality. Relationships with his friends, the other sex, and authority figures are also influenced by your child's standard of morality.

A child's moral development is the process by which he learns to make decisions about right and wrong, learns to feel guilt when it is called for, and feels the necessity of confessing misdeeds. Your child will be morally mature when he takes into account his own sense of conscience and principles when making a decision and when these principles include the good of others.

Moral Progress. Psychologist Lawrence Kohlberg of Harvard University contends that a child goes through six stages of development to reach full moral maturity. As he progresses from Stage 1 to Stage 6, a child performs certain acts because he:

(Stage 1) will be punished if he doesn't obey,
(Stage 2) will be better off if he does them,
(Stage 3) is a good boy or girl and wants to please people,
(Stage 4) is told to by those who know better,
(Stage 5) should honor the rules and laws of society, or
(Stage 6) knows it is right in his own mind.

At each stage he learns new reasons for his conduct, incorporating them with and modifying his moral principles.

We should say rather that children *may* go through these six stages and reach the highest moral level. What actually happens is that many children get "frozen" at a certain stage and use that stage as their primary motivation for morality. Everybody knows at least one fellow who obsequiously obeys policemen or employers in order to please them (Stage 3), or the fellow who declares that he does everything by the book (Stage 5). In contrast, the person at the highest level is the one typified by the old saw "A man's gotta do what a man's gotta do." (This should also be read, "A woman's gotta do what a woman's gotta do.") Actually, levels of moral development are much more complex than indicated here. Even the highest-minded person occasionally does things because he wants approval or because he fears authority. But, in any case, his life is lived *mostly* at Stage 6. Many children can understand Stage-6 morality quite early in their development—at age nine or so.

Father—A Different Moral Creature. Your role in helping your child's moral development is both unique and vital, because the kinds of moral decisions you make may be different from those his mother makes.

In families in which the father works and the mother cares for the family during the day, the mother handles most of the business of the family. She deals with tradesmen, handles interpersonal disputes, and thus offers a vital model for personal moral development to the children.

The father, however, usually makes more of these decisions that deal with manipulation of people and goods governed by the laws of society. For instance, when the furnace breaks down, the mother usually calls the repairman and supervises his visit. However, if the repairman gyps the family and the case must be taken to court, it may often be the father who handles the job. In some families, the father steps in even sooner on the interpersonal-manipulative line, to authorize large repairs or to assess the repairman's competence.

Whether or not the mother works, even today she is still far less likely to be a "creature of laws and contracts" than you are. Men have traditionally been by far the most prevalent makers, interpreters, and enforcers of law in our society. Recent statistics show that only 5 percent of lawyers, 5 percent of judges, and 3 percent of police officers are women. And men are party to far more business contracts than women.

We are not at all applauding this difference, only pointing it out as a fact that must be reckoned with. Fortunately, there are promising signs that more and more women will be lawgivers in our society in the future. A recent survey found that 16 percent of the present enrollment in law schools is women, and the percentage is rising every year.

But still, we must be realistic. It will be a long time before women are equally represented in the law-giving, contract-signing end of society, so we expect the father to be the representative of the rules of society in the family for a good many years to come.

As a result of the differences between men's and women's traditional roles in society, the mother has tended to be a more directly moral person. She is adept at and used to deciding whether Fred was right in hitting John, on the basis of what her conscience and internal principles tell her—case by case. You, the father, are more used to having your conscience expressed through business contracts and codes governing professional conduct.

To be a successful moral person, a child needs a sense of time and schedules. He must have the patience to delay gratification and be able to resist the temptation of the moment in order to gain a reward later. For instance, to get a good grade at the end of the term he must be able to stick to his schoolwork; he must be able to keep appointments because he realizes that it is not responsible of him to keep people waiting.

Just as you are a different person from your wife in being more involved with the laws of society, you are also different in being more concerned with timetables and intervals of time imposed by society.

While the mother at home schedules her duties largely as she sees fit, you are more often a prisoner of the clock, having to be at work at a certain time or having to meet a deadline for some project. The many cartoons that show a husband impatiently waiting for his wife to get dressed for a party do have a basis of truth. The husband tends to see the evening as a schedule to be met; the wife may see it as a chance to enjoy herself and relax, regardless of schedules.

Psychotherapists have observed that their father-absent patients often have a lack of accurate time perception. They have been deprived of experiencing the regular comings and goings of father, the parent who is on a schedule.

Psychologist Walter Mischel, now at Stanford University, conducted an interesting study in the mid-1950s with a group of children in Trinidad that showed the impact of father absence on a child's ability to delay gratification. After asking the children a few questions, Mischel told them he would reward them with some candy and that they could either have a smaller piece right then or a larger piece a week later. Mischel found that among the younger children, those who were father-absent chose the smaller, more immediate reward in significantly larger numbers than those who had fathers living at home. Such father-absent children, besides having a reduced ability to delay gratification, may simply not trust others to do what they say. Other psychologists have suggested that father absence in the first few years of life can interfere with the development of the child's sense of trust.

Father and Morality. In aiding your child's moral development, you should recognize the difference between being morally authoritative and being morally authoritarian. A morally authoritative father is one who is able to guide the child in what is right but who allows the child's own conscience to be the deciding factor. He may even change his own moral thinking if, after hearing him out, he decides the child is right. The morally authoritarian father, on the other hand, dictates morality to his child. Many studies have linked immature moral development in children with such authoritarian and excessively punitive parents.

In sharp contrast, recall the study we discussed earlier by psychologists Paul Mussen and Eldred Rutherford in which they asked four-year-old boys to share some candy with their playmates and found that the more generous boys had fathers who were warm, nurturant, affectionate, and comforting. In fact, other studies suggest that the father's nurturance is one of the keys to internalized moral judgment in children.

In addition to the emotional qualities we've discussed, to develop morally your child also needs certain intellectual advantages that you can give him. For instance, you should make it a practice to tell the child about the ramifications of his actions. Sit down with him and discuss what he has done, whether it is something morally right or morally wrong. In the process, you should keep in mind where your child stands on the six levels of moral development that we discussed earlier so that you won't be talking on a moral plane too high for him to understand. Psychologists theorize that children progress in a fairly straightforward fashion from Stage 1 to Stage 6 as they grow morally. There is also fairly good evidence that a child's development is most helped when he is exposed to reasoning at the stage just above the one he is currently at.

For instance, your infant will begin life at Stage 1. He will understand only that he may be punished for doing certain things, not the reasons behind their prohibition. So, if your eighteen-month-old refuses to heed your warning, you can help him progress by pointing out to him that he should mind you because he may get hurt if he does not (Stage 2). Later still, at age three or four, he may come to understand the value of pleasing people (Stage 3). Then you would explain to him that certain things should be done because you and his mother have had more experience in the world and want to give him the benefit of it.

As he goes from level to level, he will integrate each level with the preceding one. Thus, when he is at full moral development, he will understand not only the nature of punishments in his society (Stage 1) but also the role of authority (Stage 4) and the meaning of personal conscience (Stage 6).

This does not mean that your entire relationship with the child should be predicated on helping him through these six levels, one by one. We believe that children actually benefit after the fact from being exposed to levels of moral thinking far above their present level. For instance, your young child might not quite understand at first why you reported the shoplifting incident you witnessed, but in later years he might look back on the incident with a new perspective. In effect, he will have a backlog of incidents of moral behavior to draw upon. This is especially important if, for some reason, you are not with him in later life. He will have memories to guide him in his development.

Make sure you realize your true feelings toward your child's moral behavior. We know one father, a clergyman, whose child had become involved in several scrapes with authority. His child had stolen money from a schoolmate, had broken windows, had defied a policeman who had gone to his school to question him, and had sworn at the principal. The clergyman took his son to Henry to discuss the problem. As they sat there with the son telling what he had done, Henry watched not the boy but his father. He saw this clergyman, supposedly a moral authority, smiling as his son recounted his misadventures.

In a session alone with the clergyman, Henry helped him discover that all the time the father was telling his son how bad he was being the man was really nonverbally approving the boy's actions by smiling at him, giving him attention, and making him tell every detail of his defiant actions. It turned out that the clergyman himself was resentful at having been transferred to another parish, and his subtly encouraging his son's delinquency was his way of getting back at the world.

Another common example of a father's words being different from his attitude is the father who tells his daughter that he deplores her promiscuity with boys but makes her recount in detail her sexual misadventures. The daughter will soon realize that what Daddy feels is very different from what he says.

Moral Dilemmas. This brings us to our next point in discussing moral development—exposing your child to your own moral dilemmas. Because you are probably away from home more than the mother, you usually do not have the background of information she has when coping with some childhood problem. Thus, you offer a good model for your child of gathering information and using it in a moral judgment. You will frequently find yourself in the situation of coming home from work and being confronted with some moral question on which your wife wants your collaboration. If your child sees that you carefully gather information on the question and then make your decision on the basis of facts, he will have a good start in learning to make his own moral decisions and also in doing abstract moral thinking. This step-by-step process of gathering information on whether Johnny should be allowed to go on a camping trip, or whether it would be wise for Suzy to take an after-school job, can have a great impact on your child, especially if he is an active participant. When you run into situations in which you simply cannot make a decision, explain them to the child. He must learn to live with ambiguity if he is to reach Stage 6.

In developing a sense of morality in your child, just as in developing his other traits, the key is to *expect* competence. Show your child that you have the highest moral expectations for him and that it deeply disappoints you for him to falter.

Father and Authority Figures. You and your wife are obviously the first representatives of authority your child will encounter. You are his first policeman, his first judge, and his first boss. In fostering his moral development, you are helping develop his attitude toward authority figures.

At the same time, he will also be watching how you yourself deal with authority figures, whether it be the policeman giving you a traffic ticket, your boss at work, or any other representative of society and its rules. Remember this next time you encounter authority. Are you subservient? Rebellious? Accepting, but discriminatingly so?

The way you support your child in his relationships with authority is also very important. Don't say, "Do what the teacher says; she is the boss." Rather, you should say, "Listen to the teacher and think about what she says. *If* she is right, do it. Remember that she has had more experience than you."

When the teacher or other authority figure is wrong, you must help your child to understand the mistake and try to remedy it, but not reject the teacher as an authority figure. You may either simply explain why you thought the teacher erred or you may act as a questioner to help your child himself realize why. For instance, you would ask the child why the teacher punished a student too harshly. Was the teacher tired? Had the whole class been bad? Was the boy or girl a perpetual problem? Did he or she do something especially annoying to the teacher?

The intolerance of error by those subject to authority is one reason why there is widespread disrespect for the law in our society. The child who has grown up learning to appropriately accept authority would demand that bad laws be changed but would not reject all laws because of the ill-conceived ones.

FATHER AND DISCIPLINE

Your major role as an authority figure lies, as does the mother's, in the function of disciplining your child. We stress that punishment is not the only form of discipline or even the principal one. In fact, if you are an effective parent, punishment of your child will be a minimal part of your relationship with him. Other more major facets of discipline involve teaching by using rewards. Confidence, achievement motivation, independence, nurturance, and conscience should all be encouraged by giving the child appropriate rewards. By being, above all, nurturant toward the child, you will make discipline a much more positive force in his life.

Your overall disciplinary role is to use the various appropriate means at your disposal to channel the child into a workable relationship with the world around him. Remember this tenet and you will broaden not only your idea of discipline but also your general philosophy of childraising. To some extent, fathers today have abdicated their role of setting limits for their children. In more than half of American families, fathers play only a minor role in setting such limits.

Since we have discussed reward in other sections, punishment will be the main focus here. The way a child is punished often determines his relationship with authority—whether he is comfortable with it, rebels against it, or is subservient to it.

Both you and your wife punish your children, but are apt to do so in very different manners and for different offenses. Before we talk about "the right punishment" for your child, let's discuss various kinds of punishment and how mothers and fathers use them.

Physical Punishment. While both fathers and mothers use physical punishment, mothers may have to resort to it more often than fathers for several reasons. Mothers are generally a more everyday part of a child's life and may often be physically less imposing than fathers. Thus, a mother may feel more of a necessity to underline her admonishments with a whack on the backside. You may only have to threaten physical punishment in order to be listened to. Women have also been brought up to be less inhibited about using physical punishment on someone smaller than themselves, while you have probably been imbued with a strict code of honor that precludes "bullying." Mothers who are at home all day, of course, are also more exposed to the constant daily stress and frustration of dealing with a child.

The Abusive Father. When fathers do use corporal punishment, however, they may tend to hit harder and be more likely to lose control. Fathers or stepfathers perpetrate nearly two-thirds of all incidents of child abuse, often inflicting serious injuries. There are two principal hallmarks of the potentially abusive father. First, abusive fathers were themselves abused when they were children—subjected to physical punishment that was actually injurious to them. Secondly, the abusive father usually lacks the ability to nurture his child; he feels uncomfortable about holding the child or showing him affection.

Additionally, abusive fathers cannot accept their child's defects or mistakes and demand that the child always do the correct thing. Such fathers also possess the absolute certainty that they are always right and the child is always wrong. If you *ever* find yourself punishing the child to the extent of injury, do not hesitate to seek help from a clergyman, family doctor, psychologist, or other professional. It may save your child from having his bones broken, his body bruised, or even from being killed.

"I Don't Love You." Besides physical punishment, parents might use the withdrawal of love as retribution for transgressions or for failure to obey. "I won't love you if you don't . . ." is more often used by mothers than by fathers, because they have traditionally been closer to the child emotionally and can more effectively threaten the child with this loss of security.

Disapproval. Parents, especially fathers, may also use disapproval of a child's actions to induce him to behave correctly. Since you are seen by your child as being a powerful figure and a representative of society, such disapproval can be very effective. Somewhat akin to disapproval is the withdrawal of privileges in order to impress upon the child the gravity of his actions. Fathers seem to use this more than mothers, perhaps because they are more often seen as the dispenser of privileges, at least to the older son or daughter. The father often decides who gets the family car or whether a major purchase for the child should be made.

Bribery. Both fathers and mothers may also use outright bribery to induce the child to do well. Bribery consists of something given to the child *before* he accomplishes the desired behavior, while contingency rewards are privileges promised to the child *after* he performs.

Parents may also try to shame a child into behaving, telling him he is innately bad or hateful.

Fathers often punish for different kinds of offenses than mothers do. Because they are around less, fathers tend to be less involved in punishment for specific instances of misbehavior, such as hitting a friend or stealing a toy. The father is likely to become involved in discipline when the behavior develops into a chronic problem—the child constantly hits others or becomes a habitual thief. Fathers also take responsibility for the punishment of offenses committed outside the home, particularly in offenses that involve society at large and particularly as the child grows older. Ideally, both parents would share in the discipline of chronic misbehavior or social offenses.

The Right Punishment. To make decisions about what kinds of punishment you will use with your child, you must first decide what kind of child you want him to be. Of course, you want him to possess the several traits we discussed earlier—confidence, achievement motivation, independence, assertiveness, nurturance, and, of course, a comfortable relationship with authority.

Constant corporal punishment is not an answer, because such punitiveness may make the child overly aggressive and either rebellious against authority or subservient to it. It may undermine his confidence and in some cases make him overly dependent, because his security may be threatened. Liberal use of the belt or the hairbrush may also result in a child who is unable to be nurturant himself, just as you are failing to be nurturant when you punish him harshly. Physical punishment may also make the child feel that outside forces and not an internal conscience are supposed to govern his behavior.

We're not saying that you must never lay a hand on your child. Speaking realistically, the child is occasionally going to make you quite angry. To emphasize the extent of your anger and perhaps to get the child's attention you may have to resort to a slap on the backside. Children are not as logical as you are, and sometimes all the logic in the world simply will not work on them. The parent who doesn't allow himself to lay a hand on his child may become so frustrated that his anger may turn into resentment. Frankly, the emotional release afforded by a cuff to the child may be a real relief. We think it is quite difficult for a father to refrain from such punishment in anger, and we don't think he should.

This isn't a sadistic viewpoint, for we are not talking about physical punishment that will hurt the child. Physical punishment need only be quite mild to be effective. If it comes from someone he loves and whom he knows loves him, the emotional impact will be enough to make the child think about what he has done. The father who does not lay a hand on his child may be the same one who never kisses him either.

Because you have probably been brought up with the strict admonition "not to be a bully," physical punishment of your child could disturb you more than it does your wife and lead to more problems in relating to your child.

For instance, we knew one father who had a very quick temper. Whenever he became angry at his children, he would usually slap them, and then when his temper cooled, he would feel very sorry and ask their forgiveness, showering them with candy or toys. Of course, the children learned to milk their father for all he was worth. At even the slightest cuff they would bawl uncontrollably, knowing that it would mean more presents for them later.

This father didn't realize how much his children had used him until one day he saw his son push a little girl in front of their house and then try to bribe her to be quiet by giving her money from his bank. The father saw his own punishment-bribery pattern mirrored in his son.

In any case, physical punishment should be nowhere near the top of your list in dealing with your child.

Withdrawal of love should not be on your list at all. By telling the child, "You have done a bad thing and, thus, you have lost my love," you are endangering his security. And security, as we said earlier, is one of the prime goals in raising a successful human being.

The danger of trying to shame your child into obeying you—by telling him he is bad or incorrigible—is that he might come to believe you. He may then set out to justify your faith in his evilness, and your attempts at discipline will have very effectively accomplished just the opposite of what you intended. Try not to threaten your child's self-respect when you punish him.

Using bribery with your child is putting the behavioral cart before the horse. You want your child to expect reward *after* achievement, not to be expected to work for something he already has. A major consideration in all your punishment of the child should be to approximate social reality. Grown-ups seldom get a reward, salary, or commission before they accomplish something, and neither should your child. On the other hand, if you ask your child to behave in a certain way—to pick up his toys or brush his teeth—and if he does it, a promised reward will reinforce the behavior.

Be Specific. The trick to successful reward is to make the reward contingent on some concrete piece of behavior. Don't tell the young child to be "good" and you will give him something. If you feel strongly that the child should conduct himself in a particular way, *be specific about the behavior you expect.* Philosophers ponder interminably over what the word *good* means, so don't expect your five-year-old or even your ten-year-old to know all the subtleties of the word.

Also, don't make rewards contingent on something your child should be expected to accomplish anyway. For instance, continually giving a child a reward for being polite is not very adequate training. Use reward only when he will have to make a particular effort to achieve something and when he simply cannot be expected to understand the ultimate reward of his actions. A child who buckles down and keeps his room clean when he hates to clean up after himself has really achieved something. And when a child bravely goes to the dentist when he is scared stiff, it is a red-letter day. Both achievements deserve praise and perhaps even an unexpected trip to the movies. Even if he has only made it part way, he may be in for a reward.

Withdrawal of privileges should also be contingent on a specific act the child has done, and not simply because he gave you a hard time. One type of privilege-withdrawal—sending a child to his room for ten or fifteen minutes—can be used not just as a punishment as such but to give the child a "time out" period to think about what he has done. Tell the child this when you do send him to his room. Both contingent reward and withdrawal of privilege, though useful, take a back seat to the punishment that is the most effective by far for your child—your disapproval. Reward or punishment may tend to make the child feel that he is off the hook, not responsible for his actions. Once he has either the candy or the spanking, he may feel his responsibility to you and himself is ended.

In showing disapproval of your child's actions, talk to him and explain clearly what it is he has done that is wrong and why you disapprove of his *actions*. Make it clear to him that you believe the misbehavior was merely a temporary slip for him and that you still hold him in high regard. If he is not at the stage where he clearly understands the situation, then impress upon him the impropriety of his deeds by withdrawal of privileges or withholding of a reward because of lack of achievement of the standard you set.

To give your child a framework for your actions, make it a standard practice throughout your fatherhood to tell your child your opinions on behavior, morals, and society and your reasons for them. Children cannot develop a value system in a vacuum. They must have a frame of reference. One side benefit of explaining your actions to your child is that you may find out you really don't have very good reasons for some of them.

More important than telling your child what you disapprove of and why is providing him with an effective model of approved behavior. If you find yourself scolding your child for something you do yourself, you are not being an effective disciplinarian. You may produce an abiding cynicism in your child. One very blatant example of "Do what I say, not what I do" is adults' berating their children for smoking when they may be two-pack-a-day smokers themselves. Keep in mind that your child is more affected by what he sees than by what he hears.

Allow for the Child. In some cases, the reasons for doing or not doing something are just too far above your child's head to be grasped at all, and you should not expect him to function at a level he just doesn't understand. This is especially the case for very young children. A two-year-old cannot grasp why he shouldn't call somebody an "asshole," and thus any punishment is inappropriate. In such cases, it is better to simply divert the child's attention from the behavior or provide him with something else to concentrate on. Teach the child a different word to use. When he is more intellectually developed, he will learn the appropriate use of various words.

Just as you should allow for your child's less developed rationality, also allow for his lack of impulse control. Children have a less articulated time sense than adults, so ten minutes to them is like a much longer period for an adult.

Children are also clumsier than adults, so allow for honest accidents, and when possible, alter the child's environment so that such accidents won't happen in the first place. The parent who leaves a delicate piece of crystal on the coffee table has nobody to blame but himself when his boisterous four-year-old breaks it.

Incidentally, we know many parents who would simply smile and say, "That's O.K." if a guest broke even a precious heirloom, but if a child spills a glass of milk, they will read the child the riot act.

Be flexible in your approach to making the child's world an

easier place to live in. For instance, if your child has trouble making it to school, wake him a little earlier or get him to lay his clothes out and take his daily bath the night before. If your child doesn't like to admit he's tired and resists bedtime, let him play quietly or read in bed rather than fighting him tooth and nail about it. Remember, as with adults, all children do not require the same amount of sleep.

Because fathers tend to differentiate between the sexes more than mothers, they also tend to discipline their sons and daughters differently. Sons are subjected to corporal punishment for misbehavior more than daughters, but sons are given more freedom to explore before they are punished for straying too far. Fathers are usually more tolerant of such traits as sloppiness and aggressiveness in their sons, but they may let their daughters get away with more in other areas. Be careful not to be a disciplinary sexist.

The best route to follow is to take various aspects of your child into account when disciplining him. Before you punish a child for a certain act, ask yourself about how the child's physical and mental development may be related to the "crime." Remember that your child may be capable of different levels of responsibility at different times. The tired, cranky child is a very different creature from the rested, happy one. Your child will also mature at rates that are uniquely his. Just because one of your children understood moral rules at a certain age doesn't mean another will.

It is much better if you emphasize the progress your child has made, rather than punish him for his backsliding. What counts is that he is making progress—he is making successive approximations toward more mature behavior.

8 / Father and Social and Sexual Relationships

All the individual traits we have discussed combine to help determine how successful a child is in his social relationships—how easily he makes and keeps good friends, how much he is respected by others, and how easy and natural a relationship he has with the other sex. As we've discussed, you profoundly influence the basic personality traits that help your child be successful socially and you also influence *directly* how your child relates to others.

A child's friends are a vital part of his development at any age, for they give him an opportunity to try out all the talents and values he has learned from his first socializers—his family. He will find out if he is good-looking, likeable, funny, athletic from the way in which his peers relate to him. If you have done your work well, he will already be realistic about his talents and about what to expect from others. He will also have a strong set of values to contribute to his social group, so in this and many other ways, you not only affect your own child but also his friends.

When your child is still an infant, you, his mother, and the rest of his immediate family are practically his entire social world. As he grows to kindergarten age, his friends begin to mean more and more in his life in terms of social stimulation. But even when he is an adult, you and his mother will remain strong psychological forces in his life.

Just because your child may prefer being with his friends at certain times does not mean your "power" has lessened.

Psychological studies of children consistently reveal that throughout a child's life his parents' opinions are usually regarded more highly than those of other adults or his friends in matters ranging from the setting of rules to personal grooming. Even during stages of normal adolescent rebellion, your teen-ager will still value your opinions if they are fair and well thought out (assuming that you had a meaningful relationship with him before the teen-age years).

Parents play an important role in encouraging their children toward mature social relationships. For instance, children, particularly adolescents, frequently form into groups or gangs for support. This tendency has a certain valuable function during adolescence, because it allows a son or daughter to try out new ideas and fads on others who are also at a trying-out stage and who are likely to be encouraging. If, however, the child lacks a strong enough self-concept, he may continue to cling to "the gang" even after high school graduation or marriage thrusts him into the adult world. Some men especially retain the "old gang of mine" sentiment and center their lives almost exclusively around such groups, neglecting their adult duties as fathers.

The Isolated Child. Children tend to leave out of their groups those who are too intellectual, too awkward, or too unattractive. (These are qualities that teen-agers, in several studies, assert lead to unpopularity. They were asked to list what qualities they liked or didn't like in friends. They consistently said friends should be "regular guys," "smooth," "pretty," or "good-looking." Friends shouldn't be "too smart," "klutzes," "sloppy," or "ugly.") If your child is in one of these categories, you can help him to be relatively unaffected by his "handicap" by pointing out the temporary nature of such cliques and the importance of other qualities in which the child is really special. Tell him that the quality of his friendships are far more important than the quantity. Help him gain self-confidence in his strengths and individuality no matter what his peers think. For instance, tell him how special he is if his peers consider him "too smart."

Father-absent children, particularly boys, are usually less

popular and have less satisfying relationships with their friends than children with highly involved fathers. Many father-absent boys and girls have trouble maintaining friendships because they don't feel comfortable about themselves and therefore lack confidence. A boy who feels unmasculine, for instance, is less likely to assert himself when playing with others. He may then be rejected for not being active enough in play or may simply be ignored by the others. Alternatively, his feeling of insecurity may cause him to become a "tough guy" in order to compensate. He may end up pushing the other children around, berating them, and continually challenging them. This is obviously not the road to the development of positive relationships, either.

Boys who are insecure in their masculinity may seek out older boys as father images and try to model themselves after these older boys. Since they cannot keep up with this older group, their insecurity and feelings of inferiority may become even greater.

The father-absent or -neglected boy may also be forced to seek his definition of masculinity totally outside the family, which means that his development will be subject to the influence of whomever he happens to encounter. Security and a chance to define one's masculinity are the chief reasons for the existence of street gangs in our inner cities. Such gangs demand strict conformity and make acceptance by others the governing factors in a boy's life; they act as collective "fathers" for each gang member.

Father, the Unique Socializer. Regardless of whether your child is male or female, there are several things about you as a man that make you unique in aiding your child's ability to get along with others.

You are likely to be the biggest, most imposing member of your family. You thus have the potential to threaten your children more and produce feelings of inferiority in them. So, if your children have a comfortable, nonthreatening relationship with you, they will tend to feel confident that they can have a comfortable relationship with others.

You are also likely to go to places quite different from those your wife goes to—a rough part of town, for instance, or to a bar alone, or a football game. In many cases, you may actually have more freedom in your movements than does your wife. She may feel more vulnerable to the possibility of violence, especially when with a child. This threat is quite real, because as a woman she is under threat of rape and, as a less physically imposing person, she is more likely to be robbed or assaulted. Many women confess that they plan their lives according to a "rape schedule." They avoid certain areas, don't go out at certain times, or curtail certain activities because of the fear of attack.

Besides offering a child experience with a wide range of places, a father can comfortably seek out a wide range of personal relationships, often wider than can a mother at home. In your work and your play you have dealings with other men and women of many social levels, whereas, realistically speaking, your wife may not usually have such contact. A businessman, for instance, is likely to deal with a wide variety of people—the wealthy and the poor, the married and the unmarried, male and female. A housewife, however, even one involved in bridge clubs, PTA meetings, or scouting or religious groups, is more likely to meet people very similar in background to her own, so she can't offer the child contact with as diverse a group as you can.

Contact with different kinds of people can be particularly useful in preventing racial or religious prejudice in your child. Fear of another racial or ethnic group, based on ignorance of them as human beings, is a major cause of discrimination. If you are white, your child is more likely to be exposed to blacks through you; if you are black, he is more likely to get to know whites through you. With the greater integration of different ethnic groups in the schools and neighborhoods today, contact among diverse groups is a bit more prevalent, but you still offer your child a secure base from which to experience many kinds of people. Obviously, you also offer him an important model for his attitudes toward such groups.

A father who helps his child learn about other people in society will also help the child to be more confident when he deals with them and to be more sophisticated in analyzing their motives and personalities. Through the father, he is more likely to see people engaged in the give and take of commerce, science, or industry—a side of people that is probably different from the side he sees when with his mother. For example, he is more likely to see people bargaining for a financial advantage, arguing over a technical point, or dealing with a complex piece of machinery when he's with you and will therefore get an introduction into the diverse problems that he will have to learn to deal with as he gets older. By watching you and others negotiate he will begin to learn to analyze the intricacies of dealing with people on a more sophisticated level.

A Child's Friends. Knowing your child's friends well is another way you can aid his social development. Of course, the purpose of this familiarity is not necessarily to keep tabs on the child, but to show him that you are interested in his life and to allow you to help him understand his friends better. For example, you might be better able to explain to him why one of his friends is afraid of water or why another has difficulty expressing himself. You not only give your child insights into his friends' behavior, but also into how their behavior is affected by their own parents. This recognition of the effect of parents on children's actions will help your son to be a better father himself when he grows up, for boys today are seldom exposed to such notions.

If you know your child's friends, you can also advise him as to what kinds of friends you think he should avoid. While it is often difficult to forbid your child to see certain people, you can, rather, phrase criticisms of his friends in terms of their impact on you: for example, "Carol disturbs me because she is destructive of others' property." You will be surprised how effective such a respecting approach will be in aiding your child to form helpful friendships.

An excellent way to get to know your son's or daughter's friends is to take them on occasional outings, especially if the outing involves one of your particular hobbies or interests. Not only will you have a chance to observe your child getting along with others, but they will have a chance to observe you in action. If your child sees you as being considerate of his friends, for example, it will vividly bring home to him how much you value consideration. If several fathers in a neighborhood had these kinds of outings, the children would have a chance to compare adult males' styles—something they may rarely get to do in everyday play.

One particular problem fathers sometimes have is sharing their children with others. If Dad isn't home much, he may get especially jealous of his children's friends because he has so little time himself with them.

One such father, Fred R., consistently ignored his daughter's friends, pointedly refusing to talk to them when they were in the house. He would not hesitate to criticize them to his daughter, saying, "Suzy has got to be the sloppiest girl I've ever seen" or "Jane is really not too bright." Finally one day one of his daughter's friends spilled a soft drink on the rug. "Don't you ever come back!" Fred shouted at her. That night his daughter, ashamed and angry, ran away from home and was found several miles away in a diner. It was only after a long talk with her that Fred found out that she was ashamed because of the way he treated her friends. And it was only after several sessions with Henry that Fred and his family discovered why he did this—that he felt jealous of his daughter's attentions to others.

Father's Friends. Let your child get to know your friends too. When a friend visits, don't concentrate on him alone while shooing the child out to play. Let the child listen to the conversation and even interrupt occasionally to ask a question or make a comment. He does not have to be the center of conversation, certainly, but neither should he be excluded from adult social gatherings, especially those including adult males with whom he normally may not have much contact. Though sometimes you may not want the child along when you go fishing, golfing, or on other excursions with friends— and this is a legitimate wish—let your son or daughter participate in these activities when the opportunity presents itself.

Brothers, Sisters, Fathers. Among the first really close social relationships your child establishes are those with his brothers and sisters, and thus, how you act toward your various children can set the tone for their interaction with one another. For instance, if you have one chosen child who is clearly your favorite, the others may come to resent him. On the other hand, a father's scapegoat could become the center of abuse from the whole family.

Father neglect can also be a root cause of intense sibling rivalries in a family, as each child fights for a piece of the father's scant time and affections. In helping to prevent this and to get to know your children as individuals, take time to be with each of them separately, in addition to spending time with the family as a whole. Some fathers fall into the habit of taking their children somewhere as a group or giving them attention as a group, feeling that this satisfies their duty as a parent. Though it may be quite difficult, if you have several children, try consistently to give each of your children "special time" that is theirs alone.

Father: Friend or Foe? In developing a rewarding social relationship with their children, fathers sometimes experience an identity crisis. They are not sure whether they are supposed to be a friend to the child or a disciplinarian. We know some fathers who go too far the former way, insisting their children call them by their first names and trying to avoid having to discipline their children. Other fathers feel they must maintain a certain distance between their children to be effective disciplinarians.

If you try to be the kind of father we have outlined, you should have little problem with such an identity crisis. You will feel comfortable not only being friends with your child but also being the disciplinarian, because both roles stem from the same force, your sense of effectiveness as a parent.

RELATIONSHIPS BETWEEN THE SEXES

A son's or daughter's relationship with the other sex represents a special kind of social relationship, not just the mechanistic sexual technique that is emphasized by some popular books on sex. Many psychologists stress sexual inhibition as an all-important basis of sexual problems. Actually, even if there were no sexual inhibitions in our society, people would still have difficulties in relating to the other sex, because a large contributor to sexual problems is interpersonal difficulties. The boy who is shy with girls, we contend, is not necessarily sexually inhibited. He probably lacks a basis for dealing with girls on a person-to-person level.

In our society, there are some subcultures, such as lower-class, inner-city groups, where there is relatively little inhibition of youthful sexual exploration. But many individuals in these groups still have sexual problems because they lack a mature basis of dealing with members of the other sex as people.

Just as you affect the social development of your children, you also affect this special area of socialization—sexual development. A child with a strong sense of father- and mother-fostered self-esteem, assertiveness, nurturance, and sex-role pride is very likely to develop healthy relationships with the other sex.

Your direct influence on your child's sexuality includes your personal attitudes toward sex, how you handle your half of the husband-wife sexual relationship, and your sex education of your children.

Allowing your child his natural early childhood sexuality is a key factor in giving him a healthy attitude toward sex. Parents tend to forget that they once played "doctor" themselves or were curious about another child's genitals. They also tend to forget that sex was an object of *active* interest by *both* boys and girls. There is no sexually passive gender. (If you have thought about your own childhood—as we suggested in the section on fatherhood and pregnancy—you will realize that sex was a natural part of your childhood exploration.)

Some fathers may see childhood sexuality as a subtle threat to them—a different kind of threat from that sometimes perceived by mothers. A little boy's burgeoning interest in sex may be seen as a sign that the child is escaping control or is out to "replace" his father. Daughters' interest in sex may especially worry some fathers, because they fear that their daughter may turn out to be "bad," a traditional worry of fathers.

Because as a boy you were probably exposed to fewer inhibitions about sex than your wife, you may be in the best position to foster openness about the subject—to "detoxify" sex. You were probably never cautioned about being "taken advantage of" or in danger of social ostracism for being "that kind of boy." You may have to overcome both your own and society's attitudes about male sexual exploits as "conquests," but if you can view sex as a natural part of a special social relationship between a man and a woman, you will be well on your way to giving your child a healthy attitude about sex.

The relationship between you and your wife is, of course, the most important model for your child of a healthy sexual relationship. How you exhibit your affection for one another—whether you are aloof or loving, formal or relaxed—will be closely watched and modeled by the child in his own relationships. How you react if your child walks in on you when you and your wife are making love will be remembered all his life—whether you are ashamed or harsh with the child, or merely annoyed but accepting. Even sexual difficulties between you and your wife—which are usually seen as affecting only yourselves—can have a profound effect on your children. So for everybody's sake, sexual problems should be remedied quickly, for they can endanger an entire family.

Your four-year-old daughter's declaration of "romantic" love to you or your five-year-old son's "marriage proposal" to your wife is perfectly natural. Young children are learning about adult roles and are particularly fond of imitating their same-sex parent.

Freud made much out of the so-called Oedipus complex, and it definitely does occur in many families. However, strong, persistent rivalries between a son and father for the mother's love or between a daughter and mother for the father's love are by no means a necessary part of the child's development. For instance, sons usually have chronically rivalrous feelings toward their fathers only when a strong father-son attachment has not developed in the first few years of the child's life, or when a previously absent father suddenly seems to be competing with the boy for the mother's attention. Such parent-child conflicts often seem to be sublimated during the elementary school years only to reemerge when the child becomes an adolescent.

The Sensuous Father. Fear of their own sexuality has been a barrier to many fathers in relating to their children, and one reason has been the confusion of sensuality and sexuality. There is a difference between these two parts of your personality. Sensuality in the parent's case includes the physical enjoyment of being close to his child—of touching and fondling him—and is *not* the same as sexuality. Sensuality and sexuality are more like two facets of personality, each contributing to the other. Many fathers have felt guilty and uncomfortable about enjoying caressing their child, believing that such enjoyment is somehow unmanly or even sexually perverted. Actually, such sensual enjoyment of children is a natural part of mothering and fathering.

In fact, both mothering and fathering do contain a more overtly sexual sensuality than most people think. Mothering certainly has a physical, erotic component to it, which is one method nature uses to draw the mother close to the child. Her baby is born from her vagina and often nursed at her breasts, both centers of erotic pleasure. Though it is probably more subtle, fathers may have a certain physical attraction to their children too.

In any case, do not reject your child unconsciously or consciously because you find that the sensual nature of your relationship with him may occasionally manifest itself as sexuality. The father who becomes mildly aroused when taking a bath with his young son may reject any further closeness with the child from then on. A father may similarly reject his daughter because he feels a subtle erotic attraction to her. Some fathers are afraid to even touch their children, so anxious are they about the possibility of producing sensual or sexual pleasure in themselves.

By accepting your own sexuality and recognizing the sensual component of fatherhood, you will make it easier for both you and the child to remain close. Only in disturbed or immature people does such natural sensuality lead to overt sexuality. You must have confidence in your own ability to distinguish between the two.

The most effective antidotes to a variety of problems with a child are a hug and a kiss. Use both of them liberally. They are part of your father power.

Sexual Fear. Your dealings with both your sons and daughters in sexual matters should aim at heading off fear of the other sex, including fear of disease, of injury to the genitals, and aversion to the genitals of the other sex. Thus, while you should certainly tell your children about pregnancy or venereal disease, you should not cite their dangers as reasons for not having sex. Nor should you present sex in terms of the dangers of getting hurt by a sexual partner, or of sex organs as being "nasty." None of these ploys, which are often used in our society, is constructive to a child's sexuality.

Rather, you should explain the danger of pregnancy in terms of a responsibility on your son's or daughter's part. If they engage in sexual intercourse, you should point out they have a responsibility to avoid having a child who may likely be unwanted and therefore ultimately unhappy.

You should explain venereal disease as you would any other infection, telling how to avoid it, what to look for, and to be unafraid to seek medical help. Make it clear that the disease has nothing to do with the morality of sex—morality comes from conscience, not from microbes.

Basic Sex Education. Another way to head off fear of sex in your child is by proper sex education. Sex education has frequently been a source of unease and embarrassment to parents, and you must try to overcome such feelings if your child is to be comfortable in his sexuality. Some parents may avoid talking to their child about sex altogether, thinking they can avoid sex education. In reality, you are giving sex education to your child even if you never mention it to him. By not mentioning the subject, you are giving him precisely the worst sort of sex education he could have. Besides being subject to whatever notions he learns from his friends, he may adopt your attitude that sex is not a fit thing to discuss and so be forced to keep his unanswered questions and fears to himself.

Fathers in our society have traditionally been responsible only for the sex education of their sons, and mothers for their daughters. Because of our nervousness about possible sexual attraction between fathers and daughters or mothers and sons, any switching of these roles has been socially discouraged. Actually, both you and your wife should be involved in the sex education of both your sons and daughters. There are unique roles in sex education that only a father can assume with a daughter and a mother with a son.

Since sexuality is one important channel of communication between males and females, it is absurd not to employ every appropriate means possible, including sex education, to increase the ease with which your children can learn to communicate with the other sex.

Proper sex education should begin at birth. An infant is naturally curious about all parts of his body, including his genitals. To start off his life by punishing him for this curiosity will be bad for both you and him. When a young child asks a question about sex, if you answer him truthfully and honestly, you will make it much easier for both yourself and him to discuss sexual matters when he is older. When you find him exploring himself or others, you may remind him that it's not proper to exploit or embarrass others, which he may be doing, but don't scold him for the exploration as such. In such cases you may not want to interfere, unless the child is doing something physically harmful, is about to hurt another child, or if the other child's parents might object.

Though children are curious about sexual matters throughout their development, they are in particular need of information before and during adolescence. A father and mother who have not laid a groundwork for sex education early may find themselves completely unable to cope with adolescent sexuality.

Here are a few general tips on sex education:

Don't lecture to your child and cast him in the role of the passive listener; let him do the questioning. This doesn't mean you shouldn't take the initiative occasionally; there are some topics that he might be reluctant to discuss. You can bring up these topics in a subtle way yourself. But give him the confidence to take the lead by allowing him to bring up the subject himself as much as possible. For instance, if you see your child showing attentive curiosity about a pregnant woman, you can say, "It sure is interesting the way babies grow inside their mothers." By saying this you can convey to your child that you are open for discussion.

If he is keenly attentive to a love scene in a movie, you could say, "Gee, they look as if they are going to make love." Again you are leaving it open for your child to ask questions or make further comments.

As we said previously, sex is more than a physical interaction. Your talks should include the moral basis from which you are operating, whether it is a religious standard or one of individual conscience. Tell your children how love can be expressed through sexuality and how being sensitive to another person's feelings is important. Children and adolescents are just as interested to know the why of sexual behavior as the how. Many parents, however, think all their children want to know is what goes where.

Books on sex can be useful in sex education in several ways, not the least of which is to help you bone up on sex yourself. Many fathers are bashful about sex education because they don't want to admit they don't know everything about the subject. Don't be afraid to do a little studying on sex or even to look things up with your child when he asks something you don't know. If you are bashful about talking to him about sex or if you don't consider yourself a good teacher, buy some sex-education books especially for children and invite him to read them and ask you questions. This is a good way to break the ice on sex education. Learn together!

Father and His Son's Sexuality. Your son's relationship with girls is aided not only by the quality of masculinity, which is influenced by you, and by your model of the father-mother relationship, but also by his observing you in society. Your son will watch how you treat other women besides his mother, including his sisters, other girls his age, your wife's friends, and your own female associates. If you treat other women as fellow humans, rather than as members of the stereotyped category "female," you will encourage your son to do the same.

Your son will also observe how you react to the sexual attractiveness of women besides your wife. Your expressed admiration for an attractive woman walking down the street or a beautiful dancer on television will show your son that you value your sexuality as a natural, prideful part of your being, rather than as something to be hidden from others, especially children.

From the previous discussions on the father's general importance in sexual development you might well imagine how father absence or neglect might damage a boy's relationship with girls. Without a secure sense of his masculinity, for instance, he might well adopt a form of "hypermasculinity" called Don Juanism. To make himself feel "unqueer" he might feel he has to conquer every girl he meets. True, a normal young man is sexually attracted to many girls, but he will not feel the compulsion to prove himself by having sexual intercourse with all of them.

Studies of father-absent boys and men reveal that they often have more trouble with courtship behavior, less satisfying sexual relationships, and more unstable marriages than do father-present males. Studies of unwed fathers show that they were more likely to be from father-absent families or the sons of unwed fathers themselves. (The sexual double standard, however, casts the spotlight more on unwed mothers who, as we shall see, are also more likely to be father-absent.)

Male Homosexuality. Father absence or neglect is also a major factor in the development of homosexuality in males. It is popularly believed that homosexuality stems from a boy's overintimate relationship with his mother. Actually, this overnurturance that often results in homosexuality is usually in the context of a cold, aloof relationship between the father and his son, a relationship in which the father either ignores or dominates the boy and does not encourage the boy to assert himself or be independent.

Besides depriving the boy of an adequate male model and encourager of normal sexuality, the indifferent or hostile father may thrust his son into a continuing search for a father figure. This search, together with the boy's lack of masculinity, may lead the boy to search for a father figure in the form of a male lover.

Psychiatrist Irving Bieber of the New York Medical College, who along with his colleagues conducted a nine-year study of homosexuals undergoing psychotherapy, asserts that he has never interviewed a homosexual who had a close and warm relationship with his father. On the contrary, it was found that many homosexuals had hostile or indifferent fathers.

In some cases Dr. Bieber studied, though, the mere absence of hostility in the father-son relationship is not enough to protect a boy from homosexuality. As well-meaning as some fathers are, they still don't provide their sons with an assertive, involved model of masculinity. One criticism of Dr. Bierber's research has been that he studied only homosexuals with psychological problems. Other researchers have found that even well-adjusted homosexuals usually describe their fathers as having had little to do with them during childhood and as having been weak or hostile.

The father-son relationship is a two-way street. The boy's personality and physical build may affect the way his father and mother treat him. For example, the athletic father with a frail son may not value his son, because the boy doesn't live up to the father's concept of masculinity. This may result in the boy's lack of sex pride and possibly make him more vulnerable to homosexuality.

In our opinion, though both boys and girls have a natural capacity for homosexuality, they have a powerful innate tendency toward heterosexuality. Except in unusual cases, the capacity for responding to the other sex is inborn. The specifics of interpersonal relations between the sexes and sexual techniques are *learned*. Homosexuality is often learned as a defense against a fear of the other sex.

Nevertheless, some homosexuals have learned to live relatively happy and productive lives. Just as all heterosexuals are not well-adjusted simply because they are heterosexual, all homosexuals are not maladjusted simply because they are homosexual.

Incidentally, don't plunk your son or daughter into the category "homosexual" because he has a few homosexual episodes before or during adolescence. Many children go through such episodes during the social "trying out" period of adolescence but later adopt a consistent preference for heterosexual relationships.

Son's Sex Education. Because you have experienced many of the same feelings and the same kind of physical development, you can be particularly effective in telling your son what to expect as a growing male. What you tell him will carry more weight than something he learns from his friends, or even something learned in school. For instance, you can better assure him of the normality of the spontaneous erection that embarrassed him in class or the "wet dream" that he experienced. Many boys go through such episodes, and, if you are sensitive enough to your son's development to foresee such things, you can assure him that such erections or ejaculations are a normal part of his development. You may also find occasion to assure your son that his penis is of normal size and shape. Boys can be quite overawed by the size of their father's genitals, and your assurance that he will also develop normally will help his confidence.

When your son asks you about male-female genital differences, you can start him off with the right attitude by explaining that women have their sexual organs inside, *not* that they "don't have a penis." Your explanation will carry weight with your son, because you have a penis and if you don't see yourself as somehow superior because of it, neither will your son see himself, or other males, as superior. These expressions of genital equality, along with your other egalitarian attitudes toward women, will impress upon your son the concept that women are to be valued as persons and as equal sexual partners.

You can also assure him that masturbation, which is engaged in by almost all males at one time or another, is usually perfectly normal and harmless. (According to a recent survey, over 90 percent of men and over 60 percent of women masturbate at some time in their lives, though men do it about twice as frequently as women. About twice as many boys as girls have masturbated by the age of thirteen.)

Because females are not as likely to masturbate, or do it as frequently as males, your wife may be more anxious about the practice than you are. She may see it as more unnatural and may be more likely to punish your child for it. You can protect your son from being punished by his mother for masturbating and can help him understand why Mother may be more nervous about it. You can also talk with your wife about any discomfort she may have about the practice.

You may find it feasible to alleviate the guilt and tension surrounding masturbation by joking about it. An uncle of one boy was heard to ask his nephew laughingly whether he was "loping his mule around the bathroom nowadays," conveying to the boy that the practice was not one to be considered dangerous or shameful.

Because of your "extensive" experience with women, your son will also benefit from your role as a dispeller of sexual myths. You can assure him that "oversexed" women who take all a man can give, or the sexual schemer who ensnares men, are usually only the myths of scared, neurotic men. Other facets of womanhood, such as what makes a man attractive to a woman or how female organs function, may best be explained by your wife.

Besides the specifics of physiology, you can also help your son in his social relationships with girls. When he "bombs out" with a girl, you can assure him that it doesn't mean he is inferior or unattractive. When he hits it off with a girl, you can help him see his success in terms of a personal, equal relationship, and not as a conquest.

Father and His Daughter's Sexuality. Fathers are also vital to their daughters' sexual development. As we have said, you are the first man in your daughter's life, and she will see you as a model for the whole species. During her early sex-role development—the first few years of her life—she will begin to realize that she is a girl and that you are a man. As she grows, she will look to you—as the most important man in her life—for a reaction to her feminine development. As she enters adolescence, both your roles as male prototype and as judge of femininity will intensify. A good relationship with your daughter during this period will help her weather the emotional storms of her relationships with boys. You also help your daughter get to know other adult males, including your friends and business associates. With your "protection," she can enter into many meaningful relationships with males.

Research done on the father-daughter relationship reveals that father involvement has very positive effects on a daughter's sexual development. College women who have long-term romantic relationships, for instance, report closer relationships to their fathers than those who are not romantically involved. On the other hand, women who have unstable sexual associations and broken marriages are more likely to report poor relationships with their fathers or a high degree of father absence in childhood.

Surprising to many is the idea that a woman's childhood relationship with her father plays an important role in her ability to have an orgasm. In a major study, Dr. Seymour Fisher, a clinical psychologist at the Upstate Medical Center of the State University of New York, analyzed the personalities and behavior of over three hundred middle-class housewives. Dr. Fisher conducted in-depth interviews of the twenty-five- to forty-one-year-old women and gave them comprehensive psychological tests. He found that a woman's confidence in herself and others relates very strongly to her ability to have an orgasm. The high-orgasm women in Fisher's study recalled their fathers as having a definite set of values, being demanding, and having high expectations for them. Women who rarely achieved orgasm reported their fathers as being casual, permissive, and unavailable for deep involvement. They were more likely to say that they could not set up a relationship with their father either because he had died early in their lives or was away from home because of his job.

By having high expectations for your daughter you are showing that you care about her development and that you are trustworthy, respecting, and caring. This naturally prepares her for a satisfying sex life later with another trusted, respecting, caring male.

Sex and the Father-Deprived Girl. Just as father presence or involvement has positive effects on girls' relationships with boys, so father absence or noninvolvement can injure a daughter's sexual development.

Father-deprived girls are more likely to become "boy-crazy" —completely obsessed with boys—as they desperately seek affection from a male father figure. Other father-deprived girls may idealize their absent fathers and spend their lives in search of a male who fits their fantasy.

Several studies have suggested that women who reject the role of mother or who are insecure in their femininity are likely to come from father-deprived or broken homes. Delinquent girls, and those pregnant out of wedlock, are also more likely to come from broken homes, in most cases meaning father-absent homes.

A problem found in many father-absent homes is that the mother may bequeath derogatory attitudes toward males to her daughter. Such girls may very likely grow up with the attitude that men are worthless and untrustworthy. There seems to be particular danger of this in lower-class communities, where girls are less likely to be exposed to an involved, successful male model inside or outside the family.

When the father is absent, girls, like boys, are more likely to become overdependent on the mother, but it may injure girls more than boys because traditionally girls are not encouraged to be independent as much as boys are in the first place. The result of mother-permitted dependence may be a girl who is overdependent on those around her and at the same time not able to fully trust her husband or other males.

In 1972, psychologist Mavis Hetherington, of the University

of Virginia at Charlottesville, reported an extensive study with father-absent girls, illustrating their problems in dealing with males. In part of her study, Dr. Hetherington played a game of "psychological chairs" with seventy-two teen-aged girls, twenty-four each from intact, widowed, or divorced families.

An assistant ushered each girl into a room containing a male interviewer at a desk with three chairs. One chair was at the end of the desk very near the interviewer, another was directly across the desk from the interviewer, and a third chair was across and about three feet down from the interviewer. The psychologists found definite differences among the groups of girls in terms of which chair they took. The girls from intact families usually took the chair that was a medium distance away from the male interviewer and were fairly at ease with him. The girls from divorced families tended to take the chair closest to the interviewer and to assume a more sprawling, open posture. They talked more to him, sat closer to him, leaned forward more, and smiled more. The girls whose fathers had died took the farthest chair, sat stiffly upright, tended to turn away from the interviewer, avoided looking at him, and spoke very little. Both groups of father-absent girls were more nervous than father-present girls, plucking at their clothes, pulling at their fingers, and twirling their hair.

Dr. Hetherington found that the attitudes so vividly portrayed in the interviews also appeared in the girls' social lives. Girls with divorced fathers sought out boys more and tended to be seductive toward them. For instance, at a dance observed by the psychologists, the daughters of divorced fathers were usually found near the boys' stag lines, constantly trying to get their attention. Such girls also tended to be sexually promiscuous, engaging in more and earlier sexual relationships than did father-present girls. In their insecurity, they seemed to feel forced to use their bodies in order to attract boys. The girls whose fathers had died, conversely, generally avoided boys, refusing to date and remaining very inhibited around them. At the dance described previously, these girls avoided the male areas of the dance floor. Two such girls even hid in the ladies' room for the entire evening.

Besides illustrating the sexual problems related to father absence, Dr. Hetherington's study also showed how a child's attitude toward males is influenced by the reason for father absence. Interviews of the girls revealed that the daughters of divorced fathers were more likely to devalue and dislike their fathers, perhaps because of their mothers' attitudes and perhaps because they felt abandoned. The girls whose fathers had died were more likely to remember their fathers as idealized images of manhood, which no other man could equal. Though they expressed it differently, both groups were basically insecure in dealing with males. Insecurity in relating to males was greatest among those girls who became father absent before the age of five. Again, we see indications of the tremendous importance of the early father-child relationship.

Problems in dealing with men are not restricted to father-absent girls; father-neglected girls can have just as many difficulties. And when father-deprived or -neglected girls become mothers themselves, they are more likely to be "carriers" of psychologically unhealthy attitudes about men and fathers, passing them on to both their sons and daughters.

Female Homosexuality. Problems in the father-daughter relationship have also been linked with female homosexuality. Lesbians are much more likely to see their fathers as weak and incompetent. An example is the masculine "butch" type homosexual who, perhaps because of a weak father and a distant, powerful mother, rejects her femininity and men as appropriate sexual partners. Conversely, other lesbians describe their fathers as puritanical, exploitative, and fear-inducing, as well as possessive and infantilizing. Such girls, thus, may come to fear men and to reject heterosexuality because of its "sinful" nature. This may be the origin of the more passive "femme" lesbian.

Psychiatrist Harvey Kaye and his colleagues did a study comparing a group of female homosexuals and a group of female heterosexuals. Interestingly, Dr. Kaye found that female homosexuals seemed to have had much the same parental relationships as male homosexuals, except with the sexes of the parents reversed. While the fathers of male homosexuals were hostile and aloof, the mothers of lesbians were cold and distant from their daughters. Like the mothers of male homosexuals, the fathers of lesbians were close-binding, babying, and unencouraging of a normal sex role. The fathers additionally belittled the girls' boyfriends, produced fear in the daughters, and were unduly concerned about their health.

Daughter's Sex Education. Your daughter's sex education may be much more difficult than your son's, either because of a traditional male bashfulness about discussing sex with females or because of a subtle fear of an incestuous relationship. Since fathers have traditionally defined their daughters' morality in terms of being sexually "proper," you may also fear that talking about sex with your daughter will make her into an "easy woman."

Don't be afraid of this. In reality, by participating in your daughter's sex education, you are showing her an example of a male who sees sex as a natural part of the whole personality. Thus, your daughter will see that the sex act is only one part of male-female relationships, and she does not have to use it as her only attraction in dealing with men.

Just as your wife can talk about women to your son with a special kind of expertise, so you can talk about men to your daughter. You can allay the myths and fears about boys that often circulate among girls and can answer your daughter's questions about male physiology. Just as you told your son that the idea of woman as castrated man is incorrect, so you can tell your daughter.

You are a particularly good coach for your daughter on how to handle boys. For instance, you can tell her about what makes a girl attractive to boys in more than a physical sense. You can teach her that she can be active in choosing her boyfriends and still be successful with boys, that girls are not passive creatures to be manipulated by men. In a practical vein, a father's coaching in self-defense has helped many girls save themselves from rape.

Father and "The First Time." Perhaps the most vital time in the sex education of both sons and daughters is during their first sexual relationship. If you have an honest relationship with them all during their lives, you should have little trouble relating to them at this period. They should have a clear idea by now of what your feelings are about the nature of the sexual relationship. Since there is a good chance that their first "affair" will come premaritally, they should also know what your feelings are on this subject. They should also have confidence that, while you are pulling no punches in your opinions, you recognize that they have a right to control their own lives and that you can only be a concerned, loving advisor. Your high expectations of them will be much more effective than reprimands could be.

Looking at it realistically, premarital sex can be more of a problem for girls than for boys because there is still a great deal of male exploitation of females. Also, should your daughter become pregnant, she will probably be left with the responsibility of deciding whether she will abort the baby or whether she will give birth (and if the latter, whether to keep the child or give it up for adoption).

Young boys *may* have serious difficulties in their first sexual encounter if they go to prostitutes to lose their virginity. There have been many cases of young men who travel to a slum section of the city to lose their virginity and have been so shocked at what they saw there that they couldn't maintain an erection. As one young man put it, "I went into this room with all this crummy furniture and a dirty bed, and I turned around and saw this woman taking her clothes off, and I just didn't want any part of it. I thought for a while after that something was wrong with me."

Your job as a father in such cases is to decide what your attitude about your son, his virginity, and prostitutes is and to tell him about it. If you encourage your son to develop sexual relationships with girls in his own school or neighborhood, will you be accused of "letting him take advantage of nice girls"? On the other hand, if you discourage him, will he seek sex outside his own social circle or with prostitutes?

The case of Jerome P. and his son Edward shows one pitfall. Jerome told his son never to discuss sex in front of his mother.

"I'll teach you all you need to know, and I'll take you around." He did indeed take his son to a prostitute, and that's where Edward continued to go for his sexual outlet. The reason Henry learned of this case was that Edward came in for marital counseling because he was impotent with his wife. He had come to think of sex as something you only did with girls who "weren't nice." He was ashamed and nervous to approach his wife, whom he considered "nice."

In any case, we feel you should take an active advisory role with both your sons and your daughters regarding their sexual relationships. Though many parents try to ignore the developing sexuality of their teen-agers, you can probably sense when your son or daughter is about to enter into a sexual relationship and can act accordingly. If, for example, your daughter has been dating a boy whom you feel is insensitive, irresponsible, and exploitative, don't be afraid to tell her your opinion. Don't passively go along with whatever is happening because you are bashful about talking it out. On the other hand, if you feel the boy she is involved with is clearly mature and responsible, and they have a relationship based on respect, you may not feel that there is a basis for interfering. The underlying message to your child should be "I love you in any case."

9 / *Father, Physical Growth, and Body Pride*

Although there are differences in mothering and fathering in all areas of parenting, perhaps the greatest one is in the way mothers and fathers aid their children's physical development.

Because of physical differences and those fostered in our society, fathers have a unique and powerful role to play in helping their sons and daughters to develop strong and healthy bodies and to have positive attitudes toward their bodies.

Body-Build and Behavior

There is a definite, though not absolute, relationship between a person's body-build and the way he thinks and reacts to his environment—a relationship that seems clear at nursery-school age and even earlier.

According to the work of psychologist William Sheldon at Harvard during the 1930s and 1940s, there are three basic body types: the mesomorphic (muscular build), the endomorphic (round, plump build), and the ectomorphic (slender, fine-boned build).

Mesomorphs tend to be more physically assertive, have higher energy levels, be extroverted, dominating, open, and relatively fearless and impulsive.

Endomorphs tend to be less vigorous and aggressive physically, and be more cooperative and comfort-loving than mesomorphs. They are more easygoing and less apt to be upset by their environment.

Ectomorphs tend to be the most sensitive to their environment. Their reactions to it tend to be dominated by thought processes rather than by activity, as with the mesomorph, or by physical comfort, as with the endomorph.

However, most people are combinations of these types, the mesomorphic endormorph or the ectomorphic mesomorph, for instance. The former type is large, but with a less muscular and more obese build, and the latter tends to be lean but muscular. Even if a person is a relatively "pure" type, his interaction with his environment is also very important in his personality development.

Certainly, unusual or traumatic experiences will affect your child's personality uniquely, but even normal, everyday experiences affect him because of the way they filter through his body-influenced temperament. The very mesomorphic boy or girl, for instance, is more likely to have the energy and daring to go out and "meet the world," so he is likely to have the confidence that social experience brings. The very ectomorphic child, who is less physically energetic, may spend more time in contemplation and study, and this may help him to be more successful in academic pursuits.

These same boys or girls are likely to be treated differently by the adults around them, including their teachers. The mesomorphic child may be punished more for being vigorous, and the ectomorphic child may be encouraged more because he is quieter and more studious.

Early sex differences in behavior are due to more than gender per se; they may be partially determined by average *physique* differences in the sexes. Studies of young children's physiques reveal that more boys are found among mesomorphs, and more girls among endomorphs.

Children's physiques are by no means static, and you should not stereotype your young one according to his physique. Certainly, you can recall a girl who was obese as a child but who grew into a slim woman or a skinny boy who grew into a well-muscled adult.

An important function of your father power is to mediate between the world and your child in helping him adjust his physique-temperament to society, and vice versa. This means, for instance, that you caution your mesomorphic son about becoming a bully, but it also means you make sure that his teacher doesn't punish him for merely being vigorous. It means that you help your child, no matter what his body-build, gain confidence in himself as an effective person.

Be sure also to take your child's physique-temperament into account when dealing with him. If you scold your endormorphic child, he may shrug it off or accept it passively. An ectomorph is more likely to brood about the scolding and take it more to heart. A mesomorph is more likely to strike out by talking back or even by becoming physically aggressive. You may get much further by talking to a slim, ectomorphic child than by spanking him. A vigorous, mesomorphic child, on the other hand, may be more likely to require more physical discipline. An endomorphic child may need a vigorous emotional expression of your disapproval or the withdrawal of privileges to impress upon him your feelings.

Be Careful of Stereotypes. However, keep in mind the danger of stereotyping your child because of his body-build. People in our culture tend to stereotype ectomorphs (slim people) and endomorphs (corpulent people) negatively, while seeing mesomorphs (muscular) more positively. For example, males and females, even young children, tend to describe mesomorphs as having leadership ability, being friendly, and being physically strong and capable. Yet, they describe ectomorphs and endomorphs as making poor leaders, being unpopular, and being physically weak and incapable.

Children develop such stereotypes even before they enter the first grade. The negative view of very thin people is especially interesting when one considers that the slim male or female model is seen as an ideal when people buy clothes or go on diets. However, consistent with the prevalent contemporary prejudice against obese individuals, the endomorphic physique tends to be described in particularly negative terms.

It seems, then, that if your child is either very thin or rather fat, he may automatically be seen by some people in a negative light, even though his personality may not fit popular notions. "Gee, your son is skinny. Don't you think he should eat more?" was the comment by a friend to one father we knew. The father, of course, came right back with a discourse on the fact that his son was naturally that way and proud of it, and that the friend really shouldn't make snap judgments about people. In this case, the son overheard the exchange, and his body pride was thus aided by the fact that his powerful father came to his defense.

Our modern society frowns on racism or religious persecution, but we have not given enough attention to prejudice against certain physiques.

One way to avoid stereotypes is to spend time observing your child while keeping his physique-temperament in mind. Watch how he responds in play with others, with his toys, and with adults. Does he have a high level of activity or a low one? How sensitive is he to others, to their support and to their teasing? What you observe should give you insight into the child and allow you to help him feel body pride and a sense of his own power in dealing with the world.

Your Body-Build and Behavior. In learning to value your child for what he is, you have to recognize the nature of your own physique-temperament and how it may affect your relationship with your child. For example, the vigorous, muscular father with a robust son or daughter may never even have to give physique-temperament differences a thought, for both parent and child may be athletic and outgoing. The slim, delicate father with a robust son or daughter may be in an altogether different position. He may have to allow for differences in energy levels between him and his child. He must ensure that he does not stifle his son's vigor, either by failing to show him that he values exercise or by scolding him for being too boisterous.

We know one such father who was very effective in encouraging his son in athletics even though he was awkward himself on the playing field and didn't much care for sports. He attended football games with his son and set up a basketball court for the boy when the son became interested in the sport. "I really didn't care much for the game, but I could tell that what I was doing for Sammy was important," said this father. "I could tell when later he played high school basketball and, during the half-time, would look around to make sure I was there." This father realized the value of his father power in helping his child develop a positive feeling in his chosen interests.

MOTHERS' AND FATHERS' ATTITUDES TOWARD PHYSICAL DEVELOPMENT

Because of the contrast in the ways males and females are reared and their experiences as adults, your attitude toward physical development is likely to be quite different from that of your wife.

A mother's attitude toward the child's body is colored by her traditional and probably physiological role in maintaining the child in a stable environment. She gave birth to a child she held in her body for nine months and whom she physically nurtured for years afterward. She has had the profound, intimate feeling of being a source of food and early protection for the child. For these reasons the mother is likely to worry more about the child's health. She tends to be more concerned about environmental dangers and to worry more about the child's overexerting himself and about his illnesses, feeling that she should be the one to care for him during sickness.

All these attitudes, of course, can be vital to the child's well-being, but the father's attitude is also vital. Certainly, you are concerned about your child, and help care for him when he is sick, but you are probably not quite so deeply emotionally involved with the child's health. You are, perhaps, freer to encourage the child to push himself, to explore even at the risk of a hard knock or two. This greater tendency toward challenge is clearly reflected in what we overheard one father say about protecting children: "You know, there is just so much you can do. You make sure things are safe around them.

You try to remove hazards so they won't hurt themselves, and then they're walking outside one day and a wheel falls off an airplane a mile up and Pow!" A mother would probably not take such an attitude, preferring to concentrate more on the reasons why she should protect the child and less on the reasons she cannot protect the child completely.

Or, how about this father? "My daughter will be crawling along the couch and my wife will say, 'Watch it! Don't let her fall off.' and I say, 'She's just going to have to learn about what happens when you get to the edge of the couch. It's better that she learn now when she can be caught than some other time when she could be hurt.' "

Because the child may see you as physically stronger than your wife and because you may play with him more vigorously, he is more likely to test himself physically with you. Your son or daughter will feel that he can really wrestle as hard as he can, test his jumping and hitting, and unleash his aggressions on you without being afraid that you will object or be hurt. Every young child wonders what the limits to his strength are and perhaps wonders, "If I really hit somebody, would I kill him?" You can stem his fear of accidentally hurting another person because of not knowing his own strength.

You can also give your children the confidence to admit they aren't as tough as they think they are, without hurting their self-esteem. For instance, Henry's son, Cameron, likes to wrestle hard with his father. Cameron would often say, "I'm tougher than you, Dad." As he matured and gained the confidence to see himself realistically, his attitude changed, until one night sitting at the dinner table he said in self-discovery, "You know, I guess I'm not really as tough as you, but I'm going to be tougher when I grow up."

Women usually do not place as high a premium on athletic prowess as men do. There are, of course, complex social reasons for this: we have been taught that in athletics being the best is of the highest importance. Since women do not usually compete on the same level as men in most sports, and thus cannot be "the best," they have been taught that they should not even try. More important, society has never allowed women the freedom to feel that athletics is legitimately feminine.

When women do engage in physical exercise, it tends to be for a different reason than men. Women exercise mainly to become shapely because of their greater concern for appearance. Men exercise mainly to stay in shape because of their greater interest in their muscles and their greater feeling for the necessity of physical readiness. In any case, men are more likely to consistently engage in athletics, whether the game be golf, basketball, or jogging.

Fathers and mothers also differ in their attitudes toward their child's appearance. Fathers tend to be the more judging parent and, unfortunately, sometimes the more coldly critical one. The old adage "a face only a mother could love" has a large element of truth in it. This tendency of fathers to judge does have its positive side, however. It means that in your child's eyes, your appraisals of his appearance and manner will have a great deal of impact, for he senses that your opinions stem from a more objective attitude.

As we have said before, you tend to be larger than your wife and more active physically. Your child will thus see you as an impressive, sometimes overwhelming figure. It is your job to make sure that this physical father power is used to give your child confidence and his own sense of physical power.

THE DEVELOPMENT OF BODY PRIDE

Both your sons and daughters begin developing a body concept about themselves at a very early age. It comprises their basic feeling about their own body—whether it is beautiful, ugly, adequate, inadequate. Any woman who has been pregnant can tell you its effect on personality, for she has undergone an abrupt, disconcerting change in body concept as her abdomen swelled during pregnancy. This rapid change from a slim figure to a round one can be jarring for any woman, no matter how well-adjusted.

Body pride also includes a child's feelings about specific parts of his body. Everybody has had at least one episode in his life in which he was convinced that something was wrong with his body—that he had terrible acne, that his neck was too long, or that he was too fat or skinny. Adolescents are particularly vulnerable to such feelings.

And, of course, there is the oft-seen case of the parent who teaches the child that genitalia are dirty and repellent. "Don't touch that," admonishes such a parent. "That's not nice. Wash your hands." A child taught such repugnance of his genitals will likely grow up believing his own genitals, his body, and sex are all ugly, dangerous, or disgusting.

Helping Your Son's Body Pride. Using your father power to give your son a sense of body pride hinges mainly on the fact that he is a male like you. He will unavoidably compare himself to you physically and will find himself lacking. If you realize this, you can help him develop body pride by assuring him that he will grow into your shoes, and that he, indeed, cuts a nice figure himself. Compliment him on his abilities or his muscles and help him see that he represents a continuation of what you are physically; that you are what he will probably become.

Giving your son a sense of body pride may be especially difficult for you if he is unlike you physically. The slim father may subtly or unsubtly devalue his fat son's physique, or the muscular father his slim son's physique. Just by recognizing the enormous impact your attitude can have in helping your son to feel comfortable with his own body is usually enough to avoid such pitfalls.

Then there is the especially ironic case of the father who devalues his son's physique, though the father was exactly like the son when he was young. Witness this conversation we overheard between two fathers:

"Yeah, Jack's a nice kid, but I feel sorry for the little fellow. He is a chub, you know."

"I thought you were a little pudgy yourself when you were a kid. Didn't I see a photograph of you somewhere?"

"Yeah, I was myself, but I grew out of it. I remember all the other kids used to sing that song, 'Fatty, Fatty two-by-four; can't get through the kitchen door.' "

This father obviously did not realize that he was in effect singing an adult version of this song to his own son.

Helping Your Daughter's Body Pride. Your role in fostering your daughter's body pride is quite similar to that with your son, though there are definite differences. You are encouraging both your son and your daughter to feel healthy, adequate, and strong. And with your daughter, as with your son, you are the more judging parent, possibly the more critical one. However, you will inescapably see your daughter not so much as an earlier version of you but as a blossoming member of the other sex—perhaps like your wife, perhaps not. You cannot help but appraise her through the eyes of a male, and even when she is quite young, you will value her most highly for traits that you value in other women, particularly her mother.

In a previous chapter, we stressed that you should not be uncomfortable with the flirtatious, even physical attraction between you and your daughter. Rather, you should see it as a natural part of your relationship, and something that becomes *over*intimate only in people who have serious psychological problems. In terms of aiding your daughter's body pride, this attraction means that you should not hesitate to compliment her on her attractiveness and to boost her physical confidence. Just as you see her through the eyes of a male, she sees you through the eyes of a female. When you show her that you consider her physique an attractive part of her personality, you confirm for her that other men probably will too. Thus, she will feel more able to enjoy the friendship of men and not be reticent because of an imagined physical unattractiveness. Wallflowers are made, not born.

Occasionally, however, a daughter's burgeoning physical beauty may drive a wedge between mother and daughter. A mother who is sensitive about growing older may resent a father's admiration of his daughter. Be careful about over-praising your daughter and underpraising your wife in such cases.

We've stressed your appraisal of your daughter's physical

attractiveness because girls seem to place more importance on physical good looks than boys do. Boys seem to be more concerned with their musculature or the physical ability of their bodies, and girls more with the features of their faces and the shape of their bodies. But one major mistake many fathers (and mothers) make is in not allowing their daughters to test themselves physically so that they can develop a sense of pride about their bodies' functioning as well as appearance.

We know one such stifled girl, Leah H., who was terribly accident-prone. In the space of a year, she had suffered a broken wrist, a sprained ankle, and a concussion, in addition to bumps and bruises derived from colliding with almost every piece of furniture in the house. Neurological tests revealed no coordination problem, and it wasn't until the family had a talk with the school coach that they realized the basis for her problems. All her life Leah had been treated like a china doll. Her father and mother continually warned her, "Be careful; don't hurt yourself," or, "Don't climb that tree, you might fall out." Or else, "Be a nice girl now; your bones aren't that strong." Because of such warnings, Leah, who was naturally outgoing and vigorous, often became so nervous that she couldn't control her movements and thus chronically suffered accidents.

Your role in helping your daughters and sons to be proud of their bodies is a continuous one. As they grow, they need someone to help them update their body image. We know of many quite attractive people who were awkward as adolescents or children and who still think of themselves in that way. They have never had someone whom they love and respect, someone whom they feel is objective about their attractiveness, tell them, "You have really grown up; you are a very handsome person."

You are probably the best mirror your child has for continually assessing himself. You are one of the few people who has watched him grow all the way from infancy to adulthood. He will thus see you as being in an excellent position to tell him how he is progressing, and if you don't, you are not using your father power. In a sense, you are able to create beauty, because beauty can develop just as much through force of personality as through a good profile.

FATHER AND ATHLETICS

Besides helping your son and daughter feel confident in their own physical attractiveness and helping them accept their bodies, you also have a role in fostering their pride in athletic achievement. An important feature of this is your attitude toward athletic competition.

Apply the same rules to athletic achievement that you apply to intellectual achievement. Just as your child should be expected to do his best in academic endeavors but be able to live with limits on his abilities, so he should also have such an attitude toward athletic endeavors. Children should develop internal and realistic standards concerning their abilities. Unfortunately, this is often not the case. If a child cannot compete on the highest levels, with the best players, many fathers believe he really shouldn't compete at all.

Encourage your child to compete at whatever level he can. Encourage him to take pride in his ability and to obtain the greatest joy when he achieves something that is a challenge to his own internal standard and his own abilities.

If your son or daughter has problems with his body pride, athletics can be an excellent way to bolster it. For instance, many young men take up weight lifting because they feel insecure. The encouraging father might lift weights with his son and would certainly show an interest in his son's progress in lifting heavier and heavier weights or increasing his repetitions of the exercises.

Just as in the fostering of your child's emotional, social, and intellectual development, take his level of maturity into account here. When Henry, for example, first took his son, Cameron, bowling, Cameron (then four years old) tended to lose interest in the game rather quickly, fidgeting and wandering around. It finally dawned on Henry that Cameron probably liked bowling, but that the time between his turns was too long to sustain his interest. Henry let his son bowl as long as he wanted to, keeping score and encouraging him frequently, and Cameron's enjoyment increased enormously. When Henry plays baseball with his younger children, he uses a very large ball, such as a basketball, which is much easier for them to hit. The thrill the children get out of hitting the big ball is obvious. And when it comes time for an older child to bat, Henry simply reverts to the standard baseball. Similarly, in shooting basketballs, the young children get to stand closer to the basket, the older children stand at a standard distance, and Henry must stand farther back.

A major problem concerning athletics and the father-son relationship is an overstressing of athletics by the father. There is usually little danger that fathers will undervalue athletic achievement in their sons, for most fathers see their sons more as extensions of themselves and are quite proud when their sons achieve in such a traditionally masculine area as athletics.

Such was the case of Al J. who, when his son began to get quite despondent and frustrated in school, came to Henry for advice. Al described several problems with his son: His grades had dropped, he was constantly daydreaming in class, and he was generally very lackadaisical. He had even lost interest in neighborhood sandlot sports. Al seemed to be having problems too. He was very depressed and fatigued, and was on the verge of being fired from his job as personnel director for a trucking company.

The son, fourteen, had failed to make first string on his junior high school football team a month before, but when the father was asked if that had been bothering him, he assured Henry that it was not. However, when he saw Henry, the next week, the father talked more freely about himself. It seemed that Al had gotten married while quite young and in fact had been prevented from playing college football because he had had to work after school to support his wife and later his growing family. He had been a promising quarterback on the team, and he later encouraged his son to go out for the same position. When his son didn't make the team, Al told him that it was all right, but the son sensed from Al's depression that it was far from "all right."

With the whole family together in the room, the father's story had a wide range of effects. The mother realized for the first time how deeply Al resented not having been able to play football, and Al and his son realized how they had been reacting to one another. Al's new realistic attitude about his son not being a quarterback payed off. Relieved of always trying to be a quarterback, the son discovered that he was a much better guard than quarterback, and the next season became one of the key members of his team.

A particularly common problem is the father who overemphasizes athletics to his child, even though the child may not like athletics or prefers to play other sports. The obvious and chronic disappointment of the father in reaction to the child's disinterest can be a permanent crippler to a young child's development. He could grow up to hate all sports, even though he could have found enjoyment in some of them.

Daughters and Athletics. Because you probably value and participate in athletics more than your wife does, you are in a unique position to remedy the lack of encouragement women have been given in sports.

As it is now, there is widespread discrimination against women in sports, despite the fact that athletic competition would help to provide women with a means to physical fitness, a sense of body pride, and a sense of accomplishment just as it does men. There are no medical or psychological reasons whatsoever why women cannot participate in and enjoy athletics just as men do. And there is no reason why they cannot compete and still retain a basic feeling of femininity.

As a father, you could help remedy sex bias in athletics by encouraging your daughter to engage in athletics if she wants to. This means mainly helping her to have a strong feminine self-image, which will overcome any social stigma attached to women's participation in athletics. Your daughter needs encouragement from you, as a male who does not feel threatened by her interest in athletics. As the primary male in her life, you will give her a standard by which to judge other males, and she will not feel as insecure sexually if she does later encounter a man who opposes her interest in sports.

For example, there is the case of female shot-putter Maren Seidler, interviewed by journalist Nina McCain for a March, 1973, *Boston Globe* article:

> "You really have to have a pretty strong self-image," Maren says, "you can't have a weak psyche and be a woman in sports."
>
> Maren, a cheerful, articulate young woman, obviously has a strong self-image. She grew up in a family where everyone was involved in sports and no one thought it was unfeminine to win. She got interested in shot putting by watching her father work out and broke her first national record when she was thirteen. She was the national AAU champion six times and on U.S. Olympic teams in 1968 and 1972. In Munich, she was the top woman finalist of all the Western countries.

In tennis, which is considered a more traditional sport for women, Chris Evert, the famous young star, owes much to the careful, involved coaching of her father. In a 1973 *Time* magazine article she says:

> One day when I was six my dad took me to the park. He put a racket in my hand and threw balls to me. I missed them all. We did this every day. After a few weeks I started hitting a few of them back. Then I remember liking it a lot. My dad made fun out of it. He'd say, "Okay, ten over the net and I'll buy you a Coke."

Her father, Jimmy Evert, helped to give his daughter two valuable gifts—a rewarding career and a sense of her own physical power.

In fact, athletics can be a means for you and your daughter to communicate, for it is something in which you can both feel at home. When you are playing an active game, your daughter also gets to see you coping with your environment more than if her only contact with you is at home.

For both sons and daughters, the specific sport is not so important as the fact that the child sees you engaging in physical activity and realizes that his physically imposing father values and enjoys his own body. Also important, the child sees that you do not view athletics and intellectual endeavors as mutually exclusive. A well-rounded individual— male or female—can feel just as comfortable on the playing field as in the library. Though this may seem like an obvious point, many fathers, either intellectuals or athletes themselves, feel that there is a wide gulf between the academic and athletic worlds.

Self-Defense. Another outgrowth of athletic achievement and body pride is the capability of self-defense. The old tradition of the father teaching his son how to defend himself by putting boxing gloves on him gives an incomplete picture of self-defense teaching. Daughters also need to learn assertive self-defense, and both boys and girls—as we said in the section on aggressiveness—should be taught the proper role of such techniques in their social development.

We support your teaching your child to be prepared, to link in his mind the experience of being attacked and the skill and motivation to effectively counterattack. We are stressing that physical defense may be an appropriate reaction in some circumstances. Obviously, your child should also learn other ways to deal with the threat of physical attack or intimidation, but there are occasions when physical force is the only answer, or at least when your child will need the confidence of knowing how to use such force.

Your son or daughter may have to learn to live in an environment that contains a certain amount of danger of mugging or other assaultive crime. He may encounter bullies to be faced, people to be protected, and instances requiring the physical ability to control someone who is being abusive or violent. A background of self-defense teaching by a father can aid a child's confidence so that he can face such situations.

THE CHILD'S PHYSICAL GROWTH

We strongly suspect that most fathers lack a background of information on the norms for their child's physical development. At least we know many fathers who are quite disappointed that their two-year-olds can't heave a football twenty yards.

So, we've devoted this section to a few specifics as to the average child's physical abilities at various ages. First, a listing of some of the major accomplishments during infancy:

AGE IN MONTHS	ACHIEVEMENT
1	Lifts chin while lying on stomach
2	Lifts chest while lying on stomach
3	Reaches for objects (but often misses)
4	Sits with support
5	Sits on lap and grasps object
6	Sits on high chair and grasps dangling objects
7	Sits alone
8	Stands with help
9	Stands holding furniture
10	Creeps
11	Walks when led
12	Pulls self up to standing position
13	Climbs stairs
14	Stands alone
15	Walks alone

Remember that these are average ages and that before them your child is vigorously working toward the final achievements. Also remember that children differ from one another in their rate of development. Don't feel inferior because the child next-door achieves some ability before your child.

Also realize that most children will not be toilet-trained until about two years of age. Too many parents don't take this into account and so create problems for themselves and their children.

Also, children don't require the same amount of food at various ages. The eighteen-month-old who gobbles everything in sight may grow into the two-year-old who often only nibbles even at the food he likes. Both situations are perfectly normal, but if you have concerns about your child's eating habits or growth patterns, consult your pediatrician.

During the ages two through five the child is developing more complex skills as seen by the following list:

AGE IN YEARS	ACHIEVEMENT
2	Puts on hat
	Holds glass in one hand
	Walks up and down stairs alone
	Kicks large ball
3	Pours from pitcher
	Stands on one foot
	Rides tricycle
	Catches ball, arms straight
4	Easily climbs and comes down ladder
	Cuts on line with scissors
	Dresses self (except for tying shoes, buttoning)
	Makes designs and crude letters
5	Skips
	Throws well
	Catches small ball, elbows at side
	Copies designs, letters, numbers

During the ages six through twelve your child is going through perhaps the most vigorous period of physical play in his life. He is perfecting countless games of skill and testing himself against others. His strength, speed and ease of movement, and precision all increase to a large degree during this period.

Physical growth, however, peaks during adolescence, when the child gains considerably in height and weight and experiences rapid sexual development. The average boy grows eight inches in height between the ages of thirteen and fifteen and a half, and the average girl three and one-quarter inches between the ages of eleven and thirteen and a half. This is called the adolescent growth spurt.

Remember, *all this development may occur at different rates and times, according to the individual child.* The girl who develops breasts early, or the boy who remains physically immature in his mid-teens, needs the special confidence afforded by an understanding father to counteract the stigma of being "different." If your child's physical development in adolescence is extremely delayed, you should consult an endocrinologist for possible hormonal therapy.

The speed of development usually becomes most important to your child during the adolescent years. Girls may be distressed by what they feel is too little or too much development of their breasts; boys may be embarrassed by lack of height or weight or by a lack of growth of body hair and genitals. You can give your teen-ager confidence about his body by telling him about some of the obsessions you had about your own body when you were young and how you grew out of them or coped with them (hopefully!). You may have worried about your big feet, long neck, or acne but discovered they weren't as serious as they seemed then. Maybe the most important way to help your adolescent is to be sympathetic and not act as if his concerns are stupid.

During adolescence, boys continue to gain in strength and speed of running, while girls taper off. Surprisingly to some, adolescents also show an increase in coordination during these years—it appears that so-called teen-age awkwardness is due more to social ineptness than physical clumsiness.

Many changes in habit and temperament during this period may be particularly annoying to fathers. Your adolescent may want to sleep late in the morning because he stays up later at night or because he needs more sleep due to rapid body growth.

Hopefully, this outline of development, although brief, will serve to make you more aware of your child's stages of physical development and to encourage you to learn more about the subject.

FATHER'S BENEFIT

We have stressed how your child's development and your relationship with him can be aided by sports and exercise, but we should also stress that *your* health can be improved too. Your offspring-playmate constitutes the best excuse we know of for a father to take off from the daily grind and play touch football or a few sets of tennis. The embarrassment many men feel about jogging, sledding, or playing ball alone evaporates when a child's excitement and interest is added. And who else but your child would stick with you in regular exercise?—he gets a chance to play with Dad! The companionship will help you relax, the interaction with your child is a good use of father power, and the exercise could save you from a heart attack. Similarly, being able to enjoy an open emotional relationship with your child may provide the safety valve that will keep you from a stomach ulcer or hypertension.

Your concern for your children can help motivate you to take better care of yourself. Regular participation in exercise and athletics can improve your health and decrease your vulnerability to many types of illness. While fathers are the most overtly physical parents, they are also the most physically vulnerable, and we believe a child realizes this, even at an early age. Children may subliminally know that you are more likely to die younger than their mother. They may hear of other children losing their fathers and may have fears that need soothing.

In any case, children learn early that a father's sickness is usually quite visible in its effects upon a household: a physically imposing parent is transformed into a very vulnerable one; a physically active parent is changed into a less active one. The father stays home instead of going to work. In long illnesses, the economic viability of the family is threatened. In your attitude toward your health, your child senses not only your feeling of self-worth, but your valuation of him because of the importance you attach to being a healthy father.

Smoking, drinking, and the use of other drugs; your sleep habits; personal hygiene; and your attitude toward exercise are all a part of this attitude toward health. Alcoholics and heavy smokers are likely to have had fathers who suffered the same addictions. There may be hereditary factors involved in susceptibility to addictions, but what you convey by your example is probably most important.

10 / *Father, Intelligence, and Competence*

[My father's] greatest Excellence lay in a sound understanding and solid judgement in prudential Matters, both in private and publick Affairs. . . . I remember well his being frequently visited by leading People, who consulted him for his Opinion in Affairs of the Town or the Church he belong'd to and Showed a good deal of Respect for his Judgement and Advice. . . . At his table he lik'd to have as often as he could, some sensible Friend or Neighbor, to converse with, and always took care to Start some ingenious or useful Topic for Discourse, which might tend to improve the Minds of his Children. . . . He sometimes took me to walk with him and see Joiners, Bricklayers, Turners, Braziers, etc., at their Work, that he might observe my Inclination, and endeavor to fix it on some Trade or other. It has ever since been a Pleasure to me to see good Workmen handle their Tools; and it has been useful to me, having learnt so much by it, as to be able to construct little Machines for my Experiments while the Intention of making the Experiment was fresh and Warm in my Mind.

from *The Autobiography of Benjamin Franklin*

Although we've neatly separated body, mind, and emotional development in this book, there is no such separation in a living, breathing person. How your child thinks, feels, and acts are all complexly intertwined, and you affect them all. Since people erroneously believe that intelligence can be accurately measured—as neatly as one can divide a child's development into three totally separate entities—we shall begin this section by performing a small exorcism on the IQ-test myth.

IQ AND INTELLECT

We have been led to believe that intelligence is easy to assess, that one simple IQ score gives us all we need to know—a dispassionate, immutable measure of a human being. This myth may be more often accepted by fathers than by mothers, both because fathers have traditionally not been as close to children to enable them to realize the true complexity of intellect and because of the masculine penchant for numbers.

Your child's IQ is a fairly adequate predictor of success in a traditional academic setting, but it is merely the tip of the psychological iceberg. An IQ score usually indicates how well a child can use words and understand language, but it doesn't measure how well your child can solve real-life problems, which often include sorting out information and taking many diverse factors into account.

An IQ score is an after-the-fact measure of a child's intelligence, and it changes as the child develops. You and your wife are the ones who influence your child's actual development, so if you set too much store by such results, you are likely to overreact and perhaps injure his progress. Take a lesson from the father of Albert Einstein, whom we shall discuss later. He asked his son's teacher what profession he thought young Albert should study for, and the teacher answered that it didn't really matter, for the boy would not amount to much anyway, he was too slow. The elder Einstein nevertheless forged ahead, still valuing and encouraging young Albert. Or how about Pablo Picasso, whom we shall also discuss later. His father refused to force Pablo into schoolwork, at which he did poorly, but continued to encourage his painting.

But what does intelligence really mean, if it is not IQ? To give you an idea, we'll first discuss what we believe constitutes intelligence.

We define intellectual ability primarily in terms of three basic traits—problem solving, verbal ability, and creativity. You, the father, affect each of them in different ways and to varying degrees, and your impact will be different from that of the mother. In addition, these traits are affected by a child's genetic inheritance, by the influences on his growth, and by the world he encounters outside of his family.

Genetics and Intelligence. Although much thought and worry have been expended on how much of intelligence is learned or acquired, this is really not a question with which a parent has to be concerned, so we will not go into it deeply. Your job is not to worry whether or not your son or daughter inherited "good" genes from you and your wife but to help him realize his potential to its fullest.

We agree with those psychologists who assert that each person is born with a unique set of potential intellectual abilities, and that his environment—which includes his parents—determines how he will flesh out these potentialities.

Fathers are often the most concerned about how well their children will function in the world, rather than with accepting them and helping them make the best of their abilities. Thus, they have traditionally been the parent most worried about inheritance of intelligence. You may not have done as one father did, adding up his and his wife's IQ and dividing by two to find out how smart his daughter would be. But you may nevertheless have been the parent who worried most about your child's inherited intellectual potential when he was born.

Sex Differences. Basic differences in male and female intellectuality are important for the father to put in perspective, though they are no more nor less important than individual differences among children. Fathers, we contend, have been among the chief purveyors of unrealistic attitudes concerning the different intellectual abilities of boys and girls. Because many institutions in our society—in business, government, and industry—have been created and perpetuated by men, there is a tendency for men to believe that women just "don't fit in" and that there is only the "man's way" of running things. This male attitude has entered very much into family life in which the traditional father worries about whether his son will get enough education to find a good job, but worries only whether his daughter will find a good husband.

It is reasonable to believe that there are some innate differences between the thinking styles of men and women. They have differences in their physiologies and consequently may have varying ways of viewing the world and reacting to it. But we stress that these are average differences and do not apply to the extremely wide range of personalities that make up the two sexes. You should certainly take the sex of your child into account, but you should not let it dictate your behavior. You should most certainly strive to aid the development of full competence in your daughters as well as your sons.

There is a plethora of evidence having to do with sex differences in various skills; studies seem to indicate that women, on the average, are better at perception of details, rote memory, language usage, spelling, and other skills requiring the quick shifting of perception, the use of fine muscles, and the use of their better sense of touch. Men, on the average, excel at verbal comprehension, mathematical reasoning, spatial perception, mechanical aptitude, problem-solving ability, and the ability to discriminate in physical responses to the environment. However, such variation in skills between males and females is heavily influenced by differences in the way males and females are raised.

Furthermore, these neat definitions are not nearly so neat in real life, for all sorts of traits are required for even the simplest daily problem. For instance, though girls may draw and paint more accurately because of finer muscle control and sense of color, boys may be able to reproduce three-dimensionality

more accurately and organize materials better in their draw-
ings because of better spatial perception. So who's to say
whether boys or girls are naturally better artists?

Father and IQ. In spite of popular literature, which holds
that the mother is the overwhelming influence on the young
child, the father has at least as much effect on his child's
intellectual development. For one thing, psychologists have
found that the IQ scores of young children are related to how
independent and achievement-oriented the children are. We
have already outlined your important role in fostering these
traits.

Your nurturance also affects your child's IQ. In a 1972
study, psychologist Norma Radin interviewed a group of
fathers and their four-year-old sons. Dr. Radin asked the sons
to remain in the room with their fathers during the long
interview session, expecting that the sons would become bored
and fidgety. The sessions were observed and tape-recorded and
subsequently scored for how nurturant or restrictive each
father was toward his fidgety son during the long interview.
The father who said, "Show me what you're doing," was
scored as nurturant. The father who said, "Sit down, kid!"
however, was scored as restrictive.

After measuring the boys' IQs, Dr. Radin found that their
scores were significantly related to their fathers' nurturance.
On the other hand, Dr. Radin found, the more restrictive the
father was, the lower the child's IQ tended to be. She also
observed that fathers of children with higher IQs tended to
consult their sons more on a questionnaire concerning home
activities given after the interview.

True, some of this father nurturance and consultation may
have been because the child was intelligent in the first place,
causing his father to want to have more to do with him. But
many of the effects were probably due to the father's direct
encouragement of intellectual competence.

Dr. Radin did a follow-up study a year later. She found that
the amount of father nurturance shown in the initial study was
still related to the boys' intellectual functioning. She also
discovered that the father's involvement in direct teaching

activities, such as teaching his son to count or read, was significantly related to the boy's IQ at both four and five years of age.

The ability to analyze problems and to be articulate are two basic intellectual skills. The child's chances of success in life are increased if he has a good balance of these two skills. He will be able to analyze a problem thoroughly and find its solution, and he will also be able to express that solution to others. Let's examine how the father fosters and enhances these two basic abilities in his children.

ANALYTICAL ABILITY

In the majority of families you are the parent who solves the widest diversity of analytical-type problems. You are traditionally the one raised to be a problem solver. Your childhood projects included building models and figuring football strategies. Your adult career probably consists of bringing specialized skills to bear on some problem and creatively solving it. Though this trend is changing as more women enter the professional world, it is still apt to be the norm in most families.

When you change jobs or move up in your career, you are experiencing a new environment with new problems requiring new solutions. Your wife, if she is not a career woman, does not encounter such complete change; her problems usually occur in the setting of a similar home environment throughout her life. Though her problems are certainly challenging, they do not tend to demand the constant adjustment to radical changes the way yours do. This mother-father difference is by no means absolute, because many fathers do have jobs that are quite mechanical and repetitious, and many mothers either have stimulating careers or have made homemaking into a quite challenging, novelty-laden career.

Besides general differences in the problem-solving experiences of mothers and fathers, though, there are also basic differences in the way they see their parenthood. Motherhood has always been emphasized as consisting chiefly of caring for the child, protecting it, and maintaining it in a stable home environment. While this is certainly vital to the child, just as vital is the father's less protective, more exploration-encouraging attitude. The father, for instance, is likely to get more of a kick out of seeing his daughter win a math contest or his son put together a steam engine. He is in this way acting out a role important to the functioning of the family: the challenger.

Your impact on your child during your own home problem-solving sessions is potent, for the problems usually involve some "exotic," interesting feature of household functioning that the child is less likely to encounter with the mother. You might have to analyze why the heating system is not working or put up the new television antenna.

The modern father feels that he has lost much of his aura as a skilled worker at home because his chores aren't as vital to the welfare of the family as they once were. At home the father has often been relegated to the status of unskilled laborer because of his lack of competence with the complex home machinery of today. But though you may feel that your home chores aren't that exciting or important, in a child's eyes they are. He may never have seen anyone change the oil in a car or fertilize a lawn, so chores that are mundane to you may represent to him important chances to learn about the workings of the world. The attractive aura that seems lost to you may be only so in your adult eyes. Because men don't have as many home chores as they used to, there are fewer and fewer concrete problems in today's households that require solving and that give a child a chance to observe analytical functioning. Thus, you may have to find other ways, such as through hobbies or involving him in your job, to show your child problem solving at work.

Of course, it is just as important *how* you involve your child in your problem solving as the fact that you involve him. If you explain what you are doing, what various tools are for, and why you are choosing a particular method, he will be much more deeply interested than if you simply let him stand

and watch. Let him help you by fetching tools or even by accomplishing part of the job himself.

Perhaps most important, though, is that you involve him in the intellectual process. When he makes suggestions, respond to them and at least give them consideration even if you can't use them. Be enthusiastic about what he says so he will feel he is being useful. Ask him what he thinks you should do when you run into a tough spot. Even if he doesn't have any answer, he will still feel that he is participating.

And if he does come up with a good idea, accept it and use it. You may be surprised at what a young mind can do when freed from the channelized thinking of adults. This was dramatically brought home to a truck driver we heard about. In an attempt to drive his trailer truck under a low highway underpass, he became solidly stuck. Firemen and tow trucks were called out, but nothing could budge the truck. A young boy who happened along on his bicycle watched the sweating men and straining machines and told the driver, "Hey, I know how to get your truck out." The driver ignored him, but he persisted; as they were preparing to slice off the top of the truck, the boy piped up again, and the trucker, exasperated, turned to him and said, "All right, kid, if you're so smart, how would you get that truck out from under there?"

"Just let some air out of the tires," the boy replied.

Building Together. Father-child hobbies are an ideal way to aid your child's analytical skills, provided that you *both* are really doing something useful. All too many fathers building something with their child end up doing it for them. One reason is that the father may become impatient with his child's clumsiness. In building a tree house or putting together a ship model, let your child help, even if it means a few bent nails or gluey masts. It is more important that he see something finished that he knows is part his than to see something that is built perfectly.

One father we know who became involved in midget-car racing with his son is a good example of perfection taking precedence over involvement. The father bought the child an expensive, midget racing car and proceeded to tune and tinker with the machine by himself while the boy acted solely as the driver in amateur racing events. Seeing the two on the racetrack one felt that they had each become involved in his own hobby and that it was a mere coincidence that the hobbies converged in the form of the car. If properly handled, though, such hobbies could become a link for a father and child who feel they have little in common. Had the father spent his time showing his son about the car's motor and had both of them driven the car, an excellent rapport might have developed by means of this hobby.

Building such a racing car could have been an excellent example of father-child project that results in a useful toy for the child after the project is over. Whether it be a tree house, a garden, or a puzzle, such a project can be doubly rewarding. When the project is completed, not only will you have accomplished something together, but your child will have a tool for further exploring his environment, not just something to display on a shelf.

Games. Playing games with your child also aids development of his analytical ability. You need not wait until your son or daughter is old enough to master chess to play a game with him. Even when he is an infant, you can make up games with blocks or other toys, hide-and-seek or build-a-bridge, for instance. As he grows older, you can graduate to such standards as Monopoly, checkers, Scrabble, or cards. Besides teaching a child how to analyze situations in general, these games are a great way to teach spelling and mathematics.

Fathers frequently have problems in playing games of skill with their children because they don't know whether to strive to win or to let the child win occasionally. When playing a game of checkers with your daughter, you may feel that for you to win all the time will frustrate her. On the other hand, if you *allow* her to win, she may feel that you don't respect her ability. One good way to overcome this quandary is for you and the child to work out a handicap for you, which will equalize your chances. Thus, you can play to the utmost of your ability, and the child still has a chance to win.

Early game playing is more of a learning experience than an actual competitive contest. You should remove the handicap gradually as soon as the child is able to win any games at all. In the case of checkers, for instance, you should increase the number of checkers you are allowed to play with until it equals your child's number. You will find your child quite proud that he can play you without a handicap.

To handle game playing properly as a learning tool, of course, you must take the individuality of your child into account. While some children may become frustrated and lose self-confidence if they never win a game from Dad, others will flower under the challenge, as did basketball player Wilt Chamberlain:

> I'm sure some measure of my competitive instinct and urge to excel comes from my father—whether it's in the genes or just absorbed from being around him so much. He was very competitive, too, a great checkers and pinochle player, and he worked hard at it, studying his every play, studying his opponent . . . and he didn't lose very often. We were very close, and we used to play each other all the time. . . . I got so I could beat him at pinochle. But I never did beat him at checkers, not once in all the thousands of times we played.
>
> from *Wilt*
> by Wilt Chamberlain and David Shaw
> (New York: Macmillan Publishing Co., 1973.)

Father Absence and Analytical Ability. Compared to well-fathered children, father-absent and father-neglected children are more often at a disadvantage in terms of analytical ability. For instance, father-absent children tend to have more difficulty analyzing pictures to pick out hidden objects and in solving complex puzzle tasks than do father-present children.

Mathematics can be considered the purest form of analyzing, and predictably, father-absent children often show lower mathematics skills than father-present children. This problem has been found in both sons and daughters, though the effect seems more pronounced in sons. Perhaps this is because males usually do better at mathematics than girls, possibly because of innate differences, but probably more importantly because they are expected to in our society. Fathers usually encourage mathematical thinking more in their sons than in their daughters.

The Discriminating Child. Besides teaching your child how to weed out irrelevancies and solve particular problems, in involving him in your chores and other activities you are also teaching him a discriminating approach to life in general. He will be bombarded with countless requests, temptations, admonitions, and other sensory inputs during his life. To manage properly he must learn to pick and choose what he should accept.

Dennis remembers one vivid example of such analytical teaching when as a youngster he was riding with his father in the family car. Seeing the many shiny cars on the road with them, he asked, "Why can't we get a new one? Everybody else has one!" The family car was a few years old, and a new one would be a great thing, he thought.

"We don't need a new one," said his father. "This one runs O.K. and gets us from one place to another reliably. We could buy a new car every year if we wanted one, but we wouldn't have money for other things that are more important—your music lessons or a paid-up mortgage." Dennis remembers that incident clearly because after that he began to really think about why certain alternative purchases were more important than others.

VERBAL ABILITY

Watching his father and other ministers dominate audiences with artfully chosen words, the young boy tingled with excitement; and the urge to speak, to express himself, to turn and twist and lift audiences, seized him and never afterwards left him. To form words into sentences, to fling them out on the waves of air in a crescendo of sound, to watch people weep, shout, *respond:* this fascinated young Martin.

from *What Manner of Man—Martin Luther King, Jr.*
by Lerone Bennett

If you work all day and your wife cares for your young child, she will be the parent charged more with first developing the infant's verbal ability. Indeed, her effect can be a profound one. Researchers find that infants who are not talked to are likely to grow into children and adults who have difficulties using language. In our complex society the ability to express oneself fluently is very important, and adults may be accepted or rejected on the basis of their speaking ability.

Your role in your child's verbal ability during the first years is mainly to encourage the child to talk and to show your child that you value skill in verbal expression. In fact, during the first few years of a child's life there may not be all that much you or your wife can do to help him to begin to talk. Many psychologists are coming to believe that, given a relatively positive environment, the timing of verbal development in children is largely innate.

When your child begins to speak, he will attempt to use words that you give him. If you use baby talk, he will respond with baby talk, but if you use "adult" words, he is likely to respond with adult words. For example, if you reward him for saying "fafa" when he is hungry and use this word yourself when talking with him, he may have trouble communicating with others when he wants something to eat.

As your son or daughter develops intellectually, your task changes considerably. You now assume the role of *friendly* critic and debater. By pointing out to your child when he says something that is inexact or vague, you help him learn to pinpoint what he says. Ask him what he means. Tell him about new facts or experiences of your own that might change what he says, and most important, tell him he is doing well and compliment him when he says something especially perceptive. You are probably quite used to requiring this kind of precision in yourself in your job, so that this continual striving for clear speech and thinking is an effective role for you. However, *never criticize your child for stuttering, or some other speech impediment.* Don't make him self-conscious about his speech problem. This can only make it worse. Help him maintain his security. If you have questions about his speech development, don't hesitate to seek professional help but be careful not to overfocus on his difficulties while ignoring his strengths.

Father's Talk, Mother's Talk. Your role in verbal development varies somewhat from your wife's because your speech patterns may be different. While she is usually concerned about the impact her words will have on other people, you are usually more concerned that your words convey precise meanings. As an experiment, if you were to write down the major words you used during the day, they might include such words as *produce, quota, organize, commitment, contract,* and many specific technical words. A housewife, who deals with problems of a more personal nature, might list such words as *enjoy, sad, argue, understanding,* and *believe.* A career wife might still list technical words that are different from yours. So you can see how your child can get something useful from both of his parents, regardless of their occupation. The words you use at play are also likely to be different from your wife's. You may have an excellent sports vocabulary, while your wife might have a good literary vocabulary (though the reverse is also true in many cases). A good vocabulary derived from both parents can be just as important to success at play as at work.

Although among lower-class children, father-present boys and girls tend to do better than father-absent children on tests of verbal skills, father absence apparently does not affect verbal development as profoundly as it affects problem-solving ability. This can be seen in the cases of father-absent middle-class boys, who generally do as well as their father-present counterparts in tasks tapping vocabulary and reading skills. Economically deprived children's intellectual development seems to suffer more from father absence than does that of middle-class children, probably because of attitudes found in middle-class mothers, who are more likely to value verbal skills and to foster them in their children. In addition, higher socioeconomic status is usually associated with a greater degree of formal educational opportunities.

So although the middle-class father-absent child might be handicapped in analytical skills, his verbal skills enable him to get along more easily in the usually middle-class school environment than the working-class father-absent child. Furthermore, the middle-class father-absent boy's dependency on his mother may make it easier for him to attach himself to the middle-class female teacher, and this also aids his school "adjustment," but he is likely to be limited in other areas of development.

Productive Thinking. One of the most neglected facets of intellectual development is what we shall call the capacity for productive thinking. As important as it is for a child to be able to analyze and communicate, it is also vital that he be able to translate these skills into appropriate action. Everybody knows at least one person with a hundred plans and ideas who never seems to get any of them off the ground. And then there's the broad-concept philosopher who never gets around to doing anything concrete about his philosophical ruminations.

As you saw in the section on analytical ability, your role as a father is important because you give the child concrete, practical problems to work with, problems whose solution results in definite, tangible benefits. You are thus teaching him to use abstract skills to arrive at real-life solutions, an important factor in productive thinking.

Schools do not usually offer tangible benefits as rewards for work. Thus, a child may be hard pressed to understand what practical personal benefit schooling will give him. By encouraging your child to work for money at after-school jobs, by engaging in rewarding hobbies with him, and by letting him have a part in making suggestions about home chores and then carrying them out, you are linking his efforts with tangible results and rewards.

You are also more concerned than the mother with what a

child accomplishes rather than what he is, and thus you tend to get more of a kick out of it when he engages in useful kinds of thinking—when he builds something that works or organizes an outing efficiently and practically.

CREATIVITY

Don Jose [Pablo's father] proved however to be a teacher whose lessons were never forgotten by his son. In spite of his traditional outlook and his unimaginative style, he had inherited the Spanish passion for realism, and was willing to make experiments that a more restrained and conventional temperament would have considered to be in bad taste. . . .

In fact, from his childhood Pablo became acquainted with the possibilities of using materials in unconventional ways, borrowing from any source that came to hand, and making newly discovered substances obey his wishes.

from *Picasso: His Life and Work*
by Roland Penrose

Creativity is the spice of the intellect—the imaginative joining of new things never before joined and the generating of concepts that have never before existed. We won't try to define creativity any further because each definition does not really take into account new forms of it that may surface. Creativity has been traditionally thought of as having to do with the arts and literature; however, nowadays experts recognize that it is necessary in science and technology too. Yet the workings of creativity are still mysterious.

Creative potential is to some extent inborn just as are many other facets of intellect; so even if you attempt to follow our suggestions, don't expect your son or daughter to be another Picasso. However, just because you or your wife don't consider yourselves creative, it doesn't mean your child won't be a creative genius. But you as a father can maximize his creative potential in a unique way. We think several basic factors contribute to the development of a child's creativity—among them, independence, sensitivity, and flexibility.

Independence. A key factor in the fostering of creativity is that the child be allowed independence, both of thought and action.

As we discussed in the section on independence, you should teach your child that he is the final arbiter of his own actions, and that he is not wrong to question authority and traditional rules for doing things. The child will thus feel free to experiment with his environment and to discover new ways of doing things. He will not feel that there are prior restrictions on all his actions.

As a father, this means that you should not be overcontrolling. Do not bring your supervisory attitude home from the office. Make rules only when they have a definite meaning. Freely allow your child to seek out other adults and to learn from them; don't be possessive.

Many geniuses in history were not only tutored by their own parents, but encouraged to have contact with other adults who could further their education. Nobel Prize winners are much more likely to have worked for other Nobel Prize winners themselves during their graduate school days. Creativity, to some extent, is contagious.

A Special Nurturance and Sensitivity. A second important factor in developing creativity in your child is nurturance of a specific type—the nurturance required in allowing your child to explore and even to try foolish things, as Picasso's father did. Because you have traditionally been the judging parent, you present the greatest danger to the child's creativity, especially if you mock his mistakes. You tend not to be as tolerant as your wife when the child asks if he can glue on wings and fly, or if he wants to run the juicer backward and make oranges.

A third crucial contributor to creativity in your child is sensitivity to the environment. You can help cultivate this sensitivity in your child by showing him that the objects and concepts around him are very complex and that he should try to observe and appreciate that complexity. Because a young child is quite impressionable about such early sensitivity training, what he learns will stay with him all his life.

Ernest Hemingway's father offers a good example of this training for sensitivity. His brother, Leicester Hemingway, writes about that father-son relationship in his book *My Brother, Ernest Hemingway*:

> Father, extremely proud of having produced a scion, did some adroit guiding toward an interest in nature, and in hunting and fishing, the noncompetitive sports he loved so well. . . . While walking, whether down by the beach or over fields or in the yard, [Ernest] was regularly told the names of different things he saw, touched, tasted, and smelled. Our father had a way of explaining even the simplest things so that they became fascinating.

Sex-Role Flexibility. To foster creativity in your child you must also maintain flexible, sensible concepts of masculinity and femininity. Because creativity contains a feature traditionally considered masculine—independence—and another considered feminine—sensitivity—both boys and girls suffer when subjected to a parent's narrow, stereotyped views of sex roles. The father who declares that sensitive men are "sissies" or that independent women are "ball-busters" is doing great harm to his son and daughter.

Many psychologists have fallen into a similar trap. They have made the mistake of equating men's creativity with "femininity" and women's creativity with "masculinity." Actually, such creative men and women are not afraid to break out of the traditional stereotypes and to show themselves as being more well-rounded individuals.

Times of Need. There seem to be specific times in a child's life when he needs special support for his attempts at creativity because of pressure from his friends to conform. Because you as a functioning male represent someone who can successfully cope with the outside world, your encouragement of your child's creativity during these periods will have a particularly high impact on him. He will be much better able to withstand teasing by his peers if he knows that his father supports his dreaming and scheming.

The third and fourth, and the seventh and eighth grades in school are the two levels at which creativity seems particularly likely to be damaged by peer-group pressure. During the third and fourth grades, cliques—usually all-boy or all-girl—are formed as youngsters explore farther afield in their social world. During this period your child is especially sensitive to any ridicule that may damage his standing in the gang of boys or girls he plays with.

During the seventh- and eighth-grade period, your child is beginning to enter puberty and to become interested in the other sex. Changes in his body and in his teen-aged society may make your son or daughter especially sensitive about being different in any way from his friends.

Encouraging Creativity. In helping your daughter or son to feel comfortable with his creativity, the best general rule is to give him encouragement and the opportunity to view things from many different perspectives. A few examples follow:

If he has a problem with a bully, a teacher, or a friend, dramatize the problem with him, with each of you acting out a role. You be one person, let him be the other, and see how many ways you can come up with to deal with the person.

In doing a home chore, sit down with him before you start and ask him in how many ways he thinks the job can be done. How many ways, for instance, can you get a large rug into a room or remove water from a flooded basement?

Play all sorts of games with him, especially those of your and his own invention. For instance, one good game is "I spy," in which one player "spies" something, a certain color or shape, and the other guesses what it is. You can also do mathematical games, riddles, and word puzzles together. Get a book of such activities and do one a day as a contest.

Involve him if you are considering rearranging furniture in a room, encourage him to see how many different ways he can arrange the furniture and what each way means in terms of convenience.

Let him do some cooking, and encourage him to figure how changes from the recipe will help or hurt the taste of the food.

Put on impromptu shows at home in which each child can perform a little trick, tell a joke, etc. This way your child will be encouraged to think up things to do for the show, and he will have the frequent thrill of having his father applaud his creativity. Dennis remembers one such "happening" at Henry's house one night after the two had completed a day's work on this book. Sitting around the table, the two families began talking about some of the funny things the Biller children had learned. Kenneth was coaxed to do his imitation of James Cagney, Cameron sang a funny song, Jonathan told a joke, and Michael danced. All the children had a chance to perform creatively before an audience and have their creativity applauded.

If he is confident that you value his search for new ways of doing things, your child can better tolerate lack of understanding from insensitive individuals.

Parents and Genius. One myth we should scotch about creativity is that geniuses are produced solely by close relationships with their mothers. Because of the mother-oriented nature of our society, we tend to make too much of the cases where the mother was the prime mover in the child's intellectual accomplishments and to ignore the cases where either the father alone encouraged the child or both parents together helped him. Indeed, when both parents help their children the way we have just discussed, and if the child has the genetic potential, genius is likely to be fostered.

The example of Albert Einstein is a good one to illustrate the importance of both parents. Einstein's father was a warm, encouraging, optimistic man who took a great deal of interest in his son. He enjoyed taking his family on outings and showed himself both accepting of and nurturing toward his children. "Exceedingly friendly, mild and wise" was how Einstein described his father. His mother was a profound woman who had a breadth of knowledge and talent in both literature and music. Both parents were discriminating people who accepted little without analysis. As Ronald W. Clark puts it in his book

Einstein: The Life and Times, "Einstein was nourished on a family tradition which had broken with authority; which disagreed, sought independence, had deliberately trodden out of line."

In his early youth, Einstein probably suffered from perceptual problems, which made him a slow child in some areas. Apparently, he was nonetheless accepted by his parents and given that special form of nurturance that allowed him to explore his world in his own way. While his mother insisted on music lessons, which helped give Einstein an appreciation of mathematical structure, as well as a creative outlet, his father, an engineer, gave him access to scientific paraphernalia and to other adults from whom he could learn.

A story is told about young Albert when he was five years old and sick in bed. His father brought a pocket compass to show him, and seeing the iron needle always pointing in the same direction, Einstein for the first time became impressed that the space he had always considered empty was actually filled with invisible forces. When asked later in life whether such father-fostered encounters affected him, he said, "I myself think so, and I believe these outside influences had a considerable effect on my development."

How a Child Develops Intellectually

We ended the last chapter, on father and physical development, with a brief section on the physical stages children go through as they grow. We shall do the same with this chapter, outlining for you the stages of intellectual development your child experiences.

As we said earlier, involvement in fatherhood means being interested in your son or daughter from birth. We think a good way to foster this interest is for you to be aware of the exquisite, marvelous process your child undergoes as he develops his mental abilities. Like any astute observer, if you have some background on what you are observing, you will be much more interested and informed.

Many fathers inexperienced with babies are like people with no experience in art who are suddenly exposed to a museum full of abstract paintings and sculpture—they both have no background in the subject matter. They may feel very uncomfortable or else uninterested in what they see.

In discussing stages of intellectual development, we shall use the theories and observations of child psychologist Jean Piaget as our guide. Piaget sees the child as an organism continually responding to its environment, assimilating new experiences into its frame of reference, and changing or accommodating itself to learn to deal with new experiences. To effect these changes, Piaget says, the child uses methods that are remarkably similar from child to child. He theorizes that infants go through six stages of intellectual development during the first two years of life, which he labels the sensorimotor period. During the first month the infant is using only his "prewired" responses; he can only vaguely orient himself toward light or sound.

During stage two, from about age one month to four months, the infant begins to discover that the same object can be detected by more than one sense. He finds that the rattle he sees can also be reached for and grabbed and that it makes a sound when it is shaken. He still doesn't realize, however, that objects exist when he doesn't see them. He perhaps believes that he is making the objects appear and disappear by looking at or away from them. He also has no idea that his action of shaking the rattle is what produces the sound.

During the third stage—from about age four months to eight months—the child makes a monumental discovery: When he shakes his hand with the rattle in it, it rattles. By doing one thing, he realizes, he produces the other. To a father who has been astutely observing his baby, these achievements will be intriguing milestones, for the father will follow them with a background of involvement and knowledge.

The stage-three child still doesn't really have a sense of means leading to ends, but he has a beginning. The child is also starting to get the notion that objects exist apart from his own perception of them. He begins to evidence a remarkable new piece of behavior: When an object is removed from his view, he looks for it, instead of merely turning his attention to another object. He is still a primitive creature, however; he does not connect an object perceived by one sense with one perceived by another sense. If he has seen a rattle and it disappears under a blanket, he will not feel for it, and vice versa. During this stage he may first begin to wonder where an absent daddy is.

During stage four—from about age eight months to twelve months—his sense of intentionality and of the meaning and permanence of objects increases. He discovers for the first time that to get around a barrier, he must move it aside, and that to do this, he must intentionally do something to the barrier. He realizes that his shoving the barrier *causes* it to move. He learns that certain objects stand for certain things—seeing his father with his hat means that his father is leaving. His primitiveness, however, is still very much evident. If you place an object under a cover, for instance, he can lift the cover and retrieve the object. If, however, you then place the same object under another cover, as he watches, he will probably still look for it in the original place.

During stage four the child is also making progress physically. He is learning to stand and walk, which greatly increases the size of the environment available to him. During this period, and the one before and afterward, your attitude toward exploration will affect his later motivations profoundly. Your main goal should be to give him as much freedom and confidence about exploration as possible. Think twice before telling him no. If he is pulling books out of a shelf, it may offend your sense of order, but is it really hurting the books?

Exploration. Also think twice about constantly retrieving him from "danger." Infants have a built-in capacity for caution. Your child is not likely to crawl off a couch or to bang himself with a door. Of course, this doesn't mean you shouldn't take knives away from him or steer him clear of situations where his clumsiness is likely to injure him.

Fathers are usually more encouraging of infant exploration than mothers are. They have not been brought up to stress protectiveness as much as mothers and can tolerate more dirt on the child than she can. Dennis's wife's first exclamation, for instance, upon seeing a certain seven-year-old boy whom we know is always, "Lord, look how dirty he is!" Her impulse seems to be to clean up the hard-playing youngster immediately.

Infants from stage four on also begin showing a definite degree of independence. Your daughter may grab the spoon away from you and want to feed herself, though she may get more food on her surroundings than in her mouth. Allow your children these attempts, awkward though they may be.

Unfortunately, children's exploration has often been pictured as innately destructive. Destructive children, we caution, are often those who haven't been given exploratory freedom in the first place and are subsequently overactive and frustrated. Remember, your child is not inherently destructive; he is only curious about his world.

During the fifth stage—from about age twelve months to eighteen months—the child finally separates what *he* does from what *happens*. In other words, he is not part of what happens to the object. In the fourth stage, the child in throwing an object was interested only in the act of throwing. Now, though, when he throws his food on the floor, he is actually interested in watching what happens to the food. He has progressed from self-interest to other-interest as well. He also now searches for an object at the place where it has disappeared and actively begins to reach, push, and pull to get what he wants.

Speech. During this period the child is also making great progress in developing that incredible human talent, spoken language. From the beginning of his life he had been verbalizing—at first merely with cries and sighs, later with nonsense syllables and made-up words, and finally with primitive versions of real words.

Your child will probably speak his first word when he's around twelve months of age, and because of his new physical ability, his expanded environment quickly stimulates him to learn new words. During the sixth stage—from about age 18 months to 24 months—the child begins to become capable of putting words together to form simple sentences. He can also now imitate others' behavior from memory as his language and memory skills have greatly increased.

Children's Thinking. Thus, in these remarkable first two years, the child greatly expands his ability to understand and manipulate his environment. But, of course, he still has a long way to go intellectually. During his first seven years he must gain experience in new ways of manipulating his environment and thus discover many new concepts.

At age two he still does not possess the notion of reversibility. For example, if you ask your little boy who his brother is, he knows, but if you ask him who his *brother's* brother is, he will probably say his brother doesn't have one.

Other concepts also escape him. For example, if you take two equal balls of clay and roll one into a sausage, your child will probably say the sausage-shaped lump of clay is bigger. If you have two containers, each with the same volume, but one taller and skinnier, he will probably say one of two things about the container: (1) that the taller one holds more because it is taller, or (2) that the taller one holds less because it is skinnier. He cannot combine the two concepts. Until around age seven he can't sort out the intermediate steps that an object goes through when it changes in some way. To a child a ball dropping to the floor is in your hand one instant and on the floor another. To him it does not go through the many steps of falling.

He also doesn't realize the impossibility of the same object being several places at once. To him all the Santa Clauses he sees in stores and on the sidewalk around Christmas time are the same man. It's easy to believe in Santa Claus when you are only four!

The young child can also only reason from the particular to the particular. Every time you get out the hammer, he may observe you begin to curse. To your child this means that the hammer is used to curse with, and he may wonder where the hammer is if he ever hears you cursing without it.

Approximately between the ages of seven and eleven, which

Piaget labels the concrete-operations subperiod, the child begins to develop more mature logical concepts. The child finds that his brother has a brother (himself), that adding the same amount of water to two empty pitchers makes them contain the same amount of water, and that a clay sausage and a clay ball may have the same amount of material in them and simply are different shapes.

This learning of logical operations is still far short of the advanced thinking of the adult, and between the ages of eleven and fifteen years the child goes through what Piaget terms the formal-operations period. In this period, which represents the attainment of adult intellectual ability, the child begins to look for and discern general principles underlying his world. His use of logic matures, and he learns to formulate and test more sophisticated theories.

Everybody's Different. We must stress that all these ages are merely averages; your child doesn't develop intellectually with clicks, like channels on a television set, to register his progress, but rather gradually, in overlapping stages and in his own time. We know one father who heard somewhere that newborns don't actually smile and that their facial expressions are only a reaction to stomach gas. Not until they reach a certain age do they truly smile, he was told. His young son reached that age and on precisely that day the proud father was heard to say, seriously, "Aha! Today it's not gas! Today he really smiles!"

This has been but a cursory tour through the fascinating sequence of a child's intellectual development. As you observe the child, you will surely see more examples of how he progresses from a primitive infant to an intellectually competent adult. There is still considerable controversy over how much of early development is inborn and how much is affected by environmental influences. In any case, your duty is to provide the child with an encouraging and rich environment. By being consistent and supportive, you are giving him a good start in manifesting his genetic potential.

HELPFUL HINTS FOR
GENERAL INTELLECTUAL DEVELOPMENT

We have already discussed many of the ways in which you are uniquely important to specific areas of your young child's intellectual growth. We shall now give you general hints on how to help him.

Observation is very important to a child, so you should help him with this in as many ways as possible. Seeing and hearing are essentially the only contact the young infant has with distant objects; so you should make sure his world contains a rich array of sights and sounds. Hang all sorts of objects in front of him so he can touch and move them. Dennis and his wife have dangled jar tops, keys, mobiles, paper, photographs, and countless other objects for young daughter, Wendy, to learn about.

The child also needs to repeat things many times in order to grasp their significance. Because they are members of the adult world, fathers may not realize this and not repeat words or actions enough times for the child to really understand them. If your child still gets a kick out of some face or motion, don't be reluctant to repeat it again and again.

Anytime your child can watch you doing interesting things that you are enjoying, you are helping him develop his urge to explore and learn. Thus, what is fun for you is also good for the child, so don't feel you have to spend all your time with the child playing with blocks. Do things you enjoy and let him watch and participate at his own level.

Read to Him. Reading to your child is a particularly good habit. Many of the most successful individuals in life are those who can effectively and enjoyably glean information and insight from books. Giving your child an early motivation toward reading can be an enormous gift. Make it a practice to read to him regularly, even if he may be too young to understand words. If you choose a time when both of you enjoy each other's company, reading can be a satisfying emotional as well as intellectual experience. Reading to a child before bedtime can be an enormous security booster for a child preparing to face a dark bedroom.

Repeat sentences that he particularly likes as many times as he wishes. If he is too young to grasp a sentence, paraphrase it, pointing out key words and pictures. Ask him questions he can answer about the book and compliment him when he learns. Also read books over and over again that he likes—at least until *you* get bored. In his learning process he must frequently refer back to familiar stories and objects to gain a full appreciation of them.

To help him understand the story and become involved in it, paraphrase the sentences sometimes, or stop and discuss the story with him. Ask what he thinks about the story or explain or comment on something that happened in it. Using these tips can greatly enhance both the effectiveness of your reading and its interest for the child.

Reading to your son may also be especially important, because it shows him that reading is a legitimate masculine occupation. He will greatly need this confidence when he enters school and is taught reading by female teachers. Ernest Hemingway received such encouragement at the hands of his father. A masculine man who loved hunting, fishing, and the outdoors, Hemingway's father showed young Ernest that he also valued reading. According to his brother, Leicester Hemingway, "By the time he was three Ernest had been calmed with reading on hundreds of occasions. Our father used books of natural history with good color illustrations. From these Ernest learned the birds of North America." This high valuation of books, plus his mother's encouragement of his competitive spirit, were two principal factors that started Hemingway on his career as one of the world's great writers.

Father, Child, and Play. Just as you are involved with your child's reading development, involve yourself in his choice of toys. Encourage your child to choose toys that he is interested in. Toys should have many modes of use—with all sorts of knobs, buttons, faces, and noisemakers for the child to investigate.

Establish a "tear-up" room or area for your child, to give him a place where he can let his imagination go unfettered. Let him know that the room is his to do with as he wishes—a place of his own where he can play with his toys as he sees fit, use messy paints, and make noise. Give him a place to draw, perhaps a wall covered with plastic or other washable material. Add shelves, a workbench, tables and chairs, and other large objects to let him give vent to his imagination. Besides giving him a sense of property and importance, such a room will also make it easier for him to observe prohibitions about other parts of the house. Even if it is just a large closet or a divided-off portion of his own room, he will still have a "work room" to call his own, apart from his bedroom. By the same token, if you live in a house, give him a portion of the yard into which he can lug junk, dig a hole to China, or build a rocket ship.

11 / Father, School, and Education

In the last chapter we discussed how you influence your very young child's intellectual development. In this chapter we shall consider in what ways you continue to be important to your child after he enters school. We shall divide the chapter into two parts—the father and the child in school, and the father and the child outside of school.

In School. Although many fathers don't realize it, they affect the success of their child's schoolwork both directly—by teaching their child and playing with him—and indirectly—by influencing how their child's school educates him.

First we'll discuss the father's direct effects on schoolwork.

Father-absent and father-neglected children often do less well than father-present children in their grades and achievement-test scores. We would expect this, of course, in the light of what we have seen concerning the father's fundamental effects on his child's emotional strength and intellect.

But just because a child has a father at home doesn't mean that the father is effective in helping him do well in school. Several researchers who have interviewed father-present children who do poorly in school have found them much more likely to have weak relationships with their fathers. Conversely, investigators have found that boys who were doing well in school were more likely to have positive attitudes about their fathers.

Henry and psychologist Robert Blanchard, director of The Cape Cod Mental Health Center, did a study that links the father-child relationship with grades and achievement-test scores. Henry and Robert studied a group of forty-four third-grade boys, dividing them into four groups of eleven boys each, according to whether they were: (1) early father absent (before age three), (2) late father absent (beginning after age five), (3) low father present (less than six hours per week), and (4) high father present (more than two hours per day).

The high father-present boys consistently received superior grades and performed above grade level on achievement tests. The late father-absent and low father-present boys scored a little below grade level on achievement tests. The lowest scores were achieved by the early father-absent group.

This study strongly suggested both that involved fathers can help their children's schoolwork and that noninvolved fathers can hurt it.

So, as you might expect, just as you influence your child's basic emotional development and fundamental ways of thinking, you also directly affect his school performance.

The Feminized Classroom. One of the severest problems in our elementary schools is the lack of male models. Although about half the population is male, the ratio of female to male teachers in elementary schools is about six to one—and about fifty to one in the first few grades. Because a child is establishing his attitude toward intellectuality in the elementary school years, lack of a masculine model can be especially harmful. Also, considering the extent of father absence and neglect outside of school, the lack of male teachers could be devastating to the personalities of boys and girls, and not just harmful to their intellectual growth. Paternal deprivation in school is piled upon that existing in the home.

This lack of male models in the schools has not always been the case. In colonial times, being a schoolmaster was an honored profession for males, stemming both from the male's sense of responsibility toward children and from his vital role in the education of children in general. As the role of the early American father waned, child care and also child teaching came to be thought of as an exclusively feminine function.

The Female Teacher. Because teaching has evolved into a traditionally female profession, female teachers themselves are more likely to be establishment-oriented, highly conforming individuals. They are more likely to support the status quo in the classroom and to unthinkingly accept stereotypes of male and female roles (though we're not saying there aren't many creative, nontraditional female teachers). Such conforming teachers tend to value the traditional separation of traits—"men do men's work and women do women's work." They are also likely to adopt the stereotypes that boys are active and independent while girls are passive and dependent, foisting these upon their young pupils.

At the same time, the traditional female teacher may feel threatened by boys, who are usually harder to handle and more physically active than girls. Thus, she tends to devalue boys and their activities and treat them more harshly in order to achieve her goal of control and neatness. Because of this emphasis, boys who get the best grades in school often tend to be those who have been "feminized"—they have given in to the female-oriented educational system. Such boys are more conforming, polite, obedient, and neat, but not necessarily more intelligent. When we speak here of the "feminized classroom," we obviously do not mean the more modern open concept of femininity but the narrow, traditional femininity espoused by many female teachers.

Many studies show that female teachers punish their students most for being aggressive and assertive and reward them most for being quiet and sedentary. One research team observed how a group of female teachers treated nursery school children. They found that teachers complimented or encouraged boys about six times as often for traditionally "feminine" behavior as for behavior usually labeled masculine. When the boys (and girls) were quiet and sedentary, they were encouraged; when they were banging on things or being rough-and-tumble, they were ignored or criticized.

Boys in the Feminized Classroom. To a boy in such a feminized classroom, especially a father-neglected boy, the female teacher is just another woman in the long line of women who have governed his life. He may rebel against her simply to assert himself against females in general, and she, feeling threatened, may come down that much harder on him.

The boy may also begin to view school and intellectual pursuits as feminine because he never gets a chance to see a male who values learning. Desperately trying to be masculine, he may reject all such "sissy stuff," much to his own harm.

These features of the female-teacher/male-child relationship lead to definite bias against boys and their activities. Researchers have found that female teachers in general react less favorably to boys than to girls during instruction. Boys receive more negative reaction and criticism and less positive support than girls do. One study found that boys receive up to ten times as many warnings and scoldings from female teachers as girls do. And when female teachers scold boys, they are more likely to use harsh words or angry tones than when scolding girls *for the same behavior.*

Some researchers have reported that female teachers give girls better grades, even when boys have objectively achieved a higher level of performance. Another study measuring teacher reaction to boys found that the teachers made fewer requests for information and gave less information to boys when they asked questions.

Boys and Reading. The nature of boys' reading problems is a good case in point. Although girls are usually more developmentally advanced for their age, this still does not explain why four or five times as many boys as girls are referred to reading clinics.

Several of the studies we mentioned earlier showed that teachers react less favorably toward boys during reading lessons and also allow them less oral-reading time. Throughout elementary school, girls are consistently more interested in reading than boys are and consistently do better. Girls are found to attach more prestige to reading than boys, and, at least during the elementary school years, reading is not seen as a masculine virtue. This is at least partly because girls have an effective female model of reading ability in their teachers.

Boys need not have these difficulties, however. They can learn to read just as well as girls. In one study when children were given programmed, independent reading instruction, boys did as well as girls. But when children were taught in small reading groups, which featured close contact with a female teacher, girls did better.

Statistics on reading instruction in Germany vividly suggest how learning may depend upon the sex and personality of the teacher. German boys have significantly better reading scores than girls and significantly less severe reading retardation. In Germany, elementary school teachers are usually males, and reading is considered a masculine talent. Thus, the German elementary school system seems biased against the development of girls' reading competence. Another study of Japanese children, however, found no difference in the numbers of girls and boys having reading difficulties. About 60 percent of the teachers in the community studied were males.

Girls in the Feminized Classroom. Girls can be just as severely injured intellectually as boys by exposure to an imbalance of female teachers. Girls tend to be more sensitive to the attitudes of others and especially to the prejudices of a female model. Girls' independence, achievement motivation, and assertiveness may be hindered by an overconforming, traditional female teacher.

Even though they react negatively to boys, female teachers may actually be expecting more from them and may secretly downgrade the importance of girls' achievement.

A girl's impression of the school hierarchy may bruise her pride in being female, because the teacher, usually female, is the employee, while the principal, usually male, is her boss. Throughout her elementary schooling, the girl thus sees her teacher referring important decisions to a male. Is it any wonder the girl learns to accept as gospel the pattern man-as-boss, woman-as-bossed?

However, girls usually run into the most severe inhibitions of academic success in high school and college. Just as in elementary school, education was overly feminine, in high school and college it becomes overly masculine. Male teachers and professors and fellow male students may put subtle pressure on an adolescent girl to be "feminine" and nonachieving. Do you remember the study we discussed in our section on the father and achievement in which girls were "afraid" to achieve? Perhaps you will remember that when confronted with a made-up story about a successful student and told to finish it, girls often made up a story in which the student held herself back, while boys usually made up stories about forging ahead to success.

So, if a girl has been exposed only to female teachers in elementary school and has never had an adult male show her that males value learning and achievement as a natural feminine characteristic, she may be unable to resist pressures that stereotype later on. Without such early confidence, she will perhaps take the path of least resistance later in school and concentrate on becoming the "most popular" and not the "most likely to succeed."

The principal remedy to the feminized classroom is, of course, more male teachers. They would lend a sexual balance to our educational institutions and could well bring more nontraditional women into the classroom—women who presently reject teaching as being too conforming and limiting a profession. Feeling less threatened by the classroom and by the usually male principal, the male teacher could concentrate less on demanding obedience and more on encouraging performance from both boys and girls. He could also give female teachers, especially the more traditional ones, support in allowing a freer, more open classroom. It is important for children to see men and women working together cooperatively in the classroom.

Just having more male teachers is not going to remedy all our school problems. The feminized school atmosphere must become more humanized, and both male and female teachers should be selected on the basis of their social and intellectual competence. If a male teacher allows himself to be dominated by a restrictive atmosphere, he may be a particularly poor model for children.

FATHER AND THE SCHOOL

Where do fathers enter into this problem of the feminized classroom? Simply, fathers may be the only segment of our society that is really sensitized to the need for male teachers. Mothers and female teachers, because of their upbringing, often have difficulty realizing the need for males to be involved with children. Many male principals and administrators are men who see themselves as having "risen above" teaching to better jobs in administration. Obviously, such men are not the ones to crusade for more male classroom teachers.

Because the feminized classroom has been a severe and long-standing problem, we advocate radical solutions. Affirmative-action programs have been an excellent way for society to give equal opportunity to women and minority groups. We feel such a program would be an excellent way to give male teachers—a minority group in elementary education—entrance into schools. Fathers should push for a balance of men to women teachers, advocating active recruitment of men. We realize this might be termed unfair to women teachers, but schools do not exist for teachers; they exist to afford balanced, effective education to students. We believe teachers would be the first to recognize this. At the very least, fathers should advocate that classes be scheduled so that every child has frequent contacts with male teachers during his elementary school career.

. But hiring more male teachers is merely dealing with the tip of the iceberg. Teaching must be made a prestigious enough profession so that both male and female teachers need not feel intimidated because of a second-class status. Primarily, this means making teaching a financially rewarding profession. Though we emphasize here the need for male teachers, there is, of course, a corresponding need for female administrators.

And, of course, there is the old stumbling block of society's attitude that teaching and childraising are feminine functions. Although our sex stereotypes are easing, many male elementary school teachers still feel that they are not looked up to as masculine, though it is true that many other male teachers go into their profession precisely because they feel comfortably and confidently masculine and know their value to children.

Involved, confident fathers, we feel, can go a long way toward remedying these problems. The goal, of course, is for both boys and girls to feel valued by teachers of both sexes, and for the school to reflect an ideal of society.

Father-School Partnerships. You can also see to it that *every* school class has a program of bringing fathers in to describe their respective jobs and professions, and even to teach some classes themselves. Teachers should not be the only ones who teach in a school. An accountant could give a lesson, however basic, in accounting. A pilot could lecture on how an airplane flies. An insurance agent could explain what insurance is and how it works. Of course, it is important to have women as well as men in various occupations come to school and describe their activities. Both boys and girls need to become aware that women can be successful in "traditionally masculine" fields.

Although we shall talk extensively about the father and his work in the next chapter, there are several steps that business and industry can take to aid children in learning about men. Your employer could make it a standard practice to give you and other fathers time off to visit your child's school. It would be excellent public relations for business and industry to allow men and women in their employ to visit various schools in order to describe their business in an intimate, informal classroom atmosphere. Many industries encourage classes to tour their plants; and this practice encourages relationships between adults and children.

Fathers can also encourage retirees, teen-agers, and other available men to act as playground monitors, crafts supervisors, lunchtime partners, and to do other voluntary work. A father's goal should be to give the child a view of society as it really is, not as the female-dominated place portrayed in today's classroom.

Father-School Problems. Whether you involve yourself in your child's school through the Parent-Teachers Association, by working directly with his teacher, or by merely visiting at open houses and giving your views, you may run into certain obstacles.

When you arrive at school for the first time, the teacher, usually female, may react with some surprise, perhaps even with a little nervousness and defensiveness. After all, you are the parent she usually never sees unless something quite serious has happened. Thus, your initial visits to school—nursery, elementary, and secondary levels—should be only to look around and familiarize yourself with the place, so that the teacher won't be put on the defensive. Make it clear to the teacher that you are interested in what she is doing and in her philosophy about teaching. Compared with your own school experiences, you are very likely to find many changes for the better. Get to know your child's teachers, as well as the administrators of the school, so that they will know that you are available, involved, and have a definite, meaningful point of view.

Your first visit will counteract the inertia that a father often has about going to his child's school. Perhaps having unpleasant memories about his own schooldays, or being hesitant to enter a world that sometimes seems as feminine as a lingerie shop, the father may gladly put off going to his child's school. Teachers may also project an air of professional elitism; they may insist that they know what they're doing and that you are an amateur.

Of course, if you are aware of these possibilities, they are less likely to inhibit you. You should also recognize another facet of your relationship with the school. You are more apt to be effective in changing the school because you are less prone to worry about being liked. Your wife may see your child's teacher as a cohort, someone with whom she has a relationship of a social nature. She may be less willing to assert herself in calling for change. You are also less likely to be intimidated by professional chauvinism on the part of teachers. Of course, we are stressing only the pitfalls of the parent-teacher relationship. Certainly, the majority of teachers are not prone to such behavior.

In general, both you and the teacher should realize that

each of you has something special to offer the child. Neither parents nor teachers should exclusively educate the child. Their cooperation can greatly enhance a child's educational experience.

OUT-OF-SCHOOL EDUCATION

Though school occupies a large part of your child's waking hours, it is not the whole answer to his educational needs. In fact, school has several drawbacks that only a parent, in some cases particularly a father, can remedy.

The main drawback of schools is that they basically encourage passivity in children, requiring them to learn but not necessarily to explore. Though the concept of open school—in which students work at their own pace on their own projects—helps remedy this, it still cannot remedy the basic problem. In most schools a child is still expected to complete a standardized course of study at a standardized educational level, using standardized arrays of materials. Chances are that in school your child would never get to tinker with an automobile motor, visit a bustling office, go fishing, see a computer, or do a myriad other things. For instance, Dennis vividly remembers a shrimp-seining trip with his father off the Gulf Coast of Texas because of its practical biology lesson with unique "learning materials." Though he had been fascinated with animals all his life, reading about them and learning their names, never had he had a chance to see and actively manipulate the incredible array of beasts hauled up in the shrimp net that day. His father, busy culling out the shrimp, looked down to find him fascinatedly poking around among squid, flounder, shrimp, crabs, and other strange creatures—watching them move, fight, retreat, and feed on that boat under the Texas sun. In school he never would have gotten a chance to handle and play with such creatures so closely.

Even when field trips or tours are arranged through schools, they cannot have the impact on a child of a personalized adventure with a father or mother. You know your child's interests, his level of understanding, and his personality much better than a teacher can, who must deal with a class of thirty youngsters. Unlike a teacher on a field trip, you are not worried about controlling a group of other people's children. You also do not have to limit your child's exposure to displays, etc., so that "everybody can have his turn." If you have two or more children, you probably sometimes find it a bit hectic taking them places. Can you imagine the uproar and confusion of thirty children going through a zoo?

You also have a much more long-term, personal commitment to your child than his teacher does. You and his mother care that he understands an exhibit or benefits from a trip. In the final analysis, it is a teacher's job only to teach children and there is not the emotional commitment to her own offspring.

The final major basic drawback to school is that it very seldom offers a child practical benefits arising from his learning. This lack of practical reward is also one reason so many children drop out of school—they see no tangible reward in spelling, reading, or arithmetic.

You are in an excellent position to provide the link between schooling and practical benefits. After all, you are usually the person in the family who receives the most tangible rewards from your education, in the form of your salary. If it is the case, stress to your child that your family's economic well-being depends on your prior and continuing education because of the job it helps you maintain. You can also tell him that education benefits you by helping you be a participating, knowledgeable citizen and that it even provides you with hobbies, ranging from reading to mountain climbing, if that is the case.

Of course, we are not saying that you and your wife shouldn't show your child the intangible benefits of education —the ability to appreciate art, literature, and music; the wider view of society one develops through education; and the encouraging of natural curiosity. You can show your child all these things, mainly by letting him see you enjoying good art, music, or literature; and by showing him how learning is naturally pleasurable to you. But to a young child these things are perhaps too abstract. He probably will be more interested in the solid, "understandable" reasons why he should attend school.

Father and Homework. Homework can provide an important avenue for helping you and your child learn together. Because you are usually the most technically educated parent, the child may question you more often about homework, especially in such subjects as math and science.

Everybody has seen cartoons in which the poor father is pictured hunched over his child's homework, obviously baffled by it, so we will begin with the mistake such a father is making: Never do all your child's homework for him. Contribute only to the extent of answering specific questions and helping him find places to look things up. Even if he has to be helped at many points during a difficult assignment, let him go through the process to the final answer. If necessary, you can coach him by asking helpful questions. With a difficult addition problem, for instance, ask him what are the subtotals, where do you carry over, and what is the final sum.

One father we know had two sons who were assigned to prepare a written report on X-ray techniques. This father was a doctor himself and knew other doctors whom he could ask for the information the children needed. He discussed what he knew about X-rays, but he also gave his sons the names of radiologists and sent them off to the hospital to do the interviewing themselves. This father followed an excellent dictum—don't make it hard on yourself simply to make it easier on your children.

Try to answer your children's questions and show an interest in what they are doing. And don't just emphasize the answers, but also the questions they ask. Compliment them when they pose a tough question or one that gets to the heart of the matter.

When your children ask something you don't know, admit it. Tell them where they can find the answer and either ask them what the results are, or better still, join them in looking up the answer or seeking out the information from others. When you see a chance, show them how the work they are doing relates to experiences on your job. If Suzy is studying computers, tell her about the computers you work with and what they do, or tell her about the exciting aspects of computers, such as computer dossiers on criminals, or about supercomputers. Because of your wider contact with the outside world, you may be able to bring ordinary homework to life.

If you keep up with what your sons and daughters are doing in school, you won't be reduced to asking the age-old "Well, what did you learn in school today?" You can ask them if they've improved their spelling. How the report on dinosaurs came out, or whether the hamster at school had her babies.

Try not to punish your children for failing to do their homework. Rather than saying, "I understand you aren't doing your homework—no movies this month," you should say, "I am disappointed to hear that you aren't doing your homework. I know you are capable of it, and I think you will do better in the future."

On the other hand, both fathers and mothers should not hesitate to speak up when they think their children are being overloaded with homework. Keep an eye on it; ask yourself whether it really contributes to the child's understanding or is simply busywork. Don't be reticent about telling your child's teacher that you think he is getting too much. Besides homework, take into account your child's other commitments. We know many children who are overscheduled. They have religious schooling, sports activities, music lessons, and organized social-group memberships. They hardly have a free moment for spontaneous play. Remember also that children need more sleep than adults. Excessive homework is often the final insult to a child's free time. Helping your child to schedule his time can be a very effective role for fathers. Both you and your child should avoid the "frantic executive" syndrome.

Your Attitudes. In helping your child with his homework, as well as the many other aspects of fostering his intellectual growth, try to realize what your own attitudes are. If you had a bad time with school and homework when you were a child, try not to pass negative attitudes on to your child. Though he may realize that you are not interested in some intellectual activities, make it clear that you nevertheless recognize their value. Encourage him to achieve in all subjects, not just the ones in which you did well.

Dennis's father was not particularly fond of music, but when Dennis expressed an interest in learning to play the trombone, his father made sure he had an instrument and lessons. His father would often sit with him and sing as Dennis played popular songs, and his father and mother encouraged him to practice and would attend his concerts faithfully. His father did this even though he commented that he was less fond of classical music than he was of popular music. Thus, Dennis was aware that his father had certain tastes, but he did not devalue Dennis's own interests.

Parents and Reading. Parents can particularly affect their children's reading skills and habits. In fact, a major study by a University of Illinois English professor found that parents influence their children's reading preferences more than teachers do. In a nine-year study of 70,000 high school students in nine countries, Dr. Alan Purves and his colleagues found that the home reading environment was critical. They found that schools did little to develop a student's ability to read literature critically or to like literature, though teachers did teach students basic reading skills.

Dr. Purves found that the number of books and magazines in a student's home has a greater effect on achievement than does family income or educational level. A student's ability to read is affected more by home background than by type of teaching.

As we said, boys frequently get the idea that reading is feminine or unimportant as a tool or for enjoyment. Earlier we described how Hemingway's father got his son started in reading and discussed how you should read to your infant.

You should continue such practices with your school child, not only reading to and with your child but encouraging him to tell you about what he has read.

Even if you do not enjoy reading magazines or books, make sure your child has full access to them. Dennis's mother frequently took him to the library, helping him to pick out books he liked, and his father would play a game called Words with him. The two would sit facing each other, each with one volume of a two-volume dictionary, and one of them would call out a word. The other would have to spell the word, define it, and use it in a sentence. Thus, even though neither of Dennis's parents finished high school, they both showed that they valued learning and the intelligent use of words.

Incidentally, one effective way of interesting your young child in words is to tell him that when he learns to spell and define a word it is "his." Nobody can ever take that possession away. Watch how eager he is to become rich, wordwise.

One of Albert Einstein's uncles probably gave little Albert a similar impetus toward mathematics when he told him, "Algebra is a merry science. We go hunting for a little animal we don't know, so we call it X. When we bag our quarry we pounce on it and give it its right name."

Father on Vacation. The family vacation can be another excellent opportunity for you to help your child learn, both about you and about the world. We have already talked about taking your child on outings with you, but vacations offer certain unique problems. Too often the family vacation is something the family does in the company of one another, but not "together." The father who spends all his time behind the wheel of a car, visiting with his relatives, or seeing sights in the company of his family is not effectively relating to his child. When you take your children on vacation, it should be a period of interaction, not simply family members paralleling one another, each on his own trip.

On long trips, play games with the children while your wife is driving, stop and show them sights, or explain to them about the land you are passing through. Talk about the advertising along the road, how it tries to get you to buy and how good or bad the products are. Tourist attractions such as Disneyland are fun, but you should balance them with personal family experiences that will allow you to talk with your child and exchange ideas with him. Canoe trips, tours using a guide-book, sports-car rallies, or other active events offer an excellent opportunity for interaction. If you spend time talking to your child and explaining things, even a trip to the local junkyard can be better than an impersonal trip across the country.

If you have more than one child, try to take a short mini-vacation with each of them. It need only be a visit to the zoo or an overnight camping trip to make your child feel that he is something special. Other mini-vacations should be just with your wife, so that you two don't lose touch with each other.

Vacations are not just for parent-child interaction, and we fully realize this. If you continually do things that are good for the children but not pleasant for you, you are not being fair to them or yourself. Again we return to the idea that you are a many-faceted person, and your role as a father, however important, is just one of those facets. So make sure that you leave enough vacation time for those things *you* enjoy.

Television and Education. Television can have a profound impact on the intellectual development of the child. While the management of television viewing is important in the pre-school and adolescent years, it may be most important to the elementary-school-age child. He is developing his attitudes toward television and is reaching the stage where he will determine his own viewing habits. The school-age child is also beginning to progress beyond cartoon shows and to grasp the meaning of adult television programs.

Because of the pervasiveness of television watching, family interaction has decreased. Though it is not widely the case now, television can be used to bring the family closer together, but it will take a conscious effort on the part of parents.

The first step is to put television into its proper place in the home, both physically and psychologically. Television should not be a baby-sitter or a night light or background noise for conversation. The television set should be off unless there is a specific program to be watched.

Too many homes have a multitude of television sets, which tends to isolate the family members in their own rooms, each watching his own program. You may find it a good practice to have only one set so that at least you will all be in the same room. Perhaps another small-screen set could be used to prevent eruption of too many arguments over what to watch.

One good practice is to have an activity, game, or hobby room in which the television is not allowed. This way both the children and the adults can have a place to play and work with each other without its distraction. This room could be very roughly finished so that family members will not worry about attempting messy projects. Incidentally, this room can be the same one that was used as the "tear-up" room we mentioned in our section on father and the young child's intellectual development. Shelving, comfortable chairs and couches, and hobby benches would contribute to the usefulness of such a room.

Parents should set specific limits on television, both for themselves and for their children. These limits can be flexible—there may be many good programs in a given week—but they should not be lax. One good way to teach the children to plan their watching is to mark off the programs to watch on the weekly television schedule usually found with the Sunday newspaper. Both the parents and the children should be able to give fairly good reasons for watching a particular program. Make it clear to your children that television is allowed only if chores, homework, and other tasks are out of the way or are certain to be done.

Your and your wife's reaction to television programs can also help your child's learning. Though fathers who talk back to television commentators have been the subject of many cartoons, such men are showing their children a valuable trait—the habit of critical thinking. Discuss television news and editorializing with your family. Your children should be brought up to realize that what they see on television is not necessarily the correct story or the whole one. When you watch documentaries or other special programs, talk about the contents, criticize them, and discuss how the program relates to your own life. Analyze the ploys behind commercials and particularly the flaws in logic contained in most pitches to buy a product. This is another instance when you will have a chance to tell your child about your own experiences and background—how you have learned what to look for in a commercial and in the product it advertises.

12 / Father, Work, and the Child's Career Choice

TEACHER: What does your Daddy do?
FIVE-YEAR-OLD SON OF DRAFTSMAN: He drives our car!
TEACHER: When?
BOY: Every day. He just gets in the car in the morning and drives it.
TEACHER: And people pay him for it?
BOY: Yes, they give him money for driving our car.

Although, as we pointed out in our chapter on fathers and mothers, a large percentage of mothers work, their jobs are usually quite different from men's.

Because of traditional views that women should become primarily homemakers, women have not been prepared for professional and technical jobs to the same extent that men have. The result is that women in the job market have been channeled into certain occupations, such as secretary or clerk, or else they prepare for traditionally female occupations, such as nursing. Statistics of the U.S. Department of Labor show this extreme imbalance—99 percent of secretaries are women, 96 percent of nurses, 70 percent of schoolteachers, and 88 percent of bank tellers. Few women are represented in certain professions: only 5 percent of lawyers, 9 percent of physicians, and less than 1 percent of construction crafts workers and engineers are women. Working women also tend not to have as continuous or as long-term careers as men.

Thus, even though a large percentage of women work, it is

still the father who is far more likely to introduce a son or daughter to the world of the advanced professional or skilled craftsworker. Women as well as men need more opportunity to develop their occupational potential.

The typical father's failure to involve his child in his work is perhaps the most insidious contributor to father deprivation in this country. When you are at home, it is difficult to avoid your child (although many fathers become expert nonfathers); at work, however, children have been effectively excluded. The farmer-artisan, plying his trade with his children watching, no longer exists. He has been replaced by the father who goes off in the morning to do God-knows-what and doesn't return until God-knows-when.

There is, of course, a considerable amount of social pressure against consistently taking a child to work. Many men feel slightly guilty at showing off their children. They feel that fatherhood is somehow inconsistent with the image of the up-and-coming, dynamic male. Others may feel that their peers are judging them through their children and that a shy, dumb, or undisciplined child may reflect on their own abilities.

Many men feel threatened when their children visit them at work. Such men view work as a major expression of their personal power and somehow believe that a child's presence degrades it. Hence they "protect" their work from their child by keeping him strictly apart from it.

Bosses and supervisors may give fathers who want to bring their children to work or who want to take time off to be with their children a hard time. They either may not realize how important fatherhood is or may feel uneasy at the idea of a man's being so interested in his children, or they may even feel a little guilty about neglecting their own children. Usually such antifather sentiment comes out as, "I really think the kids may interfere with the office," or, "We can't spare you to go off with your kids this afternoon."

It's very important for your fatherhood that you examine the reality of these notions in your particular job situation. If such reactions don't make sense, you should be firm about involving your children with your work. You'll be proud of yourself, and your boss will think twice about demanding that your fatherhood be shunted aside.

The reasons bosses give for not bringing children to work aren't generally valid. Most businesses that would be disrupted by a father bringing his child to work occasionally may not be well run to begin with. A boss who can't allow a father an occasional morning or afternoon to be with his children is probably too dependent on that man for his own good.

At the beginning of the industrial revolution, there was good reason for excluding children from factories, for they were quite dangerous. Today, however, safety regulations are generally well-enforced and a great many fathers work in offices anyway, where the most dangerous injury a child might receive would be a paper cut.

Such excuses aside, an excellent case can be made that including your child in your work is necessary for effective fatherhood. Your work is a major part of your life. You probably spend a good portion of your waking hours at work, perhaps the most active hours of your day. On the job, unlike at home, you are neither just waking up nor resting from a day of coping with the world. Thus, if your child misses seeing you at work, he is missing a major part of your personality and your life.

As a test, ask your child what you do for a living. Whether he is five or fifteen, he should be able to tell you something about your work, and the older he is, the more detailed and comprehensive his explanation should be. He should be able to tell you what company you work for, what kinds of activities you do during the day, perhaps which ones you like best, and what you do on business trips. If he cannot tell you these kinds of things, you are not involving him effectively.

Thus, we see there exists the potential and the need for involving your child in your work. Now for the specific methods.

The Commuting Father. Obviously, the more time you spend in the car or on the bus or train, the less time you will have at home. Also, your child will have less access to you in the office if you live far from where you work. As a very general guideline, we advocate that you keep your total commuting time to under an hour per day, or as little over that as possible. This way, not only will you be able to have more time at home in the mornings and afternoons, but you can pick up your child during lunchtime for an afternoon at work or have him visit you there.

If you do have to spend two or more hours a day commuting, it may be possible for you to get some of your work done on your way back and forth from the office. Some people use a tape recorder to dictate letters and memos; others work on business matters on the train or bus. At first it may be difficult to concentrate, but such habits can allow you to spend less time at work and more time with your family.

Also, long commuting trips can be used to advantage if your children sometimes go with you. Whether they are going with you to work or spending the day in other activities, the commuting trip may provide a relaxing atmosphere for sharing and communicating.

In addition to physical access, also give your child psychological access to you at work. Encourage him to call you or to drop by if he has something important to discuss. The daughter of one man we know visited his office to tell him she had just won a tennis tournament. She was able to share this important event with her father while she was still excited about it and to receive praise from her father in the first flush of victory. Of course, we realize that you may have to limit such visits or calls for business reasons, but do so with tact. It is extremely important that you do not allow your child to be isolated in a fatherless ghetto of a suburb.

Taking Your Child to Work. The most important encounters your child has with your work will usually not be initiated by him. They will probably occur when you take him to work with you.

Practically, you can begin taking him with you as soon as he is toilet-trained, can walk and talk, and understands a bit of what is going on around him. A lot depends on your workplace and on yourself. If your coworkers don't mind having a baby in the office, and you aren't uncomfortable about changing diapers or feeding the baby, you can sometimes take your child to work when he is still quite young.

In any case, pick a day when you are not overwhelmed with work and perhaps have something to do that will be especially interesting or informative for the child—visiting a client, for example, or working with a special piece of machinery.

Even if you spend the entire day in your office, your child can bring toys along to play with beside your desk or nap on your couch. If it is not too disruptive and if your coworkers don't mind, he can also venture out with them to see other parts of the business operation. This may have the added salutary effect of encouraging other fathers to bring their own children to work when they see how successful you are with yours.

Some companies have a regular open house during which special exhibits are planned. The Monday after Father's Day might also be a good day to bring children to work—a sort of public relations gimmick for fatherhood. Don't limit your child to such special days, though, because the father-child relationship might be lost in the wonder of gadgetry or in the milling crowds.

Don't hesitate to take your child out of school for a day of going to work with you. What he learns at work may be more valuable to him, and no reputable school would allow a child to fall behind because of one missed day. Being let out of school will also underscore the importance of the day at work with father. Maybe his trips can be integrated into his schoolwork. Teachers could make it a part of the curriculum for the child to visit his father's or mother's workplace and report on the experience.

Because of the rapid growth and development of your child, you should take him to work fairly often. As he reaches new stages of mental and physical growth, he will get different things out of what you show him. At age five, he may only know that Daddy works with big machinery with lots of lights and that he puts things into the machine and gets things out. By age ten he will realize that Daddy works with computers and will have an idea of what computers do. By age fifteen he will know that Daddy is involved in systems modeling of the economics of a company and what that entails. Take your child to work frequently and watch his understanding of your job grow.

He Can Understand What You Do. Don't underestimate the ability of your child to understand what you do. Start explaining your work to him in an elementary way, relating to things he already knows. For instance, a life insurance salesman might begin by telling his child that his company gives money to a person's family when the person dies, and the insured people pay for this service of the company. Then he could proceed to explain his role in selling insurance and then, further, his role in estate planning, and so on. When he sees that his child begins not to comprehend, his explanation should cease for that time.

The child, particularly the very young child, may only be able to grasp what you do by watching you work rather than by being told about what you do. Remember that the young child may learn most by seeing and feeling.

When you first bring your child into the office or factory, let him orient himself to where you work. This will become his home territory because it is Daddy's. Show him around the plant, telling him what each section is for and how it relates to your work—who gives you work and whom you give your finished product to. Introduce him to your coworkers and encourage him to get to know them at coffee breaks or during lunch. A very young child may have difficulty staying the whole day, so you can arrange for your wife to pick your son or daughter up at lunchtime or bring them for the afternoon. If you have more than one child, remember to give each one his "special time" with Daddy at work.

Involving your child in your work is not solely your responsibility. Business, industry, and trade unions should also take an active role in encouraging such involvement. At the least, such encouragement is good public and employee relations. When one's child is interested in what his parent is doing, the parent is also likely to take more pride in his work.

In light of the fact that happy family men tend to do much better work than those with unhappy family relationships, companies also have a very practical economic reason for encouraging child involvement.

Companies should provide day-care centers and other places for visiting children to gather. For the older child, such a place may take the form of a playroom with games, books about the company, and perhaps even a chart showing where each father works. These day-care centers and playrooms, of course, would not have to be meant as long-term centers for child care. The company may want to set limits on the number of days the children could use the facilities. Such facilities could be part of a long-term day-care center for the children of working parents, too.

Management could also make it easier for the new father to establish himself by allowing him a few days off to aid in the birth of his child. Such "paternity leaves" as they are popularly called may also take the form of certain allowed days—say, four per year—during which fathers can bring the child to work or visit the child's school to teach or participate in other ways.

Business and industry could also offer courses for employees on family relations. The courses could cover the special family problems certain types of employees, such as executives, salesmen, etc., might encounter because of their work.

Working Late. Your nine-to-five involvement with your job is only part of your career. You may find yourself involved in after-hours work activities. In accepting such commitments, you should also take your fatherhood into account. If you work odd hours, you may find it worthwhile to change the family schedule of eating and even sleeping so that you will have time to spend with your children. One father we know, an airline pilot, usually finishes work about 3:00 A.M. every morning. When he gets home, his wife, son, and daughter get out of bed, have dinner, enjoy one another's company for a while and then go back to bed until the youngsters get up for school. This way the pilot sees them at dinner, and his children are able to fit into his schedule of sleeping and eating.

If you simply work long hours, your preschool child can stay up to see you when you get home and can sleep later in the morning. Your school child may be able to take a nap after school so that he can stay up and spend time with you.

Incidentally, whether you work long hours or not, you may be quite tired when you come home from the office and be in need of a nap yourself before you are ready to play with your child. We know many parents who have a rule that the first hour or so after Daddy gets home from work is his to relax and unwind in. After that comes playtime, decision-making time, or time to help resolve disputes.

If you bring work home from the office, don't feel that you should go off to do it alone. Let your child help, if only to sharpen pencils, or run errands. If you have to do reading, he can sit at the desk with you and draw or do homework. Though you may take a little longer at it, the working time can be counted doubly effective—you are getting work done *and* being involved with your child.

Henry often does some of his work at the dining-room table where the children can be involved. His younger ones (Cameron, six, and Michael, three) often climb up on his lap to watch him work or to scribble with pen and paper "just like Daddy." His older children do their homework or even help with their father's work. Jonathan, eleven, has read over some of his father's most technical papers and found errors in typing and punctuation. Both Jonathan and Kenneth, in fact, contributed to Henry's and Dennis's discussions about this book, adding their own kids'-eye-view.

Business Trips. If you spend any time at all on business trips, you should consider taking your child with you occasionally. It is economically feasible to take a child on a business trip because he usually gets reduced air fares, hotel rates, and meal costs, so money is not necessarily a drawback.

Your child can certainly get a lot out of watching you at business meetings, even if he doesn't fully understand them. During your time off, he will certainly benefit from the sights of a new city. If your child is old enough to dial a telephone, he can stay in your hotel room if he does not wish to go with you. All he has to be able to do is dial *0*. You can notify the hotel switchboard about the child and tell them where to find you. And, of course, most hotels provide a baby-sitting service if you do not feel your child is independent enough to stay by himself.

Such a father-child business trip is also an excellent way to get to know your child better. At home there are usually many distractions. On business trips, when you are alone with your child, you can observe how he reacts to many new sights and learn better how to aid his development.

Success and Fatherhood. A major myth confronting fathers in regard to their fatherhood and their work is that success in one precludes success in the other. Certainly, it is difficult to spend long hours on the job and remain a good father, and it may be just as difficult to spend a lot of time with your family and still be successful in your career.

One "successful" man, George R., whom Henry encountered at a clinic, embodied many of the problems work-driven fathers have today. George was a good example of the "driven" father, constantly involved either with his business or with some hobby or project at home. He was almost always working on his stamp collection, sharpening up his bridge game, or planning the inventory at the department store he owned.

When his children began having emotional problems and failing in their schoolwork, George declared that he knew he wasn't the cause. "I'm a damned good provider, and I'm home a lot of the time, so my kids know they have a father," he said. Only after several counseling sessions alone and with his family did George come to understand the many ways he had left his children out of his life.

A key to being successful both as a father and as a career man is to balance the two and maintain the balance. Establish a solid nucleus of things you feel you must do to be a successful father and a successful career man, and don't let anything interfere with either one. For some fathers this may mean working hard when they are at the office, but refusing to accept business calls after a certain hour when they are at home. You may even work through your lunch hour or grab a sandwich at your desk, but leave the office at five o'clock without a briefcase and spend the time at home playing with your children. Health specialists caution against taking hurried lunches, but such a habit is not dangerous if you balance it with a period of rest, exercise, or relaxation with your child.

Being successful at both a career and fatherhood may even mean refusing charity and civic work, but compared to the good you are doing your children by being a good father, you may feel civic work is expendable. The road you take depends on your own sense of priorities, but remember what we have said about the importance of fatherhood.

One good way of having time for both a career and children is to mix the two. True, taking your child to work may be enough, but if you are an eighteen-hour-a-day man, even more may be necessary. For instance, Don Shula, coach of the football team the Miami Dolphins, works monumental numbers of hours to make his team into a winning one, but he does so with a view toward the importance of his fatherhood. A recent newspaper article on him describes his efforts to include his children:

> "To compensate [for my long hours] I try to include them in any of the activities which are football-oriented and in which my family can still have a part." The Shulas attend as many scrimmages and games as they can and Don keeps finding ways in which the children can help him with the team.
>
> Says Dorothy Shula, his wife: "David, 14, has been to every one of his father's games since he was four years old, and since we moved to Miami in 1970, he has been a ballboy at every training camp. This year he . . . keeps track of all offensive plays and how many times they are run.
>
> "And one of our daughters, who just turned eleven, has been secretary for Don when his own secretary was away for a day or two. He really brings the whole family in.
>
> "He's unbelievable," says Mrs. Shula. "He takes time

for the smallest problem these children have. They get as much attention from their father, probably more, than the average children get, no matter what their father does."

Henry's practice represents a more usual case. Although he gets many invitations to speak and consult, he usually turns them down if they are on weeknights or weekends, or else he takes one of his sons with him. He limits his clinical practice to what he can handle within a normal working day. When he does have extra work, he gets up very early in the morning, so the time will not be taken away from his family. Another tactic he finds useful is to work over his lunch period but to leave his office early enough so that he can spend a meaningful period of time with his family.

FATHER, ADOLESCENCE, AND CAREER CHOICE

In the last section, we emphasized that the father's work need not interfere with his relationship with his children. In fact, we pointed out that a father can use his work as an opportunity to share more of himself with his children and expose his child to important sources of social and intellectual stimulation.

In addition to learning about the specifics of a particular job, a child can be very much influenced by your attitude toward work. Do you find it interesting and challenging? Or is it simply a means to earn a living? Is it something that keeps you apart from your family? Is it an obsession or is it a growth experience for you? Many men change careers or occupational specialties, and sharing the realities and your motivations about your job can be very important for your developing child.

Adolescence is a critical period in your child's intellectual growth and is often the time when he is having experiences and making decisions that will have a profound effect on his own occupational future. When we discussed the views of the great child psychologist Jean Piaget, we said that the last major phase in Piaget's outline of intellectual development was the formal operations period in which the child (beginning about eleven years of age) learns to grasp abstract laws and theories. Just as you provided a rich environment for the infant and many kinds of intellectual opportunities for your school-age child, you are also vital in helping your teen-ager attain a sophisticated level of thinking and in helping him make important decisions affecting his career choice.

As your child matures, your interaction with him becomes more complex. Besides security, the infant is mainly interested only in the colors, sights, sounds, tastes, and textures you can introduce him to. The school-age child is interested in the more complex things you can tell him about how his environment operates. Your adolescent demands more sophisticated thinking about moral codes, scientific laws, abstract concepts, and other more advanced facets of our world. He will use what you tell him about your experiences in the outside world in a much more sophisticated way.

Before adolescence, you and his mother, his school, and his neighborhood may have represented the boundaries of his thinking—both physical and psychological boundaries. He may have been very dependent upon you for intellectual input about the world. During adolescence, if not before, your role changes from that of facilitator to that of a person to whom he can return for intellectual stability. You have basically the same outlook throughout your adult life. Now, as your child progresses into the world on his own, he needs someone to whom he can relate his experiences. You can give him your perspective on his experiences as he establishes his own philosophy of life. Discussing the realities and your feelings about your job can be especially important to your child.

A Frame of Reference. The so-called teen-age identity crisis may be nothing more than the difficulties adolescents have in establishing a sense of reality and order *without* the aid of a solid, basic relationship with the formidable, loving creature that is the father. As author Thomas Wolfe puts it,

> The deepest search in life, it seemed to me, the thing that
> in one way or another was central to all living was man's

search to find a father, not merely the father of his flesh, not merely the lost father of his youth, but the image of a strength and wisdom external to his need and superior to his hunger to which the belief and power of his own life could be united.

You have the ability to help the child bridge the gap between your fatherhood and the child's sense of his own "fatherhood"—whether the child is male or female.

Another role in your relationship with your adolescent is that of the voice of experience, the merchant of reality. Adolescents are out to change the world to fit their own concept of perfection and may have an unrealistic perception of real-world operation. Sharing your life experiences and career development may give him a particularly valuable perspective.

Your task, and it is a touchy one, is to help your adolescent see the complexities and realities of the world and yet not put down his idealism. Puncturing grandiose schemes while helping him retain idealistic fervor is a delicate operation. You must also consider the value of his fresher outlook.

Never say that something that your teen-ager wants to do can't be accomplished; rather sum up the reasons for and against and let him come up with the decision. Hold off throwing cold water on an idea if failure of the idea will help your child get experience and won't be a devastating blow.

Be there when he fails, not to tell him, "I told you so," but to support him and to help him analyze the reasons for his failure.

An Intellect-Exerciser. Somewhat akin to this role of reality-introducer is your role as intellect-exerciser. You should see yourself as a sort of intellectual sparring partner against which your child can work to develop his sense of logic and reality, especially during his high school years. This area represents a major failure of many fathers. They do not rise to the challenge of arguing, discussing, and challenging their adolescent. Fatherhood during adolescence might also be termed a course in "Advanced Ramifications." You should continue your earlier practice of discussing with your child all the aspects of whatever he is planning or has gotten himself into. Whether the discussion is about smoking pot or taking a new course in school, it can help him bring his activities into focus.

Your child's intellectual contacts will probably be restricted to you and your wife, his peer group, and his teachers. Of the three groups, you and your wife may represent the most viable sources of intellectual conflict.

While his peers are a source of argument, they usually operate within the same framework and stage of development as your child. They are not likely to introduce new ideas or radically different ways of looking at things.

Teachers are usually necessarily concerned with teaching your teen-ager the facts of history, science, or literature and not as much with getting into philosophical discussions about them. Few high schools attain true academic freedom, at least not as much as colleges and universities do. They are not likely to be allowed to teach radical or unpopular ideas, ideas that would certainly be excellent intellectual stimulants for your child.

Your job as a father is obvious—to introduce stimulating theories that encompass both sides of the "average." Dennis remembers that his high school library, being in a conservative area of Texas, was filled with ultraconservative treatises on the Communist conspiracy. When he began thinking about politics, these were the only books available in the school library and the ones he took to represent reality. It was not until his father listened to his political theories and expressed his reaction to his views that Dennis began to evaluate political thought to the left of the John Birch Society.

In a class in political science with thirty others, for instance, your teen-ager is certain not to get the chance to express himself as much as he hopefully will at the dinner table or during the six-o'clock news. He may, in fact, be intimidated by subtle pressure from his peers not to participate in class. Being too intelligent is one "crime" for which many teen-agers are excluded from a social group.

The most pervasive problem faced by many fathers during

the high school years is breaking through what seems like an impenetrable wall surrounding the teen-age peer group. This is partly because fathers represent the rules and order of society against which teen-agers may tend to rebel. Fathers also tend to be harsher than mothers toward teen-agers for fads—their ways of dressing, their music, and their speech—because to them, working members of society, these fads seem nonproductive and immature.

If you have maintained a close, understanding relationship with your child until now, and he has learned to respect your intellectual style, you should have little trouble maintaining communication during adolescence.

As was the case during childhood, you should still openly voice your opinions. If you do not like certain clothing styles or music, you should not stifle your criticism. The key is that your teen-ager will have enough confidence not to feel threatened by this criticism. He will know that you still recognize that he is a full partner in intellectual exchange and is entitled to his own opinions. He will also know that you expect a full measure of performance from him because his self-respect will demand it. He has that important core of security and competence that we discussed earlier.

With the background of a communicative relationship, you do not have to worry that your son or daughter will become overly embroiled in his peer-group activities and will not have the benefit of adult intellectual input. The parent-teen-ager generation gap to a large extent exists only in the minds of parents who weren't comfortable with their children when they were younger.

Teen-agers, Sex Role, Intellect. Another major problem arising during adolescence is that intellectual activities become even more loaded with sex-role significance. Because your son or daughter is developing into a sexually mature human being, he or she is being pressured to assume a stereotyped social role, fair or unfair though it may be. If your son takes a course in home economics or your daughter one in "shop," they are likely to be taunted quite a bit by their friends. The taunters may not be sure of their own masculinity or femininity or may be trapped in stereotypes they absorbed from their own parents.

You should solidly support your son if, for instance, he decides to participate in glee club instead of athletics. If your daughter does the reverse, you must show her that you still feel that she is feminine. The happiest children and subsequently the happiest adults are often those who aren't afraid to try a wide variety of activities. They don't feel confined by the dictates of stereotyped masculinity. Henry's son, Kenneth, for instance, has taken up the flute and pottery making, and he also enjoys playing baseball and football, confident that all these activities are within the proper sphere of his masculinity.

We know one child, Cindy T., fourteen, who was especially good at math. Her father, an accountant, readily helped her with her homework and told her he was proud of her achievement. One day, however, Cindy came home with an F on an important math test. Her father tried to find out what she thought she had done wrong, but couldn't get an answer. Finally, she told him that the other girls had snubbed her because she was beating everybody on tests, and a boy whom she liked had scored lower than she on the previous test and had been embarrassed about it. Her father explained to her that being feminine didn't mean flunking tests and, most important, took her to meet one of his clients, a woman who was a professor of mathematics at a local university. After that, Cindy refused to let her friends taunt her into flunking. She knew that her father, an important male, valued her, and she had seen a successful woman who was also a successful mathematician.

Remember that the beginning of adolescence is a critical time, during which creativity may be injured by peer-group pressure. If you find yourself the father of an exceptionally creative child, it is important that you recognize your role of temporary bulwark against society and critical peers.

Father and Vocational Choice. Before we go into your role in the advanced schooling of your young adult, we should first discuss generally your role in his career choice. As one cognizant of the nature and requirements of many jobs, you have a duty to make that knowledge available to your offspring. He may not know the difference between a surgeon, an internist, and a general practitioner. He may not be fully aware of the requirements to become a lawyer, an electrician, or a plumber. You probably have an idea of what their everyday duties are and how they will fit in with your child's interests and aptitudes. Even if you don't know what a neurosurgeon does, for instance, you may have doctor friends to whom you can introduce your offspring.

By giving him the advantage of your knowledge and contacts, you can help your adolescent avoid many pitfalls. One major pitfall is a lack of direction in college. College counselors say that a great many students don't really know what they're doing at college. They arrive without any prior knowledge of the area they're interested in and may spend years in a field that completely frustrates them.

You can help your young adult gather information on careers that interest him or perhaps even help him take time off from school to try a few fields if he is not sure of his interests. You may want to help support him financially or just encourage his exploration. But don't be afraid to throw him out of the nest if he's not actively involved in some useful pursuit.

You can also help your offspring avoid the common pitfall of overspecialization. With your encouragement, he will not feel trapped into college, vocational school, or any other set course. Encourage experimentation for two reasons: (1) Schooling is certainly not aimed only at a particular vocation; it also aims at producing a well-rounded individual, and (2) being well versed in many fields will enable your teen-ager to readily change occupations if he so desires or is forced to. So, if your child seems dead set on a career in science, encourage him to take a few humanities courses. If he is studying to be an auto mechanic, encourage him to take a few extra courses in commercial art if he wishes.

Father and His Daughter's Career. Your daughter's choice of vocation may offer a more delicate problem for you. Although your son will probably enter some full-time specific career, daughters may be more varied in their career aims. Some may want a full-time career, others may want something they can enter and leave as their life-style changes. Still others may want a job only to earn money until they marry. Nine out of ten women work at some time during their lives. Since one of the prime goals of your fatherhood is to encourage competence, you must do your utmost to help your daughter have the best career that she can. How she uses her talents must be dictated by her own standards and abilities and not by what Daddy is willing to pay for in the way of schooling.

We have seen two principal syndromes with regard to father and the daughter's career: First of all, there is the father who blatantly aims his daughter into dead-endedness at an early age. At around twelve or thirteen years of age, the father (and the mother as well) seems to say to her, "O.K., you've edited the school newspaper and been a debating champion, but now it's time to settle down and prepare yourself for a 'feminine career.' " The girl, subtly or not, is then channeled into home economics or typing courses.

The second type of father is quite nurturant of his daughter's intellect, but not demanding enough. She is encouraged to complete college, but is not given an orientation toward accomplishing something with her education. This type of girl is encouraged to major in art, literature, or philosophy, but she is not expected to contribute seriously in these fields and certainly not to take up a more practical field such as business management. If she does receive a degree in chemistry, for instance, she may be aimed at high school teaching rather than research. Thus, her parents have encouraged her development, but only half-heartedly—they have not given her the dignity of fully valuing her career possibilities.

Of course, we recognize that the daughter is likely to be strongly influenced by her mother. The mother is often highly important in encouraging her daughter to work or to go into a profession. But at the same time, right or wrong, we recognize that women are still overly influenced by male "approval." You are the most outstanding male in your daughter's life, and thus your approval is crucial.

You also affect your daughter indirectly by influencing your wife. Whether she has a career or not or encourages it in her daughter is certainly a joint parental decision. But it is ridiculous to deny that you do not influence your wife's attitudes considerably. In fact, you exercised a judgment of the type of woman you value by marrying your wife, just as she exercised a judgment in her choice of you. Thus, be careful that your daughter, having a certain set of talents, is not stifled by the attitudes of both her parents—attitudes formed in an earlier day.

We are in no way deprecating the role of housewife and mother. In fact, such a role can be much more challenging than many careers. Also, the housewife, more than the wage earner, can schedule her time much more flexibly and fulfill herself with a wider variety of activities, including charitable work, home business, professional consultation, and the fine arts.

Another point we should make is that some fathers fear and resent the fact that their daughters may surpass them intellectually. Though an achieving son may be a chip off the old block, an achieving daughter may be a splinter in a traditional father's male ego.

Father and College. Practically speaking, the first step into college or any other training is in choosing an institution. You are probably a major provider of funds for this venture and know realistically how much the family can afford. Thus, you should certainly involve yourself in the choosing process.

We shall not go into the mechanics of choosing a college, trade school, or business school. There are many good books on the subject. But we shall outline ways in which you can contribute to an effective choice.

Read any college literature your son or daughter wishes you to, and give your opinions when asked. You should consider yourself an active consultant in the selection—not its arbiter, however. Just as investors do not have a say in the actual management of the company, so you do not have authority in choosing a college except to put your own limits on the resources you are willing to provide.

Make clear to your son or daughter what monetary restraints exist in his choice. Too many fathers see college financing as a way of making up for personal noninvolvement with their child and consequently give them a blank check. As we said before, you should not be a martyr to your child's wants, and that includes college financing.

There is no reason your son or daughter should not help meet college expenses. Saving for college, working for his money during college, or seeking scholarships can be a good way for him to feel independent. Most college students, we believe, would rather have it this way, if their study schedule allows it.

Rather than telling your college student that you will open-endedly finance his attending a certain institution, have him make up a budget to which you will both adhere. Allow him to budget food, clothing, tuition, books, etc., and decide upon a standard check that he can expect monthly or biweekly—and no writing home for money. Once this is done, never inquire into his finances, open his checking-account statement, or attempt to monitor his expenditures. He is to be considered an adult, accountable only to himself. As in your earlier dealings with him, he is to feel that he is the final master of his own actions.

You may not, in fact, be able to help with college expenses at all. Even if this is the case, you are still immensely important to your college student. By encouraging him in his desire to further his education, you are helping him to stick to his goals.

In many ways your adolescent's entrance into a college or other training represents an entrance into the adult world. He is in the process of becoming an intellectual and social equal to you, and your job now is to learn to accept and encourage him as such. For many fathers this acceptance can be quite a shock. Used to being the intellectual masters of the house, they resent their child's growth and achievement. Your son or daughter, home from college for the first time, may encounter special problems in their relationship with you as they challenge your long-held beliefs with new ideas of their own. If you have followed our guide thus far, your and your young adult's mutual respect should be well established. You will be able to maintain a warm relationship with your college student and at the same time cope with the welcomed onslaught of a young, inquiring mind.

Once your son or daughter is in college, you may become an even more meaningful reference point to him. Much more than in high school, your young adult may exist within a student ghetto. He may eat, sleep, work, and play only with people of his own age and general background. Students often complain they get caught in a deadly triangular rut—from dormitory to dining hall to class and back to dormitory. College students may even reproduce a portion of the youth ghetto in portable form during the summer vacation as they take a youth group tour to another country or congregate where fellow students gather.

One of your roles is to see to it that the adolescent ghetto does not limit your son or daughter in college. You can help by aiding him in finding a summer job or volunteer work away from campus. You can give him the chance to be involved, as an adult, in your social life when he comes home on holidays.

You can also keep up a steady correspondence with him during college. This correspondence can and should be more than a simple "How are you; we are fine." If he is taking a course you are interested in, you may be able to discuss or argue various points of it with him. You may want to get the reading list for one of his courses and learn right along with him. However, recognize that writing long letters home may be difficult for your college student. He may be neck-deep in schoolwork.

Another way of keeping adult-adolescent communications open and of aiding adult education as well is for colleges to conduct student-parent courses in popular subjects. Though you may not be able to participate if the college is far from home, other parents will, and the interaction between generations will still help your son or daughter. The University of Rhode Island, for instance, has offered evening courses for students and parents in journalism, mathematics, American history, Shakespeare, the twentieth-century American novel, and elementary speech. The courses, offered one night per week, enable parents from quite a distance away to conveniently come to campus. A minimum fee is charged the parents, unless they wish college credit for the course. Investigate the opportunities your son's or daughter's college offers.

Section Three

FATHER POWER—
CRISIS AND
CHALLENGE

13/Divorced Fathers, Stepfathers, and Single Fathers

Throughout this book we have shown that father power is imperative to the family, that it is a built-in feature important for the best development of the child. Our contention holds true even for the special types of fathers we shall discuss in the next three chapters—those with certain problems or circumstances that make their fatherhood especially difficult. They must have an awareness of the particular nature of their father power, for it can still be quite a potent force in their children's lives.

THE DIVORCED FATHER

For a large group of fathers in this country, divorce presents the greatest threat to their fatherhood. Over 1.5 million people in this country get divorced each year, and more than 4 million people are currently divorced. Almost two-thirds of divorces involve children. Because of the discrimination against the father in divorce and the father's lack of a sense of father power, divorce is a major cause of father-neglected children in this country, second only to the chronic father neglect in intact American homes.

The Child of Divorce. Although divorce is initially between a father and mother, after it is finalized, the principal players are you and your child, because unlike your marital relationship, your parenthood remains a vital function. Children of divorced fathers are particularly vulnerable to damage from father absence. A father who is away on business may at least be trying to provide for his family economically; he is showing indirectly that he cares. The child of a dead father usually realizes that it is not Daddy's fault that he is not there. But the child of a divorced father who is absent has none of these rationalizations. Daddy is alive, is perfectly able to see him, and has no apparent reason for not being around. It can be quite confusing and quite dangerous for a child.

Besides maintaining the everyday tenor of your relationship with your child, which we shall discuss later, there are several other things you can do to help him adjust to your divorce. Some of these guidelines are applicable for mothers as well as fathers.

The first step in retaining your place in your child's life is to help him adjust to your divorce. In presenting the nature of your divorce to your child, do not describe it as if it were some sort of disease, but rather as if it were an unfortunate development that sometimes happens between two people. Your child may be stigmatized to some extent by having divorced parents. Teachers may treat him differently, friends may taunt him, other adults may become pitying of the "poor child." If he realizes that divorce is not fatal, he will not be as likely to feel disturbed by the stigma others may attach to him. Of course, the extent to which your child is stigmatized by the fact that his parents are divorced depends a lot on the subculture in which you live. In the more affluent sections of the Northeast and West, divorce may be quite common and accepted, while in a rural Midwestern town a divorce may be very unusual and frowned upon.

Be appropriately truthful with your child about your divorce—that it is not his fault, that his parents love him, and the way in which his life-style will change. He probably has no need to know about infidelities, personal faults, or things said between you and your wife in the heat of argument.

Be realistic about what your child is capable of understanding about your divorce. You wouldn't tell a fifteen-year-old that "Mother and Father didn't like each other anymore," nor would you tell a four-year-old that "Our main problem was that we both had outside relationships that drew us apart." Answer your child's questions at his level of understanding and according to how much he wants to know.

Overall, your strategy should be to continue to foster in the child the two principal goals of father power that we discussed earlier—security and competence.

Security and Competence. If you were involved with your child before your divorce, you will have a sound basis to help him feel secure after it. You are a powerful protector in his life, and the idea of your not being a part of his family will probably greatly frighten him. The best way you can allay these fears is to begin seeing him as often as possible as soon after the breakup as possible, preferably even during the initial separation. If you and your wife are able to agree on the importance of this, you can each have equal access to the child, but whatever the case, do the best you can. Make it clear by frequent special times with your child, such as bringing him to work or having supper together, that you are a continuing part of his life—that he still has two parents. This way he will come to expect you to return when you must temporarily leave him. Separated fathers are frequently advised to stay away from their children and home while divorce proceedings are under way. True, seeing your wife may be a strain on both you and her, but you should not stop seeing your children. If seeing them at home is impossible, arrange meetings at friends' or relatives' houses or pick them up after school and drop them off at home after your visits.

Ironically, divorce may help you become a better father. You may spend more time with your children after the divorce than before. Perhaps before the divorce you avoided coming home at night. Now the children are "on your list of things to do," as one father put it. The individualized time you will have with the child may be particularly fruitful in terms of aiding his development while he is adjusting to being a "divorced child."

Just as you fostered competence in him before you were divorced, you should not fail to do so afterward. Many divorced fathers feel that in order to hold on to their children they must refrain from disciplining them, so Mother is thus cast in the role of the "heavy." Mom has to see to it that your child's teeth are brushed, that he sees the doctor, or that he doesn't stay out too late, while you take him to the movies or buy him candy.

But if you suddenly become the permissive parent, your child will become confused about how he is supposed to act. He may become a problem both to himself and others.

Discipline your child when he needs it, and show him that you still expect him to do as well as he can in school and in his other activities. Continue also to be his mentor, his model, and his friend. Your father power to help him in these areas is unabated. Be confident in it.

The Quitting Syndrome. The children of a divorce are much more likely to become divorced themselves when they marry than children who have grown up in intact homes. They may continue to feel that their parents let them down by getting a divorce, and it may be particularly difficult for them to develop a sense of security and trust in their own marriage relationship.

You can help your child have a better marriage when he becomes an adult by remaining close to him after the divorce. Daughters will learn that they can trust and love men, and sons will see a responsible man who doesn't abandon his children.

Children of a divorce may also develop a more generalized "quitting syndrome" about personal relationships, because early in life they saw their parents call it quits. This syndrome doesn't apply only to a child's future marriage but also to school, friendships, and other areas of life. You can guard against this syndrome by maintaining a close regular relationship with your child and by discussing, openly and honestly, the reasons for the divorce with him.

Father-Child-Mother. Although after divorce your relationship with your wife becomes secondary to the one between you and your child, how your wife defines you to him is another matter. Because she was probably with the child more before the divorce, she had many opportunities to define you to him, telling him what kind of man you were, how much you loved him, why you were cross sometimes. In divorce American-style, she has even more of this kind of opportunity after the divorce because she is usually awarded the lion's share of his time, and she can do it in particularly negative terms. After all, even if you didn't initiate the divorce proceedings, you are usually the one who "left," in that she and the child remain in the home. The child probably sees you as the more formidable parent, which may lend credence to a mother's portrayal of herself as the bullied woman.

The problem of an ex-wife denouncing her children's father to them is unfortunately quite common in divorced families. The animosity frequently present in divorce feeds it, but so does society's emphasis on the mother role for women: because a woman is usually brought up to believe that if she fails at wifehood and motherhood, she fails as a woman, she may desperately seek a scapegoat for the breakup of her marriage and the children's subsequent "loss" of a father. And naturally, the father becomes that scapegoat.

There are, however, several positive tactics to combat such bad-mouthing.

First of all, you might point out to the mother the necessity that the children have an involved, respected father, perhaps using some of the points we raise in this book. Calmly, understandingly, and without accusing her of anything, explain that it would be very bad for the children if they should come to believe that Daddy is evil, that it could endanger the adequacy of their self-image and their ability to relate to other men. Try to begin any discussion with her by pointing out where you think she shines as a mother and asserting that you only want an equal chance to be a good father.

If your children are having some particular problem, you might analyze with your wife why this might be due to their need for a father. She might say, "Well, that's not because they need a father," whereupon you counter with, "How can you be sure? Why endanger their development on a hunch?"

"How would you feel if I said those things about you?" is

another approach to showing your ex-wife the import of her degrading you to the children. We assume, of course, that you have not been denouncing your ex-wife to your children.

A more direct, personal way of gaining your ex-wife's understanding is to ask her, "How would you feel if somebody said those things about your father?" The assumption here is that your ex-wife had a close relationship with her father. If she was alienated from him, this approach is obviously not the one to use. You might instead ask how she would feel if somebody said those things about her mother.

There are times, though, when it is in the child's best interest for a father or a mother to picture the other parent in a bad light. For instance, it could do your child a great deal of harm if you consistently neglected him and your ex-wife continually pictured you as a wonderful, loving father. The child would feel that somehow something was wrong with himself for you not to be interested in him. Don't allow your wife to portray you as a bastard when you are not, but don't expect her to portray you as a saint if you are a bastard. The same goes for your portrayal of your wife. It is important for both of you to remain effective in the child's eyes.

Father and Stepfather. One major time of reckoning in your life as a divorced father comes when your ex-wife decides to remarry. In this section we shall discuss the stepfather from the natural father's point of view; later in the chapter we shall discuss the stepfather's particular problems.

Generally speaking, *if* both you and the stepfather are attached to the child, *if* neither of you feels interfered with by the other, and *if* the child is attached to both of you, a joint fatherhood is feasible. You can both feel comfortable fathering. This assumes a great deal of consistency between you and the stepfather; both of you should agree generally on matters of discipline and childraising, and you must make it a point to talk to each other about the child. Optimally, you and the stepfather should get together at least monthly to discuss the child's progress.

Unfortunately, such a balance is rarely able to be achieved. One or the other of you will probably be more attached to the child, and furthermore, the child may not be able to attach to two fathers. Assess your situation realistically. If the child's stepfather is successful and encouraging with him and they are developing a close relationship and if you have never been close to the child, don't let your vanity stand in the way of the child's having an effective father. Hopefully, you can even help him get closer to his stepfather, perhaps by emphasizing to the child that the stepfather loves him or by telling him how much the stepfather is like you and how you respect and like the stepfather.

On the other hand, if the stepfather is clearly not as successful as you are with your child, don't let some misguided sense of duty cause you to walk out of your child's life. Both you and the stepfather should watch for any signs of rivalry between you for the child's affections and deal with it promptly.

The age of the child is often an important factor in his acceptance of a stepfather. Adolescents usually have an extremely difficult time adjusting to a stepfather, and you will probably be badly needed to continue to father your teen-aged child after the divorce. On the other hand, if the child is two or three years old, he may have little difficulty attaching to a stepfather, and in the case of a lack of previous involvement on your part, it might be the best thing for you to take a back seat.

In any case, it is your duty to see that the child has at least one warm, involved father figure. When you understand the importance of father power, you can see the profound nature of your responsibility.

Father and the Stepmother. When you decide to remarry, the situation is often different from when your wife decides to take another husband. With her extensive background and confidence as a mother and the advantages society gives her in encouraging such competence, there is less chance that she will "lose" the child. You must, however, see that she doesn't feel you are trying to alienate her from her children by bringing another mother into their lives.

First of all, whether you intend to marry another woman or

not, you should establish for the child what "other" women mean in your life. Explain to him that he has a special place in your life and that you love him very much. Then explain to him that since your relationship with his mother has ended, you ought to start seeing other women, because you like women and want to have them as friends. If a child wants you to choose between him and your woman friend, point out that it's not a question of choosing, that love is not a commodity that a person has only so much of and no more.

If you decide to marry, be sure that you take the relationship between your child and your intended wife into account. Many fathers do not realize that ill will between a stepmother and stepchild can affect not only the child and the father but also the marriage. Your new wife could become resentful of your child and consequently resentful of you if she is not understanding of the requirements of the father-child relationship. Certainly, your second marriage is mainly a matter between you and your new wife, and you shouldn't marry simply in search of a new mother for your child, but neither should you ignore your fatherhood.

We know one such prospective couple who went to a marriage counselor before getting married to help them better understand their relationship. Their visit turned out to be very revealing. The prospective bride had consistently made excuses about spending time with the man's children, saying, "I really don't feel well," or, "I have a lot of work to do tonight." Although she kept saying that things would be different after the marriage, the two realized after counseling that they would not be. After some soul searching, they both agreed to call off the marriage.

Whatever you do, don't get into the situation of one young divorced but devoted father who married a woman without thoroughly understanding her attitudes toward his young son. The marriage ended with the second wife in the living room pointing to the man's son and demanding, "Either *he* goes, or *I* go." Fortunately, this young man realized the profound impact his answer would have on the child, and the callous second wife was told immediately that the decision lay in the son's favor. She left forthwith.

LIVING ARRANGEMENTS, CUSTODY, AND VISITING PRIVILEGES

So far we've discussed the psychology of divorce and the father, but there are many forces outside the family that will influence how successful a divorced father will be with his children. A major problem is the way the father is discriminated against in the divorce settlement and in living arrangements.

Guilty Until Proven Innocent. The discrimination against the father is clearly expressed in the divorce court. Just as society treats fatherhood as a second-class role, so does the law.

As almost any divorced father can attest, courts today assume from the beginning that a father is innately unfit for raising a child. And even where the mother is proven unfit, the children are often sent to foster homes rather than given to the custody of the father. And on top of this basic discrimination against the father is the fact that the whole concept of custody can be both psychologically unsound and much too rigid to fit all individual cases. Since fathers and mothers are both important to a child's development, it should be assumed from the start that each parent is equally entitled to aid in raising the child. Although the child may have a home base at one parent's house or the other, both parents should have the right to equal access to the child in the eyes of the court.

The custody method of awarding child-care rights can be extremely difficult for the child. In effect, he may be asked to choose one parent *or* the other. On the other hand, by abandoning a rigid custody concept, the child's security may be boosted at a time when he badly needs it.

By beginning the division of child-care responsibilities from a basis of equality, the father who really wants the child for more time than the mother, and is able to handle it, will really have a chance. Such a father meeting resistance from a reluctant wife will have an equal basis from which to argue; he will not be considered guilty of incompetence as a parent until proven innocent.

Along with more flexible living arrangements that would benefit fathers more, courts should also allow more flexible money arrangements. Rather than assuming that the father must support the child through the mother, judges should assume that both he and the mother can contribute to the child's support directly. Thus, the father does not owe the mother money, except to provide the amount of support for the child that the father does not himself give directly. If he buys the child's clothes, that money does not have to go to the mother. The key should be that both the mother and the father share the responsibility and privilege of contributing directly to their offspring's welfare.

Because of the greater opportunities for women in the working world today, it is an anachronism for a court to award alimony to a mother, along with a house and car, so that she can concentrate on giving care to the child, and at the same time restrict the father's access to the child. Divorce can be quite an expensive proposition, and there is no reason for the father to shoulder the entire economic burden of maintaining two homes, etc. A more equitable arrangement would be for each parent to contribute to a central fund for the child, according to each parent's income. Each parent could then withdraw from the central fund as he made expenditures for the child. This would alleviate the enormous financial burden placed on divorced fathers today and at the same time allow them more time to become better fathers. Such an arrangement may be hard on the woman who has never worked, but it might also be a means to achieving greater maturity and independence for her.

Considering what we have said about the importance of the father to his children and the benign effects on them of their mother's working, the mother whose children are old enough not to require constant care should actually be encouraged to work. A job can give her a greater sense of her own worth, and the lessened financial burden on the father will allow him more time with the children.

Hopeful Signs. Fortunately, there is now a small but growing trend for the importance of fathers to be taken into account in divorce settlements where children are involved. Even though the percentage is still very small, there are more and more cases of fathers being granted custody of their children, and more judges are making attempts to ensure more equitable visitation privileges for fathers.

Of course, there are wide variations in the attitudes of judges, but there is an increasing number of cases in which fathers', rights are being recognized. Over the last few years, Henry has received dozens of inquiries from parents, mostly fathers but also some mothers, concerning custody and visitation issues revolving around the father's role. Some of the parents merely wanted information, but others were interested in having Henry participate in more direct consultation or as an expert witness. Many other clinicians are also getting more involved in court-related matters concerning the father-child relationship.

Another sign of progress is the more careful consideration of the child's point of view. For example, Henry was asked to be an expert witness on one custody case in which the court had appointed a lawyer for the two children involved. The young children did not want to be separated from their father, and the judge explicitly weighed this factor in rendering his decision to grant custody to the father.

We are not advocating that most fathers should have custody of their children. Each case is an individual one, and the relative competencies and commitments of each parent should be carefully weighed. Hopefully, predivorce discussions will also help lead to more situations where both of the parents remain actively involved with their children.

If you and your wife can work out a happy visiting arrangement, custody need not be a major issue. Henry consulted on' one case in which, although the mother had physical custody of the children, the father was guaranteed frequent and regular visiting privileges. This father has remained particularly involved and effective with his child even though he has a very demanding career and the child was less than two when the parents were divorced. The father sees his young child four or five times a week for at least an hour and they have an overnight visit every other week. They keep in contact by phone on days they don't see each other.

Two Homes Can Be Better Than One. What does the greater parental equality we advocate mean in terms of everyday arrangements for living in a divorced family? Let's discuss the case of Jack and Sylvia R., who are divorced and have a ten-year-old son and a six-year-old daughter. Because both were agreed as to the important role Jack should have with their children and because the children were strongly attached to both parents, the parents agreed they would both have generally equal access, and that both would contribute to the children's upkeep. Jack had a good-paying job at a local bank and Sylvia had a teaching career, so both were financially able to do this.

After the divorce and despite their animosity toward each other, they agreed that Jack should live near Sylvia so that the children would have easy access to either parent. The children spend three or four nights per week with Jack. The arrangement is structured so that both children and parents know where the children are supposed to be, but the schedule is flexible. When Jack wants to shop with the children on a nonscheduled night or Sylvia wants to take them to a movie, things are usually easily arranged.

The children can get to school conveniently from either parent's house, so there is little problem with their spending weeknights at Jack's. When one or the other parent has a date, or cannot take the children for that night, he calls the other and lets him know.

Sylvia is usually at home in the afternoon when the children get out of school, so they have someone to come home to. The neighbors have also realized the sometimes difficult problems of scheduling and allow the children to play at their houses in the afternoon when the parents get home late. There is a rule, however, that one parent or the other must know where the children are after school.

Both Jack and Sylvia maintain sleeping space for the children, though most of the children's clothes are kept at Sylvia's. Because maintaining two children's rooms would be quite expensive, the children's place at Jack's consists of a sofa bed and a large closet for their things. Far from disliking the arrangement, the children enjoy "camping out" at Daddy's.

The children feel that they can come and go relatively freely between their parents' homes as long as both parents are informed and agree with their plans. There is a general expectation, however, that the children get to spend an approximately equal amount of time with each parent.

Of course, Jack and Sylvia are unique. Their combined income is above average and their children are old enough not to need constant attention; and above all, they have let their concern as parents override any bitter feelings they bear toward each other. But several of the guidelines that they have worked out should apply generally to help fathers assume their important place with the children of their broken marriage.

Open House. The first is that the parents live near each other and the children feel that both houses are their home. Neither parent portrays the other one as having "left" home—both places are home. This proximity may be difficult for some divorced parents, but it does help the father stay in contact with his children, especially since he is usually the one who must travel to fetch the children and he is usually the one who works. Incidentally, there is no reason why the mother cannot help transport the children between the two houses.

Open house also means that the child feels free to telephone the parent with any problems or news. For instance, when Jack's son won a spelling contest at school, he phoned him that night to tell him the news. Jack was thus able to share the triumph with his child and also to maintain the closeness of their relationship.

The mobility of citizens in our society sometimes makes the concept of open house difficult to achieve. One parent or the other will often move because of job changes or remarriage. Before you change residences, both you and your wife must consider the importance of your child's having two involved parents. Whether you have custody of the child or your wife does, and whether you are moving or your wife is, carefully consider the possible danger to the child. The split-custody routine, whereby the child may stay six months with you and six with the mother, is a poor substitute for the open-house arrangement. In such a situation the child is continually having to break off or build relationships afresh with each parent.

Timing Is of the Essence. Jack and Sylvia both see their children frequently, which allows them to remain a part of their children's lives. Allowing long periods to go between encounters is a major mistake many divorced parents make. They believe that eight hours spent at one time with a child is equal to four two-hour sessions. In truth, the latter is much better, for young children tend to lose the thread of a relationship if the parent is not around even for a few days.

While your children are with you, you may notice that the novelty and excitement of the visit drop off after the first hour or so. After that the visit is more of a settling into a secure routine. So if you try to have intensive-but-rare four-hour communication sessions with your child, you might find they don't fit into this natural rhythm of visiting. More frequent shorter visits are more in keeping with this rhythm.

As one divorced father put it, "When my kids visit, the first hour is spent giving affection and finding out news, and then I usually let them play and try to maintain a semblance of as normal a home life with their father as possible."

So, to maintain a close relationship with your child, see him at least every other day or so, if only for a few minutes. Keep up with what the child is doing in school, what his hobbies are, and what books he is reading, so that you will not be reduced to talking about the weather when you see him. Remain a part of his everyday life.

When you, the father, are involved in settling divorce terms, remember that the frequency of your visits is much more important than the fact that they last many hours. Too many fathers try to pile up as many hours as possible in allowed visiting time, instead of concentrating on the frequency with which they get to see the children.

Incidentally, if you have more than one child, your time with the children should increase accordingly. A good rule to follow is that you should be given a basic amount of time to be with the children together, plus additional periods to spend in special time with each child.

THE STEPFATHER

Becoming a stepfather is perhaps one of the most difficult, yet potentially rewarding aspects of fatherhood. A stepfather is entering an established family, usually one in which the natural father is still around. Thus, the stepfather may meet with considerable resentment from his new children, from the children's natural father, and even resentment of his role from his new wife.

At the same time, the children in such a broken home are usually suffering from the effects of father neglect, and the stepfather can be of enormous help in their lives. We have seen children with new stepfathers change incredibly after a few years with them, from unhappy, undisciplined, unconfident children to just the reverse.

Making a decision about whether to become a stepfather calls for careful consideration. Certainly, a man's primary relationship in such a case is with the future wife, but the stepfather-stepchild relationship is also extremely important. Not only will this relationship affect both the man and his new children personally, but the relationship with the new wife as well.

Facing Realities. A prospective stepfather must be quite sure about what he is letting himself in for in terms of fatherhood. Among the questions he should ask are: Has the future wife grown too close to the children through years of being alone with them? Will she, therefore, resent the stepfather's role with the children? Does she keep the children in the background during the courtship, saying that "They are really not any trouble," or, "I'll take care of them; you don't have to worry"? Such a woman is usually either very anxious to marry or has a problem child, perhaps a problem of her own making.

Do the children have an overidealized view of their real father? This often happens in the case of the widowed mother with children, and the stepfather may find himself a mere mortal trying to live up to the image of a saintly dead father. On the other hand, are the children hostile and mistrustful toward the stepfather because their real father has treated them badly?

Of course, many fatherless families are quite healthy psychologically, and the stepfather may be welcomed by both the mother and the children.

To assess how his prospective children will react to him, the stepfather should give himself a meaningful engagement period. Whether it is a few months or a year, it should be enough time for him to get to know the children, as well as getting to know his future spouse.

He should take the children for walks or other outings to see how they react to him in the absence of their mother. He should spend time with each child individually if there are more than one, and not just participate in group outings. Each child has a unique set of problems and a unique personality. A prospective stepfather should get to know the child in a variety of settings, watching how he reacts to exciting things, boring things, or beautiful things. Much will be learned both about his fears and his areas of competence this way.

We know one prospective father who took his future stepdaughter to the circus, on walks through the park, with him to work, and on errands to the store. Only on one outing—to work—did he find that she was painfully shy about meeting men and that her natural father's occasional brutality had made her very afraid of them.

The key to assessing how successful you will be with your prospective stepchildren is whether you feel you can cope with their personalities. Even if a child has a great number of problems, if you feel you are equal to the challenge, by all means become a stepfather. When you are with the children, if you feel that you just cannot handle their particular personalities, you should consider this in your decision about joining the family.

The Child's Age. How successful you will be as a stepfather may depend a great deal on the age of the children. Up until a few years of age, a child will usually accept a stepfather, and vice versa. Beyond that age, it becomes more and more difficult for a child to accept a new father in his life. Not only might an older child refuse to relate to the stepfather as a father, but his refusal might cause the stepfather to also reject him.

A child's reaction to a stepfather is often similar to a child's reaction to his own father when they have been apart for several years. Returning war veterans, for instance, often find great difficulty in reentering a family after a close, relatively exclusive bond has developed between the mother and child.

Becoming a stepfather to a teen-ager is particularly difficult. The young person has already done a lot of maturing emotionally and has established his ties elsewhere. He is also already fighting for his own independence from the family and is not in a position to establish close ties with a new family member. He may have grown up without a father, and your attempts to break through a barrier of resentment may be fruitless. Many times about the most a prospective stepfather can expect from a teen-age stepchild is a cordial social relationship. These are, of course, generalities. There have been families in which a loving, challenging stepfather has done wonders for a teen-ager.

Examining Your Feelings and Motives. Establishing your relationship with the child means not only that you feel competent with him or that he accepts you but that you basically like each other. You will usually know whether or not the child likes you; he will probably tell you so. Plumbing your own feelings about him may be more difficult. You may put up with a child you really can't stand because you are in love with his mother. You may also feel a bit guilty about disliking a child—because you feel he can't help his own personality. Be honest about your feelings. If you are not, it could ruin your marriage and the child's life. The key is not that you necessarily love the child but that you like him enough and are motivated enough by his personality to be involved as a stepfather.

With today's more open social mores, many future stepfathers begin living with the woman and her children to test compatibility before the marriage. This can be an extremely dangerous proposition for children—if the relationship doesn't work out, such children have, in effect, experienced the trauma of losing two fathers. The guilt this could cause, not to mention the child's feeling of inadequacy, could be crushing.

Living with a widow or divorced woman with *no* thought of a stable relationship can be even worse for the children. They will learn quite early that men are not to be trusted. This could be quite dangerous for their security and could interfere with the development of many of the important traits we discussed earlier. No doubt in many cases the divorced or widowed woman might welcome your coming to live with her and her children; just look at the vulnerable situation she is in. She is trying to raise children with little emotional and sometimes little financial support from another adult. She needs the steady companionship of a man because she may not have the time or the money to socialize to a great extent. You should recognize both the children's and their mother's situation. Get to know your future stepchildren before you move into their lives full time. And don't live with a woman with children with no thought of a stable relationship.

If you have gone through the familiarization process we have suggested and believe that you can establish a relationship with the children, then do discuss your feelings with them.

In presenting to a child the news of an impending marriage to his mother, make him feel that he is part of the process. Don't present it as if it were a foregone conclusion. Make the child feel that he has a voice in the matter; ask his opinions and consider them. Assure him that his place with you and his mother is secure.

Avoid making extravagant promises or overselling yourself. Many men attempt to court their prospective child with promises of good times or gifts. "We'll go to Playland every week when I'm your Dad" is one promise we heard. This father couldn't keep his promise, and the result was a good deal of strain between him and his stepdaughter because of it. She hadn't trusted men before, and she trusted them even less after that episode.

Though you should certainly be a bit permissive in allowing the child to adjust to you, don't be indulgent. Let the child know what you expect of him.

Before the marriage, you and your prospective wife should agree that you both will have a prominent role with the children. You should not take a back seat because the children are hers.

Life Changes. Don't force the child into too much change in too short a time. People who undergo a great many changes in their life-style too quickly can suffer emotional and physical problems.

If possible, you should move into the house of your wife and stepchildren after the marriage, rather than having them move into yours. This is so that the children will not have to get used to a new home, school, and friends in addition to adjusting to a new father. Their daily schedules should remain the same, with sleeping and eating schedules only gradually adjusted to best fit both your and their needs. If the children were sleeping in the same room with their mother, they should be moved to another room as far in advance of the marriage date as possible so that there won't be the situation of your obviously coming into the house and "forcing" them out of their beds.

Even changes that you may consider are for the better may have a traumatic impact on the child. The mother of one ten-year-old boy we knew remarried a man who was much better off financially than they were. The mother and child moved to a better neighborhood, had better clothes and a better car, but the boy had a great deal of trouble adjusting, because he had come to think of himself as a working-class kid.

"I still wore the same clothes and played the same games," he said, "so I thought I was the same, but the other kids I knew kept saying, 'Gee, you're really rich now.' I kept thinking it was good to be poor, because I would work harder for my money. Then I got rich, and I didn't know what to think. I was confused."

Establishing yourself as a stepfather is a two-way proposition. You are asking the child to allow you to become a part of his life because you care for him and respect him; you are not paternalistically taking over for his own good.

Legally adopting your new wife's children after the marriage is an action you should strongly consider. If you are thoroughly committed to the children, giving them your name legally will help assure them of your dedication and will afford them a great deal of security. Adoption will also legitimize your role with the child in your wife's eyes. Subtly or not, she may feel that the children are hers not yours if you do not adopt them. When children in the heat of anger tell their stepfathers, "You're not my real father!" it is sometimes more of a lament than an accusation. The child may be wishing you had made yourself his real daddy by adoption.

A child can be quite ashamed that he does not have the same name as his father and mother, especially when he begins school and finds himself identified increasingly by his last name. One child we know who had an Italian mother and a Jewish stepfather, who had not adopted him, would change names according to what ethnic group he was with. When he thought it best to be Italian, he became Johnny Calucci, and when Jewishness was required, he became Johnny Rothstein. The parents thought this quite amusing, but in reality the child was using his lack of a name as a weapon against his parents. He was in effect saying, "I'm not really anybody, I don't belong."

On the other hand, children can be quite proud of having been adopted by their stepfathers. One such child was offered a considerable sum of money by his neglectful natural father to change his name back. But he was heard to say proudly, "My name is Samuelson, and I'm proud of it, and it's going to stay that way." One could feel in his tone the security he derived from having the same name as his beloved stepfather.

Generally, if the child is age six or younger and his natural father is unimportant in his life, you should consider adopting him. If he is ten or older, he has probably already formed a self-image that includes his original last name. In this case, the change may do more harm than good. Also, of course, you should discuss the matter thoroughly with the child. Explain your reasons for wanting to adopt him, and listen closely to his reactions. If he objects strenuously, drop the matter.

Complexities. In this section we have discussed a relatively simplified version of the process of becoming a stepfather. But there are many, many complicating factors in the process that make each case unique.

For instance, if you have children by a previous marriage, there will be the matter of balancing your involvement with your natural children and that of your stepchildren. All sorts of jealousies and conflicts may arise, and the best general advice we can give is to bring to each situation your confidence in your father power. If you know how important you are to your children, and each knows that you love him deeply, these complications will work themselves out.

THE ADOPTING FATHER

The man who with his wife is adopting a child faces much the same situation of the stepfather and of the expectant father combined. Like the stepfather, the adopting father must get to know the child well and take care not to force him into a too abrupt change of life-style among other things. Like the expectant father, the adopting father must take stock of himself and adjust to a new person in the family, which may be particularly hard if the adopted child is his first one.

The major difference between the adopting father and the stepfather is that it is the child who is the stranger in the house and the adopting mother and father who must be the "acceptors." Unlike the expectant father's situation, the new child is not the father's and mother's natural child. He may be more of an unknown quantity than a natural child. As we will see, this is one source of anxiety for the adopting father.

Like the expectant couple, the adopting couple will probably have many reasons for wanting a child, but they may be different from those of the expectant couple and also different according to whether there are other children in the family.

A man may assent to an adoption to placate a wife who wants a child. Such a man may not want one of his own and may be trying to get out of a sense of responsibility by adopting someone else's baby.

More mature reasons for adopting include the desire to have a child without contributing to the population explosion or the desire to give a child a good home who otherwise would have little chance for one. And, of course, the couple who can't have children but wants them will likely have a very positive outlook on adoption.

Chapter 2 contains a discussion of the reasons for wanting a child. Many of them apply here.

Resistance to Adoption. The father is usually the more reluctant of the two parents when it comes to adoption. Since the mother is usually the initiator of adoption proceedings, the father is cast in the role of reactor, and he often reacts negatively.

He may feel that an adopted child will interfere with the husband-wife relationship. Adopting a child may also seem to a husband to be an admission that he is somehow incompetent as a man or even impotent. Since men place a great deal of masculine pride on being potent, this kind of negative feeling may be very strong.

Because fathers do not have such a close, physiological attachment to children, they may be the more critical parents. Fatherhood may be more of an intellectual exercise than motherhood is. To a mother, a baby is a baby, and she can easily feel love for a child that isn't her own. A father, however, may have more initial difficulty in becoming attached to the child.

This initial reluctance is not necessarily all bad, however. It can be used to help a husband and wife make a better decision about adopting. For instance, many women who think they want to adopt actually only want to care for a baby. They are not prepared for a long-term relationship with a child who will eventually grow into an adult. The father may be more able to objectively analyze this desire. Still other mothers and fathers may want to help raise another child but may not want the full responsibility for it. In this case, it might be better to take in a foster child or for the mother to do voluntary child-care work.

And, of course, a father can use this objectivity to analyze his own personality in order to decide whether he has the basic nurturance, responsibility, and confidence in his father power that are required to be an adopting father.

If your other children are above the age of five or so, it is a good idea to make adoption a family decision. Henry knows that his sons were very gratified at being included in round-table discussions the family had before adopting his youngest son, Michael. They were able to voice doubts, help with the planning, and show support of their parents in the decision.

If we have seemed negative in this section, it is only because we want to help prospective adopting fathers to realize some of the problems and doubts they may have. As with natural fatherhood, adoptive fatherhood, if approached carefully, can be an immensely gratifying experience.

The great majority of men have the potential to become good fathers. Their reluctance is due mainly to their lack of experience with children. Because men have too long been expected to know everything or risk being called weak, they may have difficulty admitting this inexperience. We have tried here to give you what we believe adopting fathers need the most—support, guidelines, and alternatives.

THE FATHER ALONE—WIDOWED OR DIVORCED

The major psychological problem confronting the father who shoulders the responsibility of raising his children without their mother is that he may see it as a handicap that is insurmountable. One father, upon learning that he would have custody of his daughter after his divorce, was overjoyed at first and then, a cloud passing over his face, was heard to turn to a friend and exclaim in a panicky tone, "Now what do I do!" This father loved his daughter but his lack of confidence as a father was a serious drawback to his becoming an effective parent.

So, in this section on the father alone we shall first discuss the advantages you have over the husband-absent mother. Unlike most mothers, you have been taught to define yourself as more than a parent. You probably have a career that at least interests you, and you are more able to travel about freely in society. You have also been brought up to value independence more than many women today.

Thus, there is much less possibility that you will develop an overintense, possessive relationship with your child, building your whole life around him because of your lack of a spouse. This can be much more a problem with husband-absent mothers.

Fathers also have a much easier time getting mother substitutes for their children than mothers have getting father substitutes. Because women in our society are generally comfortable with children and confident that the children need them, you will probably be able to find a sister, aunt, housekeeper, or friend to give your children some of the exposure to a loving female that they need. Contrast this situation with that of the husband-absent mother, whose brothers, father, or friends may not be interested in children at all, because they have never been taught the male's value as a father figure. The boyfriend of a divorced or widowed woman may fear that she is trying to trap him into something when she seeks him as a father surrogate for her children, even temporarily.

You are probably more secure economically than a husband-absent mother. You don't have to wait for a monthly child-support check, nor have you been edged into a low-paying career by society or your upbringing. This is not to minimize the sometimes enormous financial burden the father alone is under. Child-care expenses can be quite a strain on a budget. However, there is less of a chance that you will be forced into poverty by trying to raise a child alone. Nevertheless, if there is a need, welfare agencies should allow aid to dependent children of fathers alone as they do for mothers alone.

Alone with a Child. Because your child either doesn't have a mother or will see his mother less than before, you should generally increase your time with the child to help him deal with the loss. Don't be like the father, however, who felt he had to double his time with his daughter to make up for the absence of her mother. This father became so resentful at having to devote so much time to the child that he developed a chronic intolerance of her, and their relationship suffered. Twice as much time with a child does not necessarily mean twice as much security or twice as much of a relationship. (Of course, if you spent little time with your child before you became a single father, you may indeed have to more than double your time with your child now.) So bring your child to work often, but not necessarily twice as much. Take him on outings more, but not necessarily twice as much.

Although, to some extent, you will have to perform chores that your child's mother did before, don't do so to the extent that you become uncomfortable about it. We know one divorced father who hated cooking but felt his son should have home-cooked meals "just like mother used to make." He did turn out some excellent suppers but gave up his golf game and the time he used to spend having fun with the child in exchange for slaving over a hot stove and a full supermarket cart.

Such resentment of certain chores is commonplace among fathers who are alone. One study of British fathers alone found that their major complaint was having to do the ironing. Another was having to do their daughter's hair.

Your time with the child is more important than the fact that he is living exactly the same life-style that he did when his mother was present. Send your laundry out, eat frozen dinners, or hire a housekeeper so that you will have time to play and talk with your child.

Mother Wanted. Although it may be relatively easy for you to find a mother substitute, there are certain pitfalls in your search. Your child is very likely to be already exposed to a female in the person of one of his teachers. However, this relationship will probably not be close enough or extensive enough to satisfy his need for mothering.

Your sister or a friend may be willing to be a substitute mother, but she may not be a stable enough model for the child. A woman may genuinely want to keep your child occasionally or play with him, but she may be so absorbed in her career or other activities that she often cops out on the child. If your child's substitute mother has a number of children herself, she may show excessive favoritism toward her natural children, or the children themselves may become jealous of her attentions to your child.

If your own mother is to be the chief female influence in their lives, she may hinder your authority with your children by continuing to treat you as "her little boy." Such ploys as scolding you in front of the children or undermining your discipline with them are signs of such a problem. She should recognize that you are an adult and the children are ultimately your responsibility.

A major mistake some fathers alone make is to completely hand over their children to the substitute mother. One divorced father we know gets to keep his two young daughters six months out of the year. When the children arrive at his apartment, he stays with them a few days, but then begins to daily send them off to his sister who lives nearby. They come back to his apartment to sleep but otherwise see very little of him. Whether he is not interested in the children or is overly concerned about their having a female model, he is practically absent from their lives, even when he is "living" with them.

New Wife, New Mother. When you bring a stepmother into your children's lives, many of the same problems may occur as those discussed in our section on the stepfather. Just as the widow's children may have overidealized their dead father, so your children may have overidealized your dead wife. The "other" women may have quite a bit of difficulty living up to this idealized mother. By the same token, the children of a divorce may deeply resent women, especially if their mother deserted them. You and your future wife should read our section on the stepfather, putting your future wife in the stepfather's place.

One particular note of caution: Do not assume that because our society has the romanticized view that women are naturally excellent mothers, your intended spouse will be a good mother. As she is getting to know the children and discovering whether she can relate to them, you should observe her as a mother and have open discussions with her about what she thinks of the children. Is she patient? Does she genuinely care about the children, or is she just getting to know them to please you? Many a marriage has broken up because the prospective mother was not such a good mother after all.

14/Fathers with Special Problems

The effects on a man's father power of a physical or social handicap can vary enormously according to both the nature of the handicap and the personality of the father. As we have said in other chapters, we cannot hope to cover the wide range of individual cases, but we can give some general guidelines.

THE PHYSICALLY HANDICAPPED FATHER

How a man's physical handicap will affect his fatherhood depends to some extent on how long he has had his disability. Men who have been handicapped from birth often adjust to their difficulty by the time they become fathers, and the principal problem may be in the child's adjustment to the disability. Men whose handicap begins while they are fathers —a heart attack for instance—may subject their children to great emotional trauma as they themselves adjust to their disability.

Although the severity of a handicap may determine the severity of a man's reaction to it, in many cases there is no relationship between the two. We have known double amputees who were excellent, involved fathers, and men with slight limps who became so obsessed with their problems that it ruined them as men and as fathers. We've known heart-attack victims who let their heart conditions become excuses for complete passivity and self-pity, while others have used such handicaps as a focus of a new mental and physical fitness in their lives.

Many handicapped men feel they will fail as fathers, because they adopt the widely held myth that father power stems from their physical abilities as such. Actually, father power rests not on your overt abilities but in your capacity to present what strengths you have to your child, to show him your values and what lies behind them, and to expect him to accept himself, his abilities, and his limitations.

It really doesn't matter so much, then, that a father can walk or see, but that he can present his strengths apart from walking and seeing. Indeed, all fathers are "handicapped" in one sense in that they all lack certain abilities that they must help a child to derive from others. The physically handicapped father is different from his nonhandicapped counterpart only in the nature of his disability.

Besides adjusting to the fact of your handicap so that it will not greatly affect your fatherhood, you should also explain it thoroughly to your child. Tell him exactly what is wrong with you, how you got that way, and explain what this means in terms of your ability to carry out everyday activities. Make sure your child doesn't think he will become handicapped too, just because his father is.

Growing with Your Handicap. While a handicap is, of course, a sad development in a father's life, it can be turned to advantage for a child. Few sights can be more awesome or inspiring to a child than seeing his beloved, respected father struggle successfully to overcome a handicap—to learn to walk with braces, to function with only one arm, or to overcome a hearing defect. We've seen many examples of sons and daughters who were deeply affected by such examples of personal courage on the part of their fathers. Realizing the effect you may have on your children may in fact motivate you to struggle to overcome your handicap even more. And we've seen fathers who, determined not to let their handicap interfere with their fatherhood, were more successful fathers than they would have been otherwise.

A handicap may also allow the father to empathize more

with his child. As we have said, your abilities as a fully matured adult may blind you to the difficulties a child must go through to achieve what you have. Whether learning to read, to throw a football, or to drive a car, children are themselves handicapped by their immaturity and lack of experience.

Besides wallowing in self-pity over their disability, some handicapped fathers also fall into other traps that injure their relationships with their children. Some handicapped fathers try to use it as a weapon to force their children into obedience. Such a father declares, "You shouldn't do things like that; you know I've got a bad heart and it hurts me more."

Other fathers have used their handicap to produce fear in their child that the same thing will happen to them. For instance, the chronically ill father may impress upon his son that he must stay in line "or you'll wind up sick like me." Such a father could turn his son or daughter into a hypochondriac, afraid to exert himself physically or mentally.

In our chapter on the father and physical development we discussed the impact a father's illness can have on his child. We discussed how it can be a loss in both economic and psychological security for a family. Similar problems can occur for the child of the handicapped father. When the father is disabled, the family can suffer severely. Generally, the less a father's handicap impinges on a child's life, the better it will be for him. Hopefully, the child will be able to live an adequate life, including as normal a relationship as possible with his handicapped father. Try to let him go as many places and do as many things as he would otherwise.

Don't Trap Your Child. The father-child relationship may be variously affected by a handicap according to the sex of the child. Daughters are more likely to become nurses to their handicapped fathers because of their greater sensitivity to other people and because of the expectations of society. To some extent, allowing a child to help in caring for a handicapped father is good, but the father should not allow himself to become too dependent on his child. A child should be allowed to grow and develop; he should not be forced into premature adulthood. Nor should a daughter be taught to define the man-woman relationship in terms of overdependence by the man. This is the complete reverse of the usual imbalance, but just as damaging a situation in our society today in which the woman is taught to be overdependent upon the man.

We know one such daughter who had a father with chronic emphysema. The mother, overworked with three other children to care for and a job to hold down, readily allowed the daughter to nurse the ailing father. After the father finally died, and the daughter was on her own, she went many years without marrying, because she could not relate to other men in an egalitarian way. She finally married a man who himself had had an overbearing mother, and the two suffered many years through a neurotic marriage in which each felt inadequate because of an inability to relate on an equal basis with the other.

A son may also cause particular difficulties for the handicapped father. Feeling especially inadequate because of his handicap, the father may deeply resent his son's physical competence. His son's physical ability may gall him terribly, especially if the handicap is a physical one and he is a physically oriented man. And, of course, there is the other extreme—the handicapped father who tries to live solely through the son's achievements. Much depends on the individual man and the individual circumstances.

Remember that father power doesn't stem from a father's ability to walk or see or hear but from his love and commitment as a parent.

THE OLDER FATHER

In discussing beginning fatherhood in older men—those over forty—we are reminded of the jokes that begin, "I've got some bad news for you and some good news." Becoming a father at middle age or after presents problems, but the older father also has advantages over younger fathers. A successful older father is one who keeps in mind that each period in a man's life brings difficulties and strengths unique to that period and that the relative number of problems does not necessarily increase with age. Younger fathers might do well to read this section too, because by contrasting older and younger fathers, strengths and weaknesses in both are revealed. In discussing the older father, we'll begin with the "bad news."

A major source of problems for the older father can be his reaction to his aging body. The father in his forties is particularly prone to depression and bouts of frenetic physical exercise as he copes with the fact that he is not a spry twenty-year-old any longer. He may feel the aging process weighing heavily on him, especially as he compares himself physically with his vigorous young child.

Older fathers, especially those of sons, sometimes become very physically competitive with their offspring, continually challenging them to some sort of contest or another. One father of fifty, with a son of seventeen, would often play tennis with his son, but instead of allowing for his bad knee, would push himself through a whole afternoon of tennis just to show himself and his son that he was as good as he ever was.

A major source of fear for some older fathers, especially those in their sixties, is that they will die before their children are grown, leaving them fatherless. This is also a frequent problem in fathers with chronic ailments. If you are in this situation, you would do well to remember what we said earlier about involving yourself with your child while he is very young. An early, deep involvement with you gives your child a sound basis of memories he can draw upon if you are not around—a sort of fatherhood trust fund. Concentrate on being the best father you can right now, and your child will have a firm basis on which to build.

Resistance to Change. An older father may also feel that his physical age makes him too old to participate fully in his child's life—that he is supposed to be too dignified to roll around on the floor with his son or daughter. Such a father is especially fearful of being dubbed "an old fool." Considering what we have said in past chapters about the importance of fathering, you should be easily confident that fathering is not only properly masculine but properly dignified, no matter what your age.

His "mental age" may also produce some problems for the older father. Because men tend to become more conservative and perhaps less flexible philosophically as they grow older, there may be a more pronounced generation gap between the older father and his offspring. The younger father, more easily recalling his own fads and errors, may be less likely to ridicule the latest dance craze or political movement.

The older father may also have more problems in changing his life-style to meet the demands of fatherhood, especially if this child is his first. He may resent the uproar and confusion that children often bring to a home. He may have a certain long-standing schedule he likes to keep—dinner at six, golf on Saturdays, a weekly card game—and he may feel resentful of a baby who upsets this schedule.

The younger father's life-style is itself undergoing more change. Such flux can give his child a chance to be exposed to more varying environments. The child may experience a great many different kinds of people as the younger father moves up in his career.

Older fathers tend to be less physically mobile, in addition to being less psychologically mobile. The older father has probably already permanently settled in an area where he wants to live and in a job he likes. He is less likely to move to other parts of the country, even to other neighborhoods. Certainly, incessant nomadism can be bad for a child, but a certain amount of moving around will teach him about differences in people and places.

The older father is also less likely to take even short trips—to a bowling alley, to a pool hall, or to a junkyard. His hobbies tend to be more sedentary and less adventuresome. There are also financial problems in old age that may interfere with fatherhood, including expenses due to illness or the cost of retirement. But realizing these drawbacks represents a giant step toward remedying them.

Many of the drawbacks to older fatherhood that we have cited can also be turned to advantage.

Some Possible Advantages. While the older father's physical condition may make him overcompetitive if he refuses to accept his own aging, it may, on the other hand, allow him to gracefully avoid overcompetition. The child can be allowed to occupy more of the limelight, with the father becoming his number one booster. We've seen younger fathers watching their sons play football and being quite envious of them as the fathers vividly remember their own football-playing days. On the other hand, we've seen older fathers, adjusted to the fact that their football-playing days are over, vigorously cheering their sons on.

Younger fathers often have problems with their own masculine confidence. They have only recently emerged from adolescence and may still feel uncertain about their competence. On the other hand, the older father, who has been around a lot longer, has had time to develop confidence that he is a fully masculine adult. He has worked out many of the problems that might have bothered him when younger, and thus, they will not interfere with his fatherhood.

For example, we know one father who when younger went through quite a deep depression because he was going bald. As he constantly, unsuccessfully tried new hair-restoring methods, his depression deepened and often resulted in his being cross with his son. This same father when in his late fifties had another son. He was by then quite bald but had reconciled himself to it, and it never led to such problems between himself and his child.

"Historical" Perspective. The age of the older father could make him overconservative in his reactions to young fads and ideas, but his experience could also allow him to take a more mature view of things. While the younger father may be disturbed that his daughter is trying out a new form of yoga, the older father may remember that over the years he has seen many such fads come and go and may not get as upset about the latest one. The older father may not be as hip to his youngsters, but he may be able to take a longer-range, more charitable view of their foibles. This charitable attitude many times appears to increase with age, the retired man often being more tolerant of youthful attitudes than the working man.

The older father's age also gives his life an historical aura that he can use to help teach his child. To know that his father was actually an adult during World War II or during some other historical event can be fascinating for a child. The older father, like the grandfather, can bring history alive for his child in a much more vivid way than he could ever experience it in school.

Because the child of an older father is probably not his first, he is more experienced at being a father, which can be to his child's great advantage. He realizes where he has made his mistakes in the past and perhaps how to avoid them with his later offspring.

Career Status. A further and particularly important advantage of the older father is that he is likely to be more settled in his career than is the younger father. He has either achieved success already or has put his career on a back burner because he has discovered it will not be a rewarding focus of his life. Either way, he is usually more adjusted to his financial status. He is less likely to have to work nights, and if he is successful, he does not have as many superiors whose schedules he must meet.

All these factors add up to more time and more mental energy that the older father can use with his family. He can take an afternoon off to take his children places and has longer vacation periods and more money to show them sights.

Having already outdistanced the hot breath of competition and financial insecurity, the successful older father can be much more relaxed than the younger father. In retired fathers, this difference in the influence of a career is most pronounced. The retired father can concentrate on what he himself wants to do, and this may make him a much mellower individual. Whether or not he is a father, the retired man who has had positive experience and competence with children has a very rich resource upon which to draw.

The Baby's Birth. All the advantages and disadvantages of being an older father can be influenced heavily by the circumstances of the baby's birth. If the child was unplanned for, many of the more negative feelings we have described might take the fore. The father will start out with doubts about the new responsibilities thrust upon him at his advanced age and may also have negative feelings about the child. On the other hand, if the child represents a desire on the part of parents—perhaps it is a first child or a child they decided to have because circumstances were at last right—then the positive aspects of fatherhood are more likely to win out.

THE UNWED FATHER

The enormous social change that has occurred during the past few years has affected unwed parenthood profoundly. Birth control is more sophisticated and more widely practiced, making the likelihood of unwed parenthood much less. On the other hand, more women are openly and purposefully conceiving children out of wedlock and keeping their babies, and more and more men and women are living together unmarried and are having children.

Because of all these changes, we shall discuss first the traditional unwed father, the one who is caught by surprise, who is still very much with us today, and then the new style of unwed father, usually an intentional partner in the bearing of an out-of-wedlock child.

Traditional Unwed Fathers. There is a sometimes humorous saying, "I come from a long line of bastards," which is quite applicable in the case of the traditional unwed father. Such men are more likely to be "illegitimate" themselves or the products of father-absent homes.

The traditional unwed father, whether he is a young teen-ager or an older man, tends to be more immature or irresponsible and to have an insecure sense of his masculinity. Considering what we have said about the importance of the father to his children, it is easy to understand why father neglect could produce such a person. The reasons a man would intentionally try to impregnate an unmarried woman are varied, but they generally center around this lack of masculine confidence. The man may feel that he is proving himself by fathering a child or that he must get his girlfriend pregnant in order to hold onto her or persuade her to marry him.

By pointing out the inadequacies that usually mark the unwed father, we are by no means excusing those of the unwed mother. Though many women plead ignorance of birth-control methods as an excuse for getting pregnant, many others have no one to blame but themselves. And a woman can be just as exploitative in getting pregnant as a man, using it to hook a husband or to get back at parents.

What this boils down to is that the traditional unwed father is very often not a very effective parent. If he or his girlfriend purposefully engineered the pregnancy to exploit the other, it is not a good basis for a marriage, and not a good basis for raising a child.

If the unwed father became so in order to show his masculinity, it is also unlikely that he will be a good parent. He is apt to be irresponsible in other areas, and the concept of masculinity he displays to the child will not be helpful. In such cases giving the baby up for adoption should be considered. A child born in such circumstances with an irresponsible mother and/or father is likely to be in severe straits.

Though unwed fathers do tend to be relatively ineffective, there are cases in which unwed fathers and mothers have effective relationships and parenthoods. Usually such cases are those in which the unwed parents were either very close or on the verge of marriage anyway and in which the pregnancy was unintentional. Most people believe that a boy who gets a girl pregnant is usually older or from a higher socioeconomic class and has taken advantage of the "poor girl." Contrary to this myth, most unwed parents are closely involved with their partners and resemble them closely in terms of age, education, and social class.

If there is no exploitative relationship involved and the unwed father has confidence in his masculinity and is committed to the child, he can be an effective parent.

The New Unwed Father. Cohabiting unmarried couples certainly aren't a majority in our society, but many do exist. Of this group, a few even opt to have children without marriage. The nontraditional or "counterculture" unwed father is often different from his traditional counterpart in terms of social class and education. The traditional unwed father is more often poor, uneducated, or young, or suffering from problems caused by his own parents. The nontraditional unwed father is more likely to be college educated and to have had a relatively more stable home life. He has *chosen* to become a father. The traditional unwed father is often an economic or social dropout from society by chance, the nontraditional unwed father by choice.

Regardless of the commitment of the counterculture unwed father to his mate, and the supposed rationality and purpose behind his decision to become a father, many such fathers are nevertheless quite irresponsible in their actions. This lies principally in that they have not assured that their child will have a stable, continuing, warm father relationship. Regardless of how much they love each other, a couple who is living together without marriage may not be as committed to one another as they may think. They are also not considerate of their child's situation, born illegitimate as he is. Although there is not nearly the social stigma attached to illegitimacy today as there was in the past, being a "bastard" could still possibly severely affect a child's sense of self-esteem. Parents of illegitimate children cannot be sure in what atmosphere their child will grow up, so it makes no sense whatsoever to give a child a legacy of illegitimacy that may cause him great sorrow or embarrassment in some unforeseen future.

Of course, there are also many counterculture unwed fathers who are quite responsible. Although they may not have taken the strictly legal steps to marriage, they may have committed themselves to a degree that, in their own conscience, equals the traditional marriage ties. Even though the counterculture father may believe he has the strongest ties in the world to his wife and child, he should seriously consider legalizing them, at least to the extent of adopting the child. He should assure that he will be allowed access to the child should the relationship with the child's mother be broken off.

THE BLACK FATHER

> My daddy never really lived
> before he died
> He could never count on justice
> or know a free man's pride
> And now it's almost certain
> that I, too will be denied
> I've got to make things better
> for my son and for my tribe

Letters to a Black Boy
by Bob Teague
(New York: Walker and Co., 1968)

There are many other socially disadvantaged fathers in our society besides the lower-class black father, and many of the problems are shared by lower-class fathers in general. To that extent, much of this section may be relevant to the plight of other socially disadvantaged groups. We are concentrating on the lower-class black father here because his problems profoundly illustrate the devastating effects of father deprivation. For even though many black fathers have achieved middle-class status, they often still suffer from the lack of father involvement bequeathed to them from the past.

The Black Father's Heritage. Of the many ethnic groups that have come to this country, blacks are unique. Generally, ethnic groups immigrating to America brought with them a strong concept of fatherhood. The German father, Italian father, Japanese father, or Russian father might all have been different, but they all had some confidence in their importance in the family.

In many of the old hierarchies of Europe, the father lost much of his authority outside the family either to an aristocracy or to a powerful dictator. The fathers and mothers who immigrated to the new world were frequently forceful, dynamic people who perhaps had a stronger motivation than their countrymen to escape such restrictions, control their own destinies, or better their lot.

These fathers who brought their families with them, shared with them a physically and psychologically difficult journey that welded the group close together. Additionally, their initial isolation as immigrants from the American mainstream turned them more toward each other for support.

A major, tragic exception to the immigrant fathers who brought with them the traditions of the old country was the black father. The black man's introduction into this country was an agonizing one, as has been so thoroughly and poignantly documented by historians and black poets and writers. The black father never had a chance to establish himself in early America, for the very nature of the slave trade legislated against him. The slave was likely to be thoroughly and brutally cut off from other members of his tribe, separated into twos and threes for easy handling by the slavers when they reached the New World. Because a male slave was more likely to be a young man, sometimes even a preadolescent, he had no experience as a family leader to draw upon. Some anthropologists also point out that in many African cultures the father had little to do with childrearing except as his sons approached adolescence.

The slave was further degraded by subjection to the will of the master, which even included the choice of his wife and the authority over and disposition of his children. The master's order to get married was nothing more than an order to copulate and reproduce. The slave's marriage could be dissolved at the master's whim. In fact, Southern law held that "The father of a slave is unknown to our law."

Slave families centered not around a father and mother contributing to their own welfare and that of their offspring, but around the mother and child. While a slave mother and child were often treated as a unit, the father might be sold without a second thought by the owner.

After emancipation, the black man still did not have the benefit of a social order that would encourage effective fatherhood. Many blacks left the plantations and wandered aimlessly, without any social or physical roots. In search of work and adventure, and relishing their freedom, they banded together in loose groups, still not sure of their identities. The vast majority of blacks during the post–Civil-War period settled into patterns much like those of their bondage.

Because of this background, as well as current social factors, the black father is likely to be unsure of his father power.

Certainly, poverty and discrimination have contributed to the continued ghettoization, crime, and other problems of many working-class black people today. We emphasize, though, that the dilemma of the black father has been a focal point that all these factors affect and from which many problems are continued.

Because the black father, like the traditional white father, was more often the parent trying to make it in society, he was the more psychologically vulnerable to discrimination—on the job, in school, and in public. All around him were white males successfully pursuing their careers, while he, the young black male seeking a place in society, was seen as the greatest threat by fearful whites. His physical vigor threatened white males, especially older ones, who held powerful positions, and also lower-class white males who were fearful of competing with him. To such whites, the subservient black man offered less of a threat, and the black woman the least threat of all.

Economic Discrimination. This social discrimination led to severe economic discrimination against the black father. Though the black man in general is hard hit by unemployment, being much more likely to be unemployed than the white man, the black father is most affected by it. When the single black male is unemployed, his lack of a job represents a problem only for him and his own pride and wallet. But the unemployed black father may feel that he has lost stature in the eyes of his wife and his children. Being an American father, he subscribes to the notion that being the breadwinner is by far the most important father function. Feeling rejected, he may in the end opt out of his family altogether. He rejects not only his wife because of the lack of self-respect he feels, but finally his children as well, because he feels that failure at economic support means failure at fatherhood.

Welfare systems also discriminate particularly against the black father. These systems expect and even encourage the unemployed black father to desert his family. Welfare departments do this in one way by giving aid more easily to families without fathers, in essence often making the judgment that the father who cannot provide for his family does not deserve to remain in it.

Welfare cases are usually handled mainly by female welfare workers who deal primarily with the mother to determine the family's needs and to allot money. The father is usually left out and comes to feel threatened by the team of wife and female social worker.

Because of welfare regulations, many black families (and white families as well) may have to hide the fact that a male is living in the home. What does this do for the feeling of worth on the part of both the black man and of the child witnessing such deception? It is no wonder that the resultant "typical" welfare mother is pictured as having been deserted by her husband whose whereabouts are unknown and who contributes nothing to the children's support.

Father Absence. Because of high unemployment among black males, and subsequent father absence, the mother heads almost one-fourth of black families, in contrast to about one-tenth of white families.

Even disregarding the economic pressures on the black father, the father-denigrating heritage of slavery has produced father absence over and above that caused by the lack of economic power. The rate of father absence among blacks appears to be about three times higher than among whites at all income levels, even among relatively affluent families.

Of course, we're not ignoring the many economically effective, deeply involved black fathers. Although one-third of blacks exist at the poverty level, obviously, there are two-thirds who do not. While many blacks are unemployed, many more are not. While many black fathers have left their families, many are highly competent parents.

Nevertheless, black children who do not live with their fathers can suffer from all the potential deficits due to father absence we have discussed in previous chapters, plus a number of problems unique to their situation. We've pointed out how a father-neglected boy, black or white, would probably be unsure of his masculinity. A father-neglected girl would be unsure of the relationship of her femininity to men and would be less valuing of men. We've also discussed how father-absent children, particularly those from the lower class, may suffer intellectual deficits and be more likely to have emotional and social problems. Add to this a value system that predisposes lower-class black (and white) males to conflicts with authority and failure on the job. This system involves glorifying toughness, hypermasculinity, daring, luck, and escaping from authority. These values are in direct opposition to qualities usually needed for job success—self-discipline, confidence in controlling one's destiny, and ability to accept rational authority. Besides being dangerous in itself, father absence adds to a general web of cultural disadvantage for the lower-class child.

Black Woman, Black Fatherhood. The problems caused in black children by father absence stem also from the way father absence affects mothers. In part because black women have often been taught to value females much more highly than males, black girls come to have higher educational aspirations and attainments than their male counterparts. Black mothers, in general, tend to pass on their legacy of competence to their daughters, but frequently devalue and discourage their sons. All of this adds up to a chronic female overdominance in the black family.

We have already seen how our female-dominated elementary schools can interfere with the optimal development of both boys and girls. In the case of father-absent lower-class black boys, the female teacher is a particularly strong threat.

The boy has probably not had any close and positive relationships with adult males and has lived in a female-dominated home—one that perhaps includes a mother, grandmother, and older sisters. Thus, he may tend to struggle even harder against the female teacher to establish himself as a "real man." Add to this the already serious intellectual deficiencies produced by father neglect, and it is understandable why the black male often has such serious academic problems, compared to black girls and white children in general.

Incidentally, this female-dominated educational system discourages the black father from involvement even more than it does the white father. Brought up by black women, taught by women in school, not effective even in his female-dominated family, the black father is not likely to feel comfortable working with female teachers to assure his children's educational growth.

Black Father Power. Besides the strengths fathers generally afford their children, black fathers can also help their children compensate for the most insidious threat to black success—racism. A black child with the warm, supportive base of a confident father from which to venture, can better fend off racial slights. A child from a strong family more often possesses a firm sense of identity and security to draw upon when dealing with such prejudice. Also, he can turn to his family for reassurance and support.

To strengthen the black father's position, the same kinds of things must be done to emphasize his importance as must be done for the white father. Social programs aimed at involving blacks could be made most effective by involving the black father.

Generally, the black father should be encouraged to realize that a family without him, with only a mother, lacks an important strength. The mother has too long had to support the lower-class black family, both economically and psychologically. Certainly, social workers should take care not to stigmatize the mother or child in a father-absent home, but the problem must still be recognized and dealt with. The educational system, especially in ghetto areas, must introduce intensive programs geared to involving the black father.

For example, welfare agencies should employ black males as well as females and representatives of other minorities to aid flexibility in dealing with the psychological needs of clients. The agency representatives should work through both the father and the mother to determine family needs. Community mental health programs must realize and allow for the importance of the father in the family.

And, of course, we cannot ignore the black father's needs for economic power in the form of a decent job. Although simply earning money does not guarantee a successful fatherhood, we realize that raising a family is much more difficult for a man without a steady job, not only for his wallet but also for his self-confidence.

Involving black fathers can have heartening results, as witnessed by a father-involvement project at the Dr. Martin Luther King Family Center in Chicago. Sociologist Samuel Tuck, Jr., reported on the project at a meeting of mental health professionals in 1970.

In the initial phase of the project, a social worker at the center worked with four black fathers to select toys that would help the fathers in educating their three-year-olds. The fathers' involvement got them more interested in their children's development and prompted them to organize a fathers' club at the center. They planned cartoon shows, fun fairs, and other activities for the children. Eventually, the fathers' group, elated at their success with their children, organized softball teams, invested in business ventures, established a community credit union, and, as the "Concerned Fathers of the Mile Square Area," expanded to include a large area of their neighborhood. The group sought control, both economic and political, of their own community. The success of this group is a good example of how such participation can affect the father as well as the child. These black fathers found that they could be competent with their children, which inspired them to strive for more influence in their community.

Black Leaders. Effective fathers have had a profound

influence in the development of this country's black leaders. Two of these leaders were Malcolm X and Martin Luther King, Jr. Although their philosophies were quite different, they both benefited from early and vivid experiences of witnessing the vitality and courage of their fathers.

In his autobiography, Malcolm X describes a life of turmoil, persecution, and deprivation. But he also describes an incredibly determined, powerful father, a lay preacher who instilled in him many of the beliefs and traits that were to make him a powerful leader. Although his father died when he was only six, Malcolm X was deeply affected by him.

Martin Luther King's father, a preacher, was also a great influence on the road to leadership his son would take. King's father and grandfather both were among the pioneers of the modern civil rights movement.

A proud man, King's father was an excellent model for his son. For instance, consider this anecdote about an incident King shared with his father:

Martin went one day downtown with his father to buy a pair of shoes. Father and son took seats in the front of the store. A white clerk approached and said:

"I'll be happy to wait on you if you'll just move back there to those seats in the rear."

"Nothing wrong with these seats," the elder King harrumphed.

"Sorry," said the clerk, "but you'll have to go back there."

"We'll either buy shoes sitting here," the father shot back, flaring up, "or we won't buy any shoes at all." King took his son by the hand and stomped from the store, fuming. Looking back on this encounter, later, the son said: "It was probably the first time I had seen Daddy so furious, and I guess I was hurt for the first time too. Daddy has always been an emotional man, and I can remember him muttering: 'I don't care how long I have to live with this system, I am never going to accept it. I'll oppose it until the day I die.' "

from *What Manner of Man—Martin Luther King, Jr.*
by Lerone Bennett

15/Fathers with Problem Children

Although our main purpose in this book is to help the fathers of normal, healthy children, we shall not neglect fathers of children with special problems. We shall briefly discuss problems in fathering the physically handicapped child, the retarded child, the delinquent child, and the emotionally disturbed child. This is by no means a complete list of the type of problem children fathers may have, but we hope our examples will provide some helpful guidelines.

To the typical father today who doesn't feel that he has much effect on his children the child with a special problem represents both a frustration and a threat. He is frustrated because he cannot really do anything to alter the child's disability, and he is also more apt to see the child as a tangible sign to society that something is basically wrong with him and that his entire family is somehow tainted.

This is an especially malevolent form of the feeling of powerlessness in fathers, for it leads the father to the conclusion that the child is inherently bad and that abandonment is really the only answer.

In reality, father power means that you, the father, can indeed be a powerful agent in helping your child—but by the same token, that you may have been a powerful agent in contributing to his problem.

The fact that you have a child with some sort of problem should immediately spur you to use your father power in his behalf. Too often the father opts out of his role with the problem child, forcing the mother into the role of seeker-of-help. In many cases, this kind of desertion of the child is one sign that the father may have contributed to the problem or at least may be aggravating it.

The father of a problem child should make it a general rule to be sure he sees his child as a complex, individual case, and not just as a statistic. Too many fathers with a retarded, handicapped, delinquent or emotionally disturbed child are ready to slap a label on the child and declare to themselves that "This one's a lost cause."

The Physically Handicapped Child

A major step in being effective with your physically or intellectually handicapped child is to empathize with his problem. If you can successfully put yourself in his shoes, you can be much more sensitive to your child's special needs—and there may be things you might otherwise not think of doing. For instance, one father of a crippled son realized after some careful thought that the child was becoming overdependent on him and his wife. Gradually, he began to teach the child how to do things on his own—to get his own milk from the refrigerator or to adjust the television set himself. He began to introduce the child to more new situations—letting him go on picnics with other families and giving him chores around the house. This way, when time came for the child to go off to school, he was not panicked by the totally new situation and the abrupt separation from his parents.

You must also realize what your child's handicap means in terms of your own values. The man who prides himself on his intellect will be more hard hit by a retarded child than a physically crippled child. While he may be willing to work hard to help the physically handicapped child, he may reject the retarded child. By the same token, the athlete may not be too disturbed by a child with a learning disability but may be terribly disturbed by one with a limp.

Because they tend not to be as deeply involved with a child, fathers tend to see a handicap in black and white terms. They may plunk a handicapped child into one category or another that defines him as hopeless. Or else they may deny a less obvious handicap, saying, "He'll grow out of it," or, "There's really nothing wrong that a little study (or practice or discipline) won't cure." Hopefully, you'll be seeking help and learning about your child's handicap, and you will generally know how he stands in relationship to other children.

Even if a father does know, for example, that little Johnny will never be able to walk, he may erroneously define the handicap in terms of what Johnny can't do rather than what he can do. One father we know was so concerned that his partially paralyzed son could not play baseball that he was oblivious to the boy's impressive swimming ability. Concentrate on what you can help your child achieve, not on what he cannot achieve.

Some handicaps that children have call for special types of parent-child activities. For example, the child who is born deaf will need certain kinds of stimulation to ensure the effective development of his speech. Parents often have to gain much knowledge in particular areas in order that their handicapped child get all the opportunities and resources he deserves.

It is beyond the scope of our book to provide you with information about specific physical handicaps, but we do encourage you to seek out the advice and cooperation of well-trained professionals. We mention some important points in seeking professional help later in this chapter.

Some fathers, because of their own insensitivity, even "create" physical handicaps for their children. For example, a teen-age boy who stops growing at five feet, four inches may be made much more self-conscious and insecure if his father continually makes reference to his son's "puny" appearance. Such a boy may go through life blaming any failure on his stature. Similarly, the parent of a child who has lost a finger or an eye may become so overprotective that the child develops a serious psychological problem where only a slight physical disfigurement existed.

Remember that the important personality attributes such as

self-confidence, assertiveness, sensitivity, creativity, etc., are not dependent on a completely "normal" body.

THE MENTALLY RETARDED CHILD

At the beginning of this chapter we discussed some general problems fathers have in dealing with problem children. Those general problems apply especially to the father with the mentally retarded child. The retarded child may seem to be much more of a reason for shame than the physically handicapped child to a father who prides himself on being a thinking, rational member of society. In fact, many parents, especially highly intellectual ones, have so much difficulty accepting a retarded child that they go from place to place until they get a diagnosis that labels their child as emotionally disturbed rather than retarded. Of course, some children have multiple problems and may be both mentally retarded and emotionally disturbed.

If your child is slow in developing language or other skills, don't hesitate to seek help from professionals in understanding his difficulty. If possible, go to a multidisciplinary clinic or hospital complex specializing in children's problems where your child can be seen by neurologists, psychologists, psychiatrists, and other professionals who all have special skills in dealing with children.

There are many reasons why a child may be functioning at a retarded level. They range from clear-cut genetic anomalies, such as mongolism, to cultural deprivation or even severe parental neglect. The underlying factors involved in the retardation are often very complex and require careful diagnosis.

Mental retardation is not an all-or-nothing phenomenon, and there are various degrees of intellectual handicap. If you do have a retarded child, make sure you understand his potential capabilities and try to challenge him to live up to them. Several studies have revealed that the majority of retarded children, those with IQs between 50 and 70, usually have problems of attitude and motivation as well as problems caused simply by their retardation. If taught well, many of them can learn to read and write, as well as master basic self-care and problem-solving skills.

Henry vividly remembers the case of Harold P., a lawyer, who, upon learning that his young son, Gerald, was retarded, became very depressed. All he could think of for weeks was that his son would never amount to anything because he wouldn't be able to go to college. When Harold was able to realize that Gerald was only mildly retarded and would probably be able to achieve at least a fifth-grade level of academic skill, he began to set his expectations more realistically and took pride in his son's persistence and obvious social skills.

If you "obsess" about your retarded child's slow academic progress, you may indirectly hinder the development of his other skills. Many intellectually handicapped individuals are not retarded in a general way, because they have developed an excellent ability to get along with others and a strong self-sufficiency.

Retardation is usually more than simply an intellectual deficit, and many retarded children learn to be far more competent than an IQ measure would suggest. On the other hand, we all have encountered individuals who have average or above-average IQs but who are grossly retarded in their emotional and social development.

Unless he has extremely severe problems, a retarded child usually does better at home than in an institution. If you and your family feel that you can cope with a retarded child, living at home will benefit the child because he will get much more personalized care and attention.

Of course, parents have to carefully weigh the potential effects that a retarded child living at home may have on their marital relationship and on their other children. In too many cases, parents shift the bulk of responsibility for the care of the retarded child onto their other children. Also, much resentment can occur if the other children perceive that their peers chastise or ridicule them for having a retarded sibling.

In contrast, in families where the responsibility is shared fairly among the mother and father and their other children, family cohesiveness can be increased, and a sense of positive involvement with the retarded child can be fostered.

The importance of the entire family's sharing in the growth and development of the retarded child cannot be overstressed. But the other children and their development should not be sacrificed. If you and your wife are in doubt, you should seek professional guidance.

Have the child retested often so that his rate of development can be assessed. He may be gaining significantly in ability yet may not be receiving enough challenge because you do not realize his growing skills. Some children with learning disabilities but normal intelligence have been diagnosed as retarded because of limited testing procedures. Also, IQ tests during the first few years of the child's life can give an indication of very high or very low intellectual development, but they are not accurate in predicting long-range potential.

Remember, retardation is a relative thing. A child with a normal IQ in a family of geniuses may feel just as retarded as a child with a low IQ in an average family. Be sure you do not make your child feel so inferior that he becomes unmotivated to develop his abilities, whatever they may be.

THE DELINQUENT CHILD

The child who is chronically malicious, destructive, and rebellious against authority represents a complex challenge to his family and society. Before pondering whether you have directly contributed to your child's delinquency, you must realize that there are many factors that can be involved in its development. First of all, many delinquents have subtle learning disabilities. If your child is lashing out at those around him, it may be in frustration at not being able to keep up with his friends. Seek professional help in determining whether a learning disability may be contributing to your child's problem.

Another major kind of delinquency not attributable to the parents is due to peer-group pressure on the child. Is he running with a crowd that you consider of questionable moral character? Hopefully, you have been enough involved with him to know his friends well and can discuss with him your opinions on the worth of his friends.

Unfortunately, too many parents use "his crummy friends" as an excuse to absolve the child of responsibility for his actions. It may be that your child chooses delinquent friends because of his own lack of communication with his family, and not that they are luring him into trouble.

In study after study the father has been identified as the parent who most contributes to delinquency in his son or daughter. Father absence, particularly when it begins early in the child's life, is especially highly associated with delinquent behavior among both boys and girls. While it must be emphasized that delinquency can stem from other causes, you should think long and hard about your own dealings with the child in searching for answers to your child's delinquent behavior.

Father and the Delinquent Son. Comparisons of groups of delinquent and nondelinquent boys have produced a frequent picture of a father who is overly aggressive toward his son. Probably a failure in his own life, he takes it out on his children, being very controlling, rigid, punitive, and often alcoholic. Together with the frequent alcoholism, a frightening picture emerges of a father, unable to be successful in his own life, brutally venting his frustrations on his children. He has perverted his natural father power into an excuse for paternal brutality.

On the other hand, when such a father is not punishing his children, he usually has little to do with their guidance. In one study of delinquents, their fathers were found to be more neglecting, giving less direction, and sharing fewer plans, activities, and interests than were the fathers of nondelinquent boys.

The fathers of delinquent boys in another study were more

likely to ridicule their sons when they made mistakes. And another researcher found that the fathers of delinquents were more likely to *support* antisocial behavior than other fathers. This conjures up a vivid picture of a bitter failure of a man, taking out his bitterness on the world through his son.

In a review of the research concerning comparisons of the fathers and mothers of delinquents, fathers clearly emerge as the more damaging of the parents. The fathers of delinquents are consistently described as being more punitive and neglecting, and in many cases the mothers appear to be no different from mothers of nondelinquent children.

How can such a father-child relationship lead to delinquency? First of all, the overly punitive father, in being hostile in his interactions with his son, affords the boy a very bad model for the control of aggression. His anger is in effect passed on to the boy. But since this aggression is turned toward the son, it also makes him reject his father's discipline and the family.

Father and the Delinquent Daughter. Boys' delinquency is frequently marked by aggressiveness and violence as they lash out at the world. Girls' delinquency is more often defined by society in sexual terms—specifically in terms of sexual promiscuity. The delinquent girl is often physically aggressive, and sometimes violent, but this is by no means the major expression of her delinquency.

Because girls are usually smaller and less muscular than boys, they are less likely to be successful at physical aggressiveness. Thus, they are less likely to use it as part of their repertoire of acting out. Society also frowns more on physical aggressiveness in girls, and they are generally not as much encouraged to such acting out as boys are.

Our sexual mores have changed considerably, making sexuality in girls a much more accepted thing. The sexual activity that today is considered normal would have been labeled delinquent ten years ago. Nevertheless, there are certain styles of sexual behavior that would still be labeled delinquent. If the girl continually engages in sexual activity without a close personal relationship, and the activity is a sign to her not of personal dignity but of rebellion and self-deprecation, she may be labeled delinquent.

The father's attitude toward his daughter, both as a parent and as a representative of society, is often the principal definer of how she will be delinquent. Fathers of delinquent daughters are likely to be cold, rejecting, and hostile. They are most often restrictive because they are anxious about their daughter's sexual misconduct. The father may accuse his daughter of sexual misbehavior, mistrust her, and become preoccupied with her sexuality long before she becomes involved in an overtly sexual relationship. In many cases, this is because the father has not accepted his own attraction to his daughter, as we described in our section on the sensuous father in Chapter 8. The daughter, frustrated at her father's punitiveness, often has sexual relations just to get back at him.

Father Neglect and Delinquency. Certainly, such poor father-child relationships as we have described can lead to delinquency in children, but what about the child who has little contact with a father in the first place? The classic case is that of the successful businessman who has given his children everything and who has a cordial relationship with them. Nevertheless, to his puzzlement, the children are caught stealing, they get hooked on drugs, or they don't respect other people or their property.

If his father is absent or neglectful, the child may interpret the father's lack of interest as a personal devaluation. "Nobody really cares what I do, so why should I?" is an exclamation often heard from delinquents. In their frustration, they often decide to *make* somebody care.

The mother can act as a buffer against father neglect, but there is only so much she can do. Whether the family is rich or poor, one involved parent simply can't give as much care and guidance as two involved parents.

In many upper-middle-class families, the mother is also neglectful, thus negating the role she could play in delinquency prevention. Ironically, this mother neglect is often caused indirectly by the father. Working hard to build a business or rise in a company, he demands that his wife do the same. As she entertains business contacts or immerses herself in civic affairs, she joins the husband in this upper-middle-class form of neglect.

In our section on the father and his child's masculinity or femininity we discussed how father absence can be especially damaging to a child's sex role. This damage often shows not just as a personal problem in the child's life but in delinquent acts against society. When a father is cruel and brutal, a boy learns to define masculinity in those terms, but he may also embrace cruelty and brutality by default. With a neglecting father, he may decide that the only way to be a man is to be tough.

We knew one such boy, Stanley J., who because of his father's lack of support and involvement was unsure that he was masculine, even afraid that he was homosexual. This boy subsequently adopted a supertough attitude to prove his masculinity. He grew his hair extra long, wore black "muscle" shirts, and often got drunk or high on drugs. "I tried to be tough, strong, and supercool—I made trouble—I went in for drugs and street fighting. I was determined to prove my manliness and my identity because I felt I never had any," he said. It wasn't until Stanley was in his mid-twenties that he settled down, took stock of himself, and realized what being a man really meant.

Similarly, a daughter may decide, in the absence of a father to teach her differently, that the only way to relate to males is to have sex with them.

This vacuum in children's lives is often filled by a peer group that supplies overly rigid concepts of masculinity and femininity. The father-deprived child, whether from the ghetto or the richest suburb, is likely to be especially vulnerable to the values of his peer group. Other father-deprived children may become influential substitutes for the family in teaching the child about sex roles and society. In addition to having sex-role insecurity, the father-deprived child is apt to lack an appropriate model for controlling aggressive impulses, delaying gratification, and for self-discipline.

Preventing Delinquency. The major step in preventing delinquency in your children is to take realistic stock of yourself. Here are some questions you might ask yourself:

If you feel that you are a failure, do you take it out on your children by being harsh and punitive with them?

Do you drink too much and subsequently punish your children while intoxicated?

Do you see your children only to punish them, or do you frequently have fun with them and take them places? When was the last time you hugged your child and told him that you loved him?

Are you away from home a lot, and when at home, do you keep to your study or watch television without really seeing your children?

Do you know who their friends are?

Do they have set curfew hours?

Do you make fun of your son when he makes a mistake?

Are you extremely fearful that your daughter will have sexual relations on her dates? Do you punish her and restrict her activities when she comes in late no matter what the reason? Do you trust her?

Many fathers have only to look in the mirror to see the major factor in their children's delinquency.

The actual label that a child receives for his behavior may be rather arbitrary. Children who act out toward others are more likely to be labeled delinquent, while those who become anxious, depressed, and inhibited are more likely to be called neurotic.

In actuality, the delinquent as well as the neurotic child is likely to be emotionally disturbed. Many times one child is labeled as delinquent and another neurotic while both manifest the same behavior. In some cases there are different causes for seemingly similar problems; the major issue, however, should not be the label but whether or not the child and his family become aware of the problem and receive adequate professional help.

THE EMOTIONALLY DISTURBED CHILD

The impact of the father-child relationship on the development of psychological problems among children is incredibly complex. In this section we shall merely paint a broad-brush-stroke picture of how the father may be directly or indirectly contributing to the emotional disturbance of the child and, more important, how he can help his family cope with the problems of a disturbed child.

There are many behavior patterns that may indicate that a child is emotionally disturbed. A child who constantly withdraws from peer-group activities and is chronically fearful of others probably has a serious emotional problem. So does the child who doesn't like himself and is constantly self-abusive. In our discussion about delinquent behavior, we described the child who is destructive toward property and frequently hostile and malicious toward others. Such a pattern of behavior can also be a symptom of serious emotional disturbance.

On the other hand, you should not overreact to very limited "behavior problems." Just because your three-year-old sucks his thumb or your four-year-old wets his bed is not evidence of emotional disturbance. Your child's isolated behavior problem is likely to give way to more mature behavior if you and your wife treat him with love and respect. Thumb suckers, bed wetters, etc., sometimes develop more serious psychological problems as a result of the criticism and abuse they receive from insensitive parents.

Remember that the diagnosis of emotional disturbance, as with other child problems, can also be a very complicated process. Whether or not a child is properly diagnosed as emotionally disturbed is often dependent on whether his behavior is brought to the attention of a mental health professional.

A child's behavior may appear very aberrant but may actually be merely a short-term reaction to a more general family problem, and not a chronic problem at all. In some cases his behavior may be a symptom of a learning disability or even a dietary deficiency rather than the result of an emotional disorder. Also, as emphasized earlier, the child may have multiple handicaps; he may, for example, be retarded, delinquent, and emotionally disturbed.

Are You Responsible? Recognizing whether or not you have contributed to your child's emotional disturbance is not easy. Of course, if your child has serious emotional and social handicaps from birth, it is likely that his condition is largely congenital or the product of a very unstable prenatal environment, and there may be relatively little you can do. If your child's problem develops later in his life, there are a few guidelines that you can apply to help determine whether you are contributing to the disturbance.

Do you have any significant addictions? Do you drink, smoke, or eat to excess? This is often an indication of some kind of pressure on you that you are seeking to alleviate. Such a strain can affect your ability to relate to your child and thus your child's mental health.

Do you have any large problems with which you are preoccupied? Sexual problems, jealousy, or severe insecurity can be profound enough to disrupt your relationship with your child and damage his mental health.

Do you find yourself consistently telling a child not to do something that you frequently do yourself? There are cases in which the parent is extremely aggressive toward the child for being aggressive, or extremely derogatory toward the child for being insensitive. Such a tug-of-war between what you say and what you do can be quite damaging to your child's emotional stability.

In your relationship with the child, if you do not give him a sense of security and competence, if you denigrate him, are jealous of him, overly dominate him, overly restrict him, or neglect him, you are tempting mental illness.

If you deviate from a basic attitude of equality and respect for your wife, thereby reducing her mother power, you are also aiming your child toward serious psychological difficulties.

If you possess none of these damaging personal traits, are psychologically healthy, and are committed to being an involved father, then there is little chance that you have contributed significantly to mental illness in your child.

Fathers can foster emotional disturbance in their children in two general ways. If the father is himself emotionally disturbed, his child may mirror his behavior by imitating him. On the other hand, if the father is neglectful or absent, his child is more likely to have low self-esteem, be overdependent (usually on his mother), be immature, aggressive, or have other such problems. Because of father neglect, the child is significantly more likely to be vulnerable to mental illness as well as other personality disorders, such as chronic delinquency.

Of course, the father's behavior is only one possible factor in the development of emotional disturbance. The child may have a hereditary disorder or a constitutional vulnerability that may predispose him to mental illness, or he may be negatively influenced by his mother or by others around him, or there may be a combination of such factors.

But the father is especially important; because he is probably the most physically and psychologically imposing figure in a child's life, he is potentially the most dangerous to the child.

The Case of Hitler. Perhaps the best-known example of mental illness produced by an aberrant father-child relationship is that of Adolf Hitler. In *Mein Kampf* Hitler mentions his family background directly only a few times, and when he does, he tries to portray it as peaceful and quiet—his "father a faithful civil servant, the mother devoting herself to the cares of the household and looking after her children with eternally the same loving care."

Walter C. Langer, an American psychiatrist who wrote *The Mind of Adolf Hitler*, discerns a very different picture. He

presents strong evidence that the following quote in which
Hitler describes a drunken, fearsome, tyrannical father is in
actuality a description of Hitler's own father:

> Among the five children there is a boy, let us say, of
> three. . . . When the parents fight almost daily, their
> brutality leaves nothing to the imagination; then the
> results of such visual education must slowly, but inevi-
> tably become apparent to the little one. Those who are
> not familiar with such conditions can hardly imagine the
> results, especially when the mutual differences result in
> the form of brutal attacks on the part of the father
> toward the mother or to assaults due to drunkenness. The
> poor little boy, at the age of six, senses things which
> would make even a grown-up person shudder. . . . The
> other things the little fellow hears do not tend to further
> his respect for his surroundings. Not a single good shred is
> left for humanity, not a single institution is left unat-
> tacked; starting with the teacher, up to the head of the
> State, be it religion, or morality as such, be it the State or
> society, no matter which, everything is pulled down in
> the nastiest manner into the filth of a depraved mental-
> ity. . . .
>   I witnessed all of this personally in hundreds of scenes
> and at the beginning with both disgust and indignation.
>
> *Mein Kampf*
> by Adolf Hitler

Hitler's father is pictured as a domineering man, a tyrant in
his own home. Langer's sources allege that the father beat the
children unmercifully, on one occasion beating Adolf so
severely that he was left for dead. Langer also uncovered
evidence that the father would get so drunk that the children
would have to bring him home, whereupon he would beat his
wife, children, and dog indiscriminately.

All this is quite different from the public appearance
Hitler's father presented. An officious, condescending man, he

wore his customs official's uniform even after he had retired from duty and insisted that everyone call him by his full title, Herr Oberoffizial Hitler. At home he demanded to be addressed as the full title of Herr Vater, instead of the German version for "Dad."

Hitler's mother, however, is pictured as a hard-working, loving woman. She is described by those who knew her as conscientious, quiet, sweet, and affectionate. But because of the father's brutality, the mother-child bond became extremely close as Hitler's mother protected him from the father's brutality. Because of this, in addition to Hitler's frailness, the mother catered to him to the point of spoiling him. Undoubtedly, this too close mother-son attachment would not have occurred had Hitler's father been a loving, challenging parent.

As a result of this family relationship, Hitler became an extremely submissive young man, especially to representatives of authority. He was quite docile to his officers in the army, even going so far as to do their laundry. True to the practice drummed into him by his father, he insisted on calling them by their full titles, a practice he continued when addressing generals and fellow heads-of-state even after he became *"der Führer."* In his own deranged way, Hitler attempted to give Germany the father he himself had never had. What remarkable and pathetic parallels can be drawn between Hitler's own experiences with his father and his personality in later life.

Of course, a combination of Hitler's overintimate relationship with his mother, a genital abnormality he was found to have, and later experiences all contributed to his madness, but we can almost certainly assume that the father-child relationship was the primary catalyst to his mental illness.

The Legacy of Inadequate Fathering. Research linking father deprivation with emotional disturbance in the child is extensive. Father absence is a frequent contributor to mental illness. Not only is the incidence of emotional disturbance higher among father-absent boys and girls, but the earlier and the more prolonged the father absence, the more serious the mental illness is likely to be.

Fathers who are absent because of separation, divorce, or desertion generally have children who are worse off than those whose fathers have died. For instance, the findings from some studies suggest that among neurotic and psychotic patients the incidence of father absence due to divorce or separation is very high in childhood but that the incidence of father absence due to death is about average. Patients hospitalized for severe depression and attempted suicide also have an especially high rate of father absence in childhood. Teen-age suicides are often closely linked to feelings of worthlessness produced by an absent or neglecting father.

The fathers of emotionally disturbed children are frequently described as maladjusted themselves—either aggressive and hostile, or weak and timid. Such fathers are often excessively rigid and dogmatic, unable to empathize with the needs of their children.

Many alcoholics have a background of family disruption, parental neglect, and harsh punishment. A high proportion of alcoholics have been found to have fathers who were themselves alcoholics. In one study, half of the female alcoholics had fathers who, unless they were drunk, were dominated by their wives. Similarly, the family histories of drug addicts frequently reveal inadequate fathers who were alcoholics.

There is also evidence that addiction to gambling is likely to be associated with having had an uncaring, or overly demanding father. Many gambling addicts are seeking to overcome a father-induced sense of inadequacy and failure by trying to outdistance others in gambling and daring.

People with emotional disorders manifested in criminal behavior are likely to have been inadequately fathered. A study of murderers by Boston psychiatrist Shervert H. Frazier revealed that father absence or brutalization was frequent in the killers' backgrounds. Eighteen of the thirty-one murderers he studied had either suffered father absence for significant periods or had been the subject of repeated violence from the father. Many other histories of assassins and mass murderers suggest that they suffer similar backgrounds of father absence or abuse. Schizophrenic behavior in the killers' childhood or adolescence was apparent in some of the cases.

Researchers studying fathers of schizophrenics have discovered that many didn't fulfill the father role effectively. Many of these fathers had severe conflicts with their wives, often undercutting their authority and showing them little respect. They were often highly illogical and egocentric, overly seductive toward their daughters and hostile and aggressive toward their sons.

Other fathers of schizophrenics have been found to have delusions of paranoid grandiosity, thinking they were one of the "chosen few." They were domineering but at the same time had a basic lack of self-esteem and unsure masculinity. Still other fathers had failed so miserably in life that they were little more than pathetic figures in the home, usually treated with disdain by their wives.

Children Affect Their Parents. Obviously, there are many types of paternal inadequacy that can contribute to severe emotional problems among children. However, we must again emphasize the complexity of mental illness. Many schizophrenics, for example, particularly those with problems that surface during early childhood, may suffer from a biological vulnerability that often leads to distorted parent-child relationships as well as to their specific symptoms.

It is clear that you can contribute to mental illness in your children, though you are only one of many factors in the child's life. Various forms of mental illness can be primarily the result of biological, social, or psychological problems, and are often an outcome of the complex interaction of many factors.

The father-child relationship is a heavily traveled two-way street. In many cases we cannot be sure how much a child's mental illness is directly affected by the father or how much of the father's behavior is a reaction to a biologically predisposed problem in the child. It is clear, however, that you can do much to help the mentally disturbed child.

Coping with the Emotionally Disturbed Child. As we said in the introduction to this chapter, the father too often cops out of taking an active role in helping the family cope with a problem child. You, your wife, and your other children should try to make helping your emotionally disturbed child a family commitment.

The first and most absolute rule in dealing with an emotionally disturbed child is not to ignore his problem. A contemporary example of such a head-in-the-sand approach is the parents who try to overlook a drug problem in their offspring, purposely ignoring obvious symptoms, hoping the problem will go away by itself. If your child is having problems with his peers, his schoolwork, or other facets of his life, actively help him grapple with them. Listen to what others say about your child; they may see aspects of which you are unaware. Don't be afraid to seek professional help as soon as you believe you recognize a problem. Too often children's problems aren't diagnosed until after they enter school, resulting in a loss of valuable time.

You can also take an active role in seeking treatment for your child and in assuring that the treatment is of the proper kind. Beware of treatment that does not include the whole family. A mentally ill child is a problem not only for himself but for those around him. Thus, the whole family must understand his problem and cope with it.

Don't fall into the trap of believing that you can put the child into therapy and thus solve your whole problem. Therapy is only a means to help the family begin working together to help the child. Recognizing your father power means recognizing that you can be effective in helping your child.

Most of the time the best place for an emotionally disturbed child is with his family. However, for some severely disturbed children, a specialized institution may be the only realistic alternative. Such a decision is extremely complex and should be made only after all other alternatives have been carefully explored. In many cases, it is better for the family as well as the child to move to a community where the child can receive adequate outpatient treatment than to send the problem child away from home.

Sometimes the most important thing you can do for an emotionally disturbed child is to stand by him, giving him the support and love he needs to pull himself together.

16 / Social Crisis and Social Fatherhood

So far we've concentrated on the father-child relationship in defining father power. We have discussed how fathers affect their children and vice versa, and we have given some guidelines to help fathers use their father power effectively.

But father power is a force not only in the family; it very much affects and is affected by society as a whole. In this chapter we shall discuss how father power and society intertwine.

FATHER TODAY—THE INVISIBLE MAN

The decline in the arbitrary power of father in the home began with the social reforms that swept our society during the early part of this century. With the growth of women's rights, the rise of trade unions, and other democratic developments, mothers and children began to demand democracy in the family too. They began to declare that the father should no longer have the right to inalterably determine their lives as he had done in the past. And they were right. In past Western societies, from the Romans all the way up to the American Puritans, the father had been an absolute ruler, almost purely because of his greater size, aggressiveness, and strength. In some societies he had the right to freely kill his sons and daughters; in most he had a considerable say in how they conducted their lives.

But in denying this tyrannical power, our society went too far. We wrongly adopted the belief that, except for being the family oppressor, the father actually had very little to do with his children. It is one thing to deny paternalism; it is quite another to deny fatherhood.

Technological Change. Yet while fathers and families now react against stifling views of punitive, autocratic fathers, they are left without a view of effective fatherhood. And besides lacking confidence that fatherhood is important, fathers also are often the victims of the very technology they helped create.

In the early days of our country, the father's home chores—chopping wood, plowing, building a smokehouse, or raising livestock—were major undertakings that contributed to the welfare of the family. All his important tasks were done at home where the children could watch, and where they could learn not only about needed skills, but also about their father as a man.

Modern technology changed all this. If you are an average father, you can't hope to repair everything that goes wrong in your house—a balky furnace, a television on the blink, a transmission problem in the car, a clogged water line, or a broken washing machine. The expert repairman is a must for such tasks. While modern conveniences have certainly made things easier for all of us, they have robbed your home chores of the aura they used to have, at least in your own eyes. Many fathers hold the belief that what they do at home is unimportant to their children.

To be effective adult models for their children, both fathers and mothers should be able to show their children what they are like at their jobs. But with the Industrial Revolution came the rise of the factories and offices. Fathers had to go away from home every day alone, all day, to work. After child-labor laws were instituted, unlike the farm or the artisan's shop, the factory and the office became no-children's lands.

As Father became a wage earner instead of being a self-employed artisan, families became used to measuring things in terms of dollars and cents, because the size of the family paycheck determined how well off they were. The

American father came to believe that if he neglected his job, it would show up in his bank account, where it counted, but neglect of his children wouldn't show up anywhere because it was not quantifiable. However, it did show up—on the ledger books of children's lives.

The final blow to the father's pride in his worth came with the passage of compulsory child-education laws. No longer did the father teach his offspring the family trade or even skills needed to get along in the world. The child learned a trade in school or went off to make his way.

Formal education has continued to grow in importance in our lives until, today, it is a child's major source of information and training. Education in social responsibility, such as sex education, has also assumed a place of prominence. Though such education is good for children, it has made parents, especially fathers, unsure of themselves, wrongly feeling they are unneeded as child educators.

Work and Leisure. The American father today is going through a difficult period of change in relating to his work. With the work ethic on one side and the lure of increasing leisure and wages on the other, fathers are having difficulty striking a balance, with some working incredibly long hours and others reducing their work load as much as possible. A father's children, ironically, often lose either way, for the father who has not become wrapped up in his work in many cases has become wrapped up in his own play.

Modern technology has also made it possible for people in families to spend more time away from one another. Our relatively convenient, high-speed transportation system has the effect most often of transporting family members away from one another. It enables you to live farther from work conveniently, and thus tempts you to spend more hours commuting in your comfortable, private car.

Modern transportation has, in effect, widened the gulf between your own and your child's ability to get around. While in earlier times children could walk to see Daddy at work, today many children are trapped in fatherless suburbs, while Daddy goes off to the inaccessible city to work.

Modern transportation has also caused a decline in the sense of community in our society. Families may have friends at the other end of the city and be strangers to the neighbors next door. They are more likely to live farther away from grandparents, uncles, aunts, and other relatives.

Because you can pick up a telephone and call your relatives or fly out to see them, you still feel a sense of continuing intimacy with them. "Telephoning is the next best thing to being there," goes one commercial for long-distance telephoning. However, this is deceptive, because physical distance still poses a barrier to communication within families. While parents can assuage their conscience about keeping in touch with relatives, they do not have to worry about the relatives dropping in and discovering a family problem. The father in today's isolated family does not feel nearly as strong a sense of accountability for his children. After all, he feels, if they get into trouble they are far removed from relatives who would censure the father for his children's behavior.

Modern man's mania for movement and modern transportation makes it easier for families to change communities. One in five of American families moves every year, usually because of the father's job. Though children learn much more about the world they live in by moving about, too-frequent moves lessen a family's sense of community and thus the father's sense of social responsibility.

Unlike our transportation system, television, another prominent technological wonder of our time, sometimes encourages family togetherness but of the worst kind. Television-togetherness is a zombielike state, with each family member caught up in his own communion with the electronic window-on-the-world. A recent sociological survey revealed that the most frequent argument in today's families is not over morals or politics, but over which television program to watch.

In many ways television has become this nation's new father figure, benignly and authoritatively presenting news, entertainment, and its own prime-time theory of the universe. The family dinner, which used to feature parents holding forth on the issues of the day, has been replaced in many families by the TV-tray supper, with a network commentator providing one-sided conversation.

If home chores or family discussions have ceased to be arenas for fathers and children to get to know one another, how about home recreation? Unfortunately, because of the father's lack of confidence in or preparation for his important role, fathers and children in our society seldom get to play together either.

Most suburban fathers say that their weekend activities are child centered. At first glance, these fathers appear to be quite devoted, but just what are those "child-centered" activities? They include chauffeuring their children to football or hockey practice, music or tennis lessons, going with them to track meets, snowmobiling, bicycle fixing, Boy Scout activities, and taking family trips. In short, these fathers often do things for their children, and do things in their company, but *seldom* directly interact with them. The activities are almost always of the kind that draw the fathers' and children's attention away from one another. Their children have become immersed in a whirl of activities without a chance to simply have a quiet talk or enjoy a one-to-one activity with their fathers.

It isn't surprising that the father today feels so trapped by responsibility that he all but runs screaming from the house to play golf or tennis on Sunday, getting his true enjoyment by *not* being with his children—not because he doesn't love them, but because he is so uncertain of *how to father them.*

Of course, many modern technological advances can also free you to spend more time with your family and to develop into a more effective father. As we have stressed, *the overall quality of your relationship with your child is more important than the specific activities that you do together.* We hope that the guidelines we have presented in previous chapters will help you to demonstrate your father power.

FATHER AND THE SOCIAL SCIENTIST

The social scientist, with his research and theories, is supposed to be a sort of Paul Revere, awakening us to the possible "redcoats" of social problems in our midst. Unfortunately, many of our social scientists have been color-blinded against the father by their own biases and those of our society. Less than 10 percent of the scientific studies of parents have taken the father's role into account, in spite of the fact that half of all parents are fathers.

Why the Father Is Left Out. One reason for this difference in the amount of research on fathers and on mothers is that social scientists are human like everybody else. They see the mother's close physiological attachment to the child, the way she gives birth, feeds, and cares for the child, and they reason that she must be the primary parent. They may ignore the fact that the period during which a child is physically dependent on the mother is very short in contrast to the time he is learning the many other things he needs to be a successful adult. They may also ignore the fact that infants are not even really dependent on the mother as such, but on her food supply, nurturance, and stimulation. A father with a bottle, properly motivated, could be an excellent "mother" as far as survival is concerned.

The social scientist may also be unconsciously affected by all the warm, tender feelings our society has woven about mothers, from the Virgin Mary to Mother Goose. Certainly descriptions of the harsh, tyrannical fathers in Western history can generate no such warmth.

Also, since the modern father's role during the last half century or so has been principally that of the breadwinner, there is a strong temptation to define him solely in those terms. Thus, Daddy goes out and makes money and Mommy stays home and takes care of the children.

There are also very practical reasons why fatherhood has not been studied as extensively as it should be. One reason is that the father is difficult for the researcher to contact and interview, for he is at work—away from his family both physically and mentally. Since mothers are more often at home, readily available and deeply immersed in raising the children, the social scientist interviews her, not the father, in his research, often even to the point of only asking her what role her husband plays in the family. When he is reached for comment, the father may not really have much to say about himself. Without any background on how important he is, he may never have given much thought to the fact that he is a father.

Ironically, the relative lack of research on the father also stems from the fact that in our male-dominated society, most social researchers are men. While they may be interested in traditionally male roles, such as worker, educator, or criminal, male researchers may be unconsciously embarrassed at examining what can seem to be a secondary male role—fatherhood.

The male social scientist is also a professional career man, which may further bias him against fatherhood. Hard at work on a career studying human behavior, he may be away from home a great deal himself and lose close touch with his own family. In a similar way, many clinicians neglect the role of fatherhood in the development of their patients' psychological problems.

All these forces separating the social researcher from the father can create a vicious circle of research and theory. When a microphone is brought too close to its loudspeaker, the sound begins to circulate round and round from speaker to microphone until the familiar squeal of feedback is heard. Similarly, primary research showing that the mother is important then generates more research showing that she is important. From this research come theories on the family showing that the mother is important, resulting in more research on the mother. Dizzying, no?

The results of ignoring the father and his role lead to some glaring misconceptions on the part of researchers. For instance, social scientists often refer to nurturant behavior toward the child as "maternal," though it should be considered a natural quality of both sexes.

FATHER AND THE MEDIA

Another profound impact of society on the father in this country comes as a result of the way he is usually treated in the mass media, because television, radio, and the press are so prominent in our lives. It is easy and tempting to criticize the media's belittling of the father if you don't stop to think that media only reflect the popular view of him. But they are powerful reinforcers of these views, for they pass on and lend credibility to them.

Part of your education as a father must be to learn how to react to the fallacies about fatherhood presented on television, radio, and in the press. These can adversely affect your sense of father power.

The TV Father. Of the various media, television has probably had the greatest effect on popular views of the family. The overwhelming majority of programs present nothing more than a superficial cartoon view of family life, created to attract viewers, not to portray reality. Television news, by its visual nature, seeks stories that are dramatic and colorful. As profound a problem as father abuse is, it stands relatively little chance of being explored by a television commentator, because it is not a "hot" news item.

Everybody has heard the standard complaint that the father is usually portrayed as a dope or a poor sucker in TV situation comedies. Being put in one of those categories is an obvious trap for real-life fathers to avoid.

Also, seldom is an ambitious or hard-driving man ever portrayed as a warm, successful father. Involved fatherhood and high career goals are not incompatible in real life, but television shows it that way. Surgeons, tycoons, and other television heroes are almost never shown as parents, much less involved ones. In fact, most programs that show the materially successful man interacting with his offspring concentrate only on how bad a father he has been. The story line of such a program usually concerns either his daughter's and son's rejection of such a father, or the young coping with problems he has caused. And who should appear to set things straight but the kindly nonfather—your friendly neighborhood doctor, lawyer, cowboy, policeman, or detective. Such dramas seem to say that dynamic, successful, warm men are not capable of becoming good fathers.

Adventure heroes are never shown as involved fathers, because as with other ambitious characters portrayed on television, cowboys or policemen should have a romantic aura about them, the producers feel. Since "everybody" knows fathers are schnooks, the hero thus can't be shown as a father because that wouldn't be romantic. Occasionally, attempts are made to "fatherize" heroes, but they are usually half-hearted and represent attempts to use the family as a prop for more exciting adventure. As one star of a police adventure series put it, "They gave me this wife for awhile, and then they cut her out. There I was in the squad car talking about this wife and child, and they never showed them. It got to be a real drag." Another incredible example of this was an episode on the long-running western "Bonanza." In a special two-hour feature, the first episode of a TV season, Michael Landon met a girl, got married, and the girl got pregnant. Before the episode was over, the wife died in a fire. Obviously, the producers of the show were afraid to marry off this tough cowboy—afraid of what it would do to Landon's image.

The true-life father is engaged in a constant juggling act to allot his time fairly among his family, his career, his civic duty, and his recreation. Many times all these things interact with one another. Very few television programs have ever accurately portrayed that juggling act.

It is ironic that some of the warmest, most involved adult males a child may see are on television. While the real father is away from his children at work, such father figures as Captain Kangaroo, the genial children's-show host, are teaching children, entertaining them, and being an accepting male model for children. (Do you remember the science experiments patiently demonstrated to children by Don Herbert in the title role of the 1950s television show "Watch Mr. Wizard"?)

The Printed Media. Narrow definitions of adult rules have also affected writing about the father in the printed media. Newspaper articles on parenthood are usually relegated to the women's page. Similarly, in magazines, articles on parenthood are usually only found in traditional women's periodicals. This discrimination by newspapers and magazines stems from editors' beliefs that if they alter traditional editorial guidelines on article content or placement their audience count for any special group will suffer, and thus advertising revenues will suffer.

Books and magazines that do purport to aim at "parents" fall prey to the same economic trap. Reflecting the popular notion in our society that the only persons interested in parenthood are mothers, they are essentially mothers' publications.

The most prominent of these, *Parents' Magazine*, greatly emphasizes the female parent. Besides articles on childraising, the magazine features beauty tips, articles on pregnancy, and women's fashions. When the father is portrayed, it is as a peripheral parent—he takes over child care "occasionally" or "gets a chance" to hold the baby. Articles on problems peculiar to the father are almost nonexistent.

The photographs illustrating advertisements and articles clearly emphasize the mother. She is either the center of action or attention, with the father looking on; or the father is absent altogether, leaving her the entire stage. In addition to the expected advertisements for children's hygiene products, the magazine is peppered with ads featuring feminine-oriented hygiene products, feminine deodorants, birth-control devices, and figure-improvement devices. The children's-product advertisements that show parents almost always feature the mother, usually without the father.

Parents' Magazine does run occasional articles featuring the father, but their examples are relatively unusual ones—a divorced father who is raising his children alone or a father who has swapped roles with the mother. The magazine's editorial stand seems to be that "normally" only the mother is an involved parent.

The magazine is so female-oriented that an advertisement for athletic supporters would be an almost shocking departure from the view of the parent as feminine that the magazine emphasizes.

To a father interested in reading about how to help his

children, "family" magazines produce an almost palpable air that he is neither needed nor wanted in the province of childraising. As a father, you must recognize that interest in and deep involvement with your children are legitimate masculine occupations and are best for your child's development, such magazines notwithstanding.

Magazines like this, as well as other areas of journalism, are caught in an almost unbreakable journalistic circle. Because childraising is thought to be a province of the mother and a feminine preoccupation, articles about childraising are almost always written with the women's point of view in mind, and this point of view is perpetuated by the journalists themselves.

Why don't male journalists write sensitively and often about fatherhood? Previously we mentioned how the social scientist's personal life-style can affect his work. This is also true of journalists, both print and electronic. The journalist, too, can become immersed in his career at the expense of his family. He can find himself a holder of a job in the city, with his family isolated in a far-away suburb. Fortunately, there have been recent indications that both the mass media and the scientific community are beginning to give more attention to the father's role. Such support for the father's potential impact is vital to the development of what we call "social fatherhood."

SOCIAL FATHERHOOD

In the first chapter we hinted at our theory of a concept of "social fatherhood"—the feeling by adult family men (the "establishment," used in a positive sense) that they have a responsibility to see to society's proper functioning. This social fathering manifests itself in ways as diverse as leading a Boy Scout troop, apprehending a purse snatcher, or perhaps demanding corporate social responsibility from one's employer.

At the beginning of the present chapter, we outlined the problems of the father in today's society, pointing out the frequent lack of recognition of fatherhood as an important role for men. In earlier chapters we discussed the effects fathers have on their children's social development, which also indirectly affects the quality of a society. Now we shall draw this link between father and society more in terms of our own society and of how father power can be used to its benefit.

It would be presumptuous of us to heap all of today's social problems—crime, environmental problems, moral laxity, urban decay—upon the lack of social fatherhood. It would also be presumptuous to say that the lack of efficacy men feel today is all due to their estrangement from the family. And, of course, social fatherhood is partially a basis for a male's personal ability to father as well as a result of his success at fathering.

We believe, though, that a significant portion of our social problems stems from the fact that males do not feel a confident sense of power over their environment. This feeling of powerlessness in turn stems in large part from their feeling of a lack of consequence in the society's basic institution—the family. Conversely, many of society's difficulties are due partly to the problem children who tend to be produced by father-neglected families.

The father-society link, we insist, is a strong one. An adult male's attitude toward society originates to a large degree from his role as a father—besides his previous role as a child. Not until he becomes a father do many employers, insurance companies, etc., assume that a man is a fully responsible member of society; although sometimes unfair, this judgment has a component of truth to it.

Concern for the Future. In growing into fatherhood, a man learns the true meaning of nurturance and gains a confidence that he can have a deep effect on others—adults as well as children. After gaining this confidence and the necessary skills from interacting with his children, the adult male tends to apply them to his dealings with his environment, his neighborhood, his city, his nation, and his world.

Social fatherhood also has a purely selfish component in that the man sees his environment as being the same one his children have to live in. "I was really shocked by the crime;

I've got kids myself, you know!" is a typical comment from a father upon hearing of some misdeed. We've all heard of a male who does a good deed for some child, saying, "I'm a father myself, and I know what I'd want somebody to do for my kid."

Fatherhood projects a man's mind into the future more profoundly and more personally than does any other role. The effects twenty or fifty years from now of what a man does are purely abstract and impersonal to him, except when he considers his actions as affecting the future lives of his children and grandchildren.

Indeed, historians have noted that for the first 150 years of our country's existence we were a very posterity-minded people. Our duty to our forebears and our descendents was very much a part of our lives. Today we have lost the sense that we have inherited our world from previous generations to improve and bequeath it to generations to come. We strip-mine the land and flush enormous amounts of waste into lakes, rivers, and oceans. We have destroyed more land, water, flora, and fauna in the last fifty years than previous generations did in a thousand. We have used more energy resources more profligately than any generation before us.

Keep in mind that you teach your daughter or son not only how to be an involved family member, but also how to be an involved social member. You show her or him that it is a proper and important role for a parent, whether male or female, to help society function.

Personal Meaning. There do exist other major sources of training for social fatherhood besides actually being a father, but they are generally much weaker in their psychological impact. Many men have resorted to these secondary sources for their feeling of social fatherhood, sources including aiding business and social protégés or performing social or charitable works.

None of these outlets usually gives a male a chance to feel as profound a sense of responsibility toward and importance to another human being as fatherhood does. They usually do not offer the same continuity of personal meaning. Male physicians, teachers, and clergymen certainly affect their constituents and feel a sense of importance in relation to them. Nevertheless, their involvement with patients, students, or congregation members is more likely to be episodic. It typically doesn't extend over a period of decades or involve as much intimate daily contact as fatherhood can.

A man's role in his family closely parallels his role in society; skills learned in one can apply to the other. Society is a delicate system, often requiring a sensitive blend of protection, nurturance, and challenge by the social father; just so are children to the family father. Unless a strong sense of social fatherhood, founded on a strong sense of family fatherhood, is encouraged in society, we shall continue to suffer from a lack of social involvement, a lack of public morality, and a plenitude of frustration.

We advocate father power. We think it can be done without the chauvinism—social, sexual, and political—that constituted the paternalism of the past.

Although earlier in this section we said that a firm basis for social fatherhood could not be founded simply on career aspirations, protégé cultivation, or social involvement, all these things can be extremely important outlets for social fatherhood.

In colonial days, the importance of personal contact between skilled men and their protégés was recognized in the institution of the apprenticeship. Today scientists who must pass on the complex and delicate talent of scientific inquiry, use a system in which protégés work closely with master scientists. But the system of one-to-one teaching has languished elsewhere, partially because of the lack of emphasis on the ability of males to personally influence and teach younger males and females. Rather, today many young people are taught in enormous megaversities where they may not even know what their social father, the professor, looks like up close.

Clearly, social fatherhood (and social motherhood) must be emphasized, not only in colleges but everywhere else in society where adult males have knowledge to impart and a role model to represent. This is over and above the bequeathing of confidence in father power from father to son.

Opportunities Outside the Family. While social fatherhood should be thought of as a male's feeling of effectiveness in society in general, there are particular opportunities for men to help children outside their own family.

In Chapter 11, "Father, School, and Education," we pointed out how the father could add a masculine touch to educational facilities. This is also true for community organizations that deal with children. The Big Brothers and other organizations that seek to give fatherless children surrogate fathers can be excellent outlets for social fatherhood. Social fathers are also needed to do volunteer work with children in schools, community centers, and charitable organizations. We particularly need to give men more of a chance to get involved with young children and infants as well as with older children and adolescents. As we have stressed in many parts of this book, men can have a strong impact on a child's development even in the first year of life.

The most well-known outlets for community social fatherhood today are in scouting and in sports organizations, such as the Little League. No doubt many men have done much good in these organizations, but these groups generally sadly lack the prerequisites for social fatherhood. In scouting, the Little League, and other sports groups, the emphasis is heavily on goal-oriented activities. Scouts are urged constantly to work for higher ranks, and young athletes, to win on the playing field. This would normally be commendable, except that the men running these organizations frequently neglect the intimate personal guidance they should be affording their charges.

This neglect isn't necessarily their fault. They have not been taught the importance of fatherhood as a personal role and thus do not see its importance as a social role. The result is that they do what they know how to do best and what they have always been taught is the masculine role—organizing. For example, while den mothers work directly with cub scouts in dens, men are usually the cubmasters, spending their time attending committee meetings or running pack meetings. And when they are involved with the cubs in the den, they are den dads, whose duties are to be an adjunct to the den mother, not usually a full-fledged partner. When a child enters boy scouting, he often encounters the organizing, rather impersonal scoutmaster.

In girl scouting the situation is even worse. Women are practically the only adults a girl sees in these organizations. They work directly with the girls, organize the troop, and administer the organization. If men feel that it is unmasculine to be true social fathers to boys in scouting, they seem to be positively horrified at social-fathering girls.

Correspondingly, in the Little League, the only times a child usually has contact with the team coaches are on the field during practice and during games. Seldom do they get to see the coach as a human being, only as a manager, manipulating the team to win games.

These criticisms are not meant to minimize the excellent work scouting and similar groups have done in teaching social skills and in promoting intellectual and athletic achievement. We are aware also that these groups allow for some social-fathering. For instance, older boy scouts become den chiefs to groups of cub scouts—an excellent means of teaching fathering, which should be encouraged and emphasized. But all this does not go deeply enough into the society.

An increase in the amount of social-fathering is much needed to help children in their personal lives, as well as in achieving specific organizational goals. We don't expect social fathers to have a close relationship with every boy or girl in an organization. Nor do we expect them to compete with the primary father-child relationship. But social fathers can give children personal experiences with other men besides their fathers, thus widening the children's experiences. They can also effectively immunize a community against father neglect, helping those children who suffer emotionally, socially, or intellectually from the lack of a father or from a damaging father-child relationship. Both Henry and Dennis sometimes extend themselves to children whom they know have absent fathers or fathers who are away from their families for long periods of time. They make it a point to talk to the children, find out how they are doing, and to show an interest in their lives.

Teaching Fatherhood. Your sense of father power should include a sense of effectiveness in teaching your own sons to be good fathers and in teaching your daughters to value fatherhood as they do motherhood.

For the father, who tends to get the biggest kick out of seeing his children function happily in the world, there can be no greater happiness than seeing them become good parents themselves.

By being an involved, loving father you have already given your daughter a sound valuation of both men and fathers. The basis for helping your son become a good father is also already established if you have been involved with him. Your son will probably have confidence in his masculinity. Thus, he will not suffer sexual problems during his wife's pregnancy or jealousy of the baby upon becoming a father. He will know that nurturance is perfectly masculine and is very important to a child, because he will remember his own childhood and father, the way you did when you became a father. He will also have confidence in his role as a challenger of the child.

Children, both boys and girls, are born with a predisposition to nurture, and they will have a good start as parents if they do not have their nurturing qualities drummed out of them. We have seen countless instances of little boys giving sympathy, comfort, and aid and being tender to other children who are hurt or crying. Unfortunately, many of these same little boys who dried tears or held hands when young were taught later that such tenderness is "sissy stuff." Like their fathers toward them, they have become tough, unyielding fathers toward their own children. Don't drum this important quality of fatherhood out of your sons.

You can also do a good deal of direct training for fatherhood with your son. Encourage him to baby-sit for extra money. If he is in the Boy Scouts, encourage him to become a den chief to a group of cub scouts. Help him to become involved with younger children; a good way to do this is to bring him in as your assistant if you are involved in youngster-oriented civic activities.

When your son shows fatherliness toward another child, encourage him to analyze how he helped the child and what an important thing it could be for the child. Support your son if other, less confidently masculine, less nurturant boys taunt him for his fatherliness.

Tell your child outright the importance of fatherhood and how much you value the role in your own life. All this training may not be evident at first, but as with most of the examples you present to your child, sooner or later the lessons you give will show themselves.

Your involvement will be rewarded one day when you find yourself the grandfather of a happy, healthy grandson or granddaughter with an involved father—a father who knows he can be aggressive and assertive and tender and nurturant and feel that all these traits are a natural part of his personality.

Politics and Father Power. Psychologists and political scientists have often commented on the tendency of citizens to perceive their male leaders as father figures. The reverse is also true—male-elected officials tend to look upon their constituents or at least the society they help govern as their "social children."

Our leaders' sense of social fatherhood (or motherhood, in the case of females) can be a major driving force leading them to seek political office. And, of course, like biological fatherhood, the reasons for social fatherhood can include not only the desire to help another human being but also a healthy helping of ego gratification.

This role of social fatherhood in political aspirations can be a valuable tool to help voters decide on the best candidate. A father's children, to some extent, represent a mini-society to him, which it is his duty to aid and foster. A politician's attitudes toward his children and toward his constituents may have many similarities.

Thus, to gain clues as to whether a politician will be

paternalistic, restrictive, avuncular, or democratic—to taste the basic flavor of what political life may be like under his aegis—take a close look at his children. What kinds of personalities do they have? Are they independent? overconforming? analytical? compulsive? Certainly, a father's effect is only one factor in a child's upbringing. And just as certainly, there are politicians otherwise perfectly capable who simply cannot relate to children. Nevertheless, analyzing a candidate's fatherhood may offer a valuable clue to his personality.

Journalists could contribute a great deal to public understanding of a candidate by not only analyzing his stand on the issues but by also exploring the personalities of his children and their relationship with their father. If used judiciously, getting to know the candidate's children through media interviews and self-written articles by the offspring would seem to be a more painless way of at least beginning to learn what makes a candidate tick.

The late President John F. Kennedy is an excellent example of the relationship between family fatherhood and social fatherhood. Himself the product of a loving, challenging father, John F. Kennedy was such a father to his own children. Major General Chester V. Clifton and Cecil Stoughton, both of President Kennedy's staff, with journalist Hugh Sidey, recalled the President as a father in their book *The Memories: JFK 1961–1963*:

> It was of constant fascination to watch the President with his children. There was no baby talk. The conversations, while fanciful and concerned with the fundamentals of a child's life, were always adult in tone and outlook. . . . While the children were watched closely and supervised critically, they were not waited on or coddled beyond infancy. They were lavished with affection and love, but in adult language and reason. . . .
>
> The President of the United States on more than one occasion was a babysitter. . . . More than once when Jackie was gone, the President had a lunchtime rendezvous with his children. It was then his job to see that they

were behaving properly, to make certain they were well, to provide them with whatever parental guidance seemed appropriate.

From this feeling of success at fatherhood and, of course, from his own upbringing, John F. Kennedy drew his feeling of social fatherhood. His term in office was marked by regard for his constituents as well as challenge—perhaps best summarized by his famous quote, "Ask not what your country can do for you; ask what you can do for your country."

The Future of Father and the Family. In our society, the one major form of the family will probably always be the essentially nuclear-family structure. The basic man-woman-child family offers some advantages that will probably never be equaled by communes or any other family form, regardless of what social utopians say.

The nuclear family offers privacy in an increasingly crowded world. Nowhere else can the individual come closer to having his life completely to his own taste, to maximizing his individual choice. Because people tend to marry those like them in tastes and aspirations, ideally, each person in a marriage has a congenial partner.

The nuclear family offers each parent and each child intimate, involved, personal contact with other people. The child will receive a small but solid base of support from the other members of the family, because he is theirs and they are his. Although divorce certainly damages a great many families, the general concept of the nuclear family remains viable.

The nuclear family offers parents the feeling of effectiveness in aiding their children. We said before that parenthood is partially a means to an ego gratification. But that is not necessarily bad, for it means that the parent will be deeply involved with his offspring for his own reasons. And, as we said in the section on social fatherhood, a firm feeling of father or mother power means a confidence in dealing with people in the outside world. For most of us, these advantages could not be equaled in communes. Individuals, regardless of how committed they are to a group, have their own ideas of how they want to live and raise their children.

But even though the nuclear family will continue, the lessons of the commune should not be lost on the American family. Father should not be expected to be the lone, isolated source of male psychological support in the family. Children should not be brought up in rows of houses where nobody knows or cares about their neighbors. Nor should a child deprived of his own father or mother be deprived of fathering or mothering in general.

Thus, we do not advocate communes, but we do advocate *communities,* complete with a firm sense of social-fathering and -mothering. Reestablishing the community of families might involve measures as diverse as a larger involvement in community social-fathering, as discussed earlier, or even the revival of the old architectural concept of houses grouped around a town square. It would mean increasing the availability of block clubs, civic groups, and special interest groups, and breaking society into geographical subgroups to which the individual family can relate as a unit.

But above all, it would mean encouraging men to become aware that they have the power as fathers and as social fathers to keep the bonds between family and society strong.

References and
Suggestions for Further Reading

Chapter 1: Introducing the Father

Biller, H. B. *Father, Child and Sex Role.* Lexington, Mass.: Lexington Books,
D. C. Heath, 1971 (Paperback edition, 1973).

Biller, H. B. *Paternal Deprivation.* Lexington, Mass.: Lexington Books, D. C.
Heath, 1974.

Biller, H. B., and Meredith, D. L. "The Invisible American Father," *Sexual
Behavior* 2 (1972): 16–22.

Jolly, A. *The Evolution of Primate Behavior.* New York: Macmillan, 1972.

La Barre, W. *The Human Animal.* Chicago: University of Chicago Press, 1954.

Lynn, D. B. *The Father: His Role in Child Development.* Monterey, Calif.:
Brooks/Cole, 1974.

Mitchell, G.; Redican, W. K.; and Gomber, J. "Males Can Raise Babies,"
Psychology Today 7 (1974): 63–68.

Nash, J. "The Father in Contemporary Culture and Current Psychological
Literature," *Child Development* 36 (1965): 261–297.

Stephens, W. N. *The Family in Cross-Cultural Perspective.* New York: Holt,
Rinehart and Winston, 1963.

Chapter 2: Preparing for Fatherhood

Arnstein, H. "The Crisis of Becoming a Father," *Sexual Behavior* 2 (1972):
42–48.

Benning, L. E. *How to Bring Up a Child Without Spending a Fortune.* New York:
David McKay, 1974.

Benson, L. *Fatherhood: A Sociological Perspective.* New York: Random House,
1968.

Biller, H. B. "Include the Father in Pregnancy (Invited Commentary),"
Sexual Behavior 2 (1972): 47.

Biller, H. B., and Meredith, D. L. "The Invisible American Father," *Sexual
Behavior* 2 (1972): 16–22.

Bradley, R. A. *Husband-Coached Childbirth.* New York: Harper and Row,
1965.

LeMasters, E. E. *Parents in Modern America: A Sociological Analysis.* Homewood,
Ill.: Dorsey, 1970.

Liebenberg, B. "Expectant Fathers," *American Journal of Orthopsychiatry* 37 (1967): 358–359.

Peck, E. *The Baby Trap.* New York: Bernard Geis, 1971.

Salk, L. *Preparing for Parenthood.* New York: David McKay, 1974.

Schaefer, G. *The Expectant Father.* New York: Barnes and Noble, 1972.

Chapter 3: Father and the Newborn

Biller, H. B. "The Father's Role," *The London Sunday Times Magazine*, 25 February 1973, pp. 48–50.

Kagan, J. *Change and Continuity in Infancy.* New York: Wiley, 1971.

Mussen, P. H.; Conger, J. J.; and Kagan, J. *Child Development and Personality.* New York: Harper and Row, 1974.

Pedersen, F. A. and Robson, K. S. "Father Participation in Infancy," *American Journal of Orthopsychiatry* 39 (1969): 466–472.

Salk, L. *What Every Child Would Like His Parents To Know.* New York: David McKay, 1972.

Smart, M. S., and Smart, R. C. *Children: Development and Relationships.* New York: Macmillan, 1972.

Spelke, E.; Zelazo, P.; Kagan, J.; and Kotelchuck, M. "Father Interaction and Separation Protest," *Developmental Psychology* 9 (1973): 83–90.

Spock, B. *Baby and Child Care.* New York: Pocket Books, 1970.

Chapter 4: Father Power, Mother Power

Bernard, J. *The Future of Marriage.* New York: Bantam Books, 1972.

Biller, H. B. "Father Absence, Maternal Encouragement, and Sex-Role Development in Kindergarten-age Boys," *Child Development* 40 (1969): 539–546. Reprinted in *Readings in Child Development and Relationships*, edited by R. C. Smart and M. S. Smart, pp. 239–254. New York: Macmillan, 1972.

Biller, H. B. "Father Dominance and Sex-Role Development in Kindergarten-age Boys," *Developmental Psychology* 7 (1969): 87–94. Reprinted in slightly abridged form in *Personality and Socialization*, edited by D. R. Heise, pp. 73–85. New York: Rand McNally, 1972.

Biller, H. B. "Maternal Salience and Feminine Development in Young Girls," *Proceedings of the 77th Annual Convention of the American Psychological Association* 4 (1969): 259–260.

Biller, H. B. "The Mother-Child Relationship and the Father-absent Boy's Personality Development," *Merrill-Palmer Quarterly* 17 (1971): 227–241. Reprinted in slightly abridged form in *Influences on Human Development*, edited by U. Bronfenbrenner, pp. 306–319. Hindsdale, Ill.: Dryden, 1972.

Blood, R. O., Jr., and Wolfe, D. M. *Husbands and Wives.* New York: Free Press, 1965.

Brothers, J. *The Brothers' System for a Liberated Love and Marriage.* New York: Peter Wyden, 1973.

Hetherington, E. M., and Frankie, G. "Effects of Parental Dominance,

Warmth, and Conflict on Imitation in Children," *Journal of Personality and Social Psychology* 6 (1967): 119–125.

Hoffman, L. W. "Effects of Maternal Employment on the Child—A Review of Research," *Developmental Psychology* 10 (1974): 204–228.

McBride, A. B. *The Growth and Development of Mothers.* New York: Harper and Row, 1973.

O'Neill, N., and O'Neill, G. *Open Marriage.* New York: Avon, 1973.

Chapter 5: Father, Masculinity, and Femininity

Biller, H. B. "A Multiaspect Investigation of Masculine Development in Kindergarten-age Boys," *Genetic Psychology Monographs* 76 (1968): 89–138.

Biller, H. B. *Paternal Deprivation.* Lexington, Mass.: Lexington Books, D. C. Heath, 1974.

Biller, H. B., and Borstelmann, L. J. "Masculine Development: An Integrative Review," *Merrill-Palmer Quarterly* 13 (1967): 253–294.

Block, J. H. "Conceptions of Sex Role: Some Cross-Cultural and Longitudinal Perspectives," *American Psychologist* 28 (1973): 512–526.

Green, R. *Sexual Identity Conflict in Children and Adults.* New York: Basic Books, 1974.

Maccoby, E. E., *The Development of Sex Differences.* Stanford: Stanford University Press, 1966.

Mead, M. *Male and Female.* New York: Morrow, 1953.

Money, J., and Ehrhardt, A. *Man and Woman: Boy and Girl.* Baltimore: Johns Hopkins Press, 1972.

Sutton-Smith, B., and Rosenberg, B. G., *The Sibling.* New York: Holt, Rinehart and Winston, 1970.

Chapter 6: Father, Self-Confidence, and Achievement

Baumrind, D., and Black, A. E. "Socialization Practices Associated With Dimensions of Competence in Preschool Boys and Girls," *Child Development* 38 (1967): 291–327.

Biller, H. B. "Paternal and Sex Role Factors in Cognitive and Academic Functioning." In *Nebraska Symposium on Motivation 1973*, edited by J. K. Cole and R. Dienstbier, pp. 83–123. Lincoln: University of Nebraska Press, 1974.

Biller, H. B., and Bahm, R. M. "Father Absence, Perceived Maternal Behavior and Masculinity of Self Concept Among Junior High School Boys," *Developmental Psychology* 4 (1971): 178–181.

Block, J.; von der Lippe, A.; and Block, J. H. "Sex Role and Socialization Patterns: Some Personality and Environmental Antecedents," *Journal of Consulting and Clinical Psychology* 41 (1973): 321–341.

Coopersmith, S. *The Antecedents of Self-Esteem.* San Francisco: W. H. Freeman, 1967.

Hoffman, L. W. "Early Childhood Experiences and Women's Achievement Motives," *Journal of Social Issues* 28 (1972): 129–155.

Horner, M. S. "Femininity and Successful Achievement: A Basic Inconsistency." In *Feminine Personality and Conflict*, edited by J. M. Bardwick; E. Douvan; M. S. Horner; and D. Guttman. Monterey, Calif.: Brooks/Cole, 1972.

Rosen, B. C., and D'Andrade, R. "The Psychosocial Origins of Achievement Motivation," *Sociometry* 22 (1959): 185–218.

Rosenberg, M. *Society and the Adolescent Self-Image*. Princeton: Princeton University Press, 1965.

Chapter 7: Father, Nurturance, Morals, and Discipline

Fish, K. D., and Biller, H. B. "Perceived Paternal Relationships and College Females' Personal Adjustment," *Adolescence* 8 (1973): 415–420.

Ginott, H. *Between Parent and Child*. New York: Macmillan, 1965.

Gordon, T. *Parent Effectiveness Training*. New York: Peter Wyden, 1970.

Hoffman, M. L. "Father Absence and Conscience Development," *Developmental Psychology* 4 (1971): 400–406.

Kohlberg, L. *Stages in the Development of Moral Thought and Action*. New York: Holt, Rinehart and Winston, 1969.

Mischel, W. "Father Absence and Delay of Gratification," *Journal of Abnormal and Social Psychology* 62 (1961): 116–124.

Mussen, P. H., and Rutherford, E. E. "Parent-Child Relationships and Parental Personality in Relation to Young Children's Sex-Role Preferences," *Child Development* 34 (1963): 589–607.

Reuter, M., and Biller, H. B. "Perceived Paternal Nurturance-Availability and Personality Adjustment Among College Males," *Journal of Consulting and Clinical Psychology* 40 (1973): 339–342.

Rutherford, E. E., and Mussen, P. H. "Generosity in Nursery School Boys," *Child Development* 39 (1968): 755–765.

Sears, R. R.; Rau, L.; and Alpert, R. *Identification and Child Rearing*. Stanford: Stanford University Press, 1965.

Chapter 8: Father and Social and Sexual Relationships

Bieber, I., et al. *Homosexuality: A Psychoanalytic Study*. New York: Basic Books, 1962.

Biller, H. B. "Father Absence and the Personality Development of the Male Child," *Developmental Psychology* 2 (1970): 181–201. Reprinted in *Annual Progress in Child Psychiatry and Child Development*, edited by S. Chess and A. Thomas, pp. 120–152. New York: Brunner-Mazel, 1970. Reprinted in slightly abridged form in *Personality and Socialization*, edited by D. R. Heise, pp. 407–433. New York: Rand McNally, 1972.

Biller, H. B., and Weiss, S. D. "The Father-Daughter Relationship and the Personality of the Female," *Journal of Genetic Psychology* 114 (1970): 79–93. Reprinted in *Issues in Adolescent Psychology*, edited by D. Rogers, pp. 106–116. New York: Appleton-Century-Crofts, 1972.

Fisher, S. F. *The Female Orgasm: Psychology, Physiology, Fantasy*. New York: Basic Books, 1973.

Freedman, M. *Homosexuality and Psychological Functioning*. Belmont, Calif.: Brooks/Cole, 1971.

Hetherington, E. M. "Effects of Father-Absence on Personality Development in Adolescent Daughters," *Developmental Psychology* 7 (1972): 313–326.

Katchadourian, H. A., and Lunde, D. T. *Fundamentals of Human Sexuality*. New York: Holt, Rinehart and Winston, 1972.

Masters, W. H., and Johnson, V. E. *Human Sexual Inadequacy*. Boston: Little, Brown, 1970.

Masters, W. H., and Johnson, V. E. *Human Sexual Response*. Boston: Little, Brown, 1966.

Thompson, N. L.; Schwartz, D. M.; McCandless, B. R.; and Edwards, D. A. "Parent-Child Relationships and Sexual Identity in Male and Female Homosexuals and Heterosexuals," *Journal of Consulting and Clinical Psychology* 41 (1973): 120–127.

Chapter 9: Father, Physical Growth, and Body Pride

Biller, H. B., and Liebman, D. A. "Body Build, Sex-Role Preference and Sex-Role Adoption in Junior High School Boys," *Journal of Genetic Psychology* 118 (1971): 81–86.

Gesell, A.; Ilg, F.; and Ames, L. *Youth*. New York: Harper and Row, 1956.

Jones, M. C. and Mussen, P. H. "Self-conceptions, Motivations, and Interpersonal Attitudes of Early and Late Maturing Girls," *Child Development* 29 (1958): 491–501.

Mussen, P. H., and Jones, M. C. "The Behavior-inferred Motivation of Late and Early Maturing Boys," *Child Development* 28 (1957): 243–256.

Sheldon, W. H. *The Varieties of Temperament*. New York: Harper and Row, 1942.

Smart, M. S., and Smart, R. C. *Children: Development and Relationships*. New York: Macmillan, 1972.

Staffieri, J. R. "A Study of Social Stereotypes of Body Image in Children," *Journal of Personality and Social Psychology* 7 (1967): 101–104.

Thomas, A.; Chess, S.; Birch, H. G.; Hertzig, M. E.; and Korn, S. *Behavioral Individuality in Early Childhood*. New York: New York University Press, 1963.

Walker, R. N. "Body-build and Behavior in Young Children: I. Body-build and Nursery School Teachers' Ratings," *Monograph of the Society for Research in Child Development*, 1962, 27:3, Serial No. 84.

Chapter 10: Father, Intelligence, and Competence

Biller, H. B. "Paternal and Sex-Role Factors in Cognitive and Academic Functioning." In *Nebraska Symposium on Motivation 1973*, edited by J. K. Cole and R. Dienstbier, pp. 83–123. Lincoln: University of Nebraska Press, 1974.

Biller, H. B. "Paternal Deprivation, Cognitive Functioning, and the Feminized Classroom." In *Child Personality and Psychopathology: Current Topics*, edited by A. Davids, pp. 11–52. New York: Wiley, 1974.

Biller, H. B.; Singer, D. L.; and Fullerton, M. "Sex-Role Development and Creative Potential in Kindergarten-age Boys," *Developmental Psychology* 1 (1969): 291–296.

Flavell, J. H. *The Developmental Psychology of Jean Piaget.* Princeton: Van Nostrand, 1963.

Guilford, T. P. *The Nature of Human Intelligence.* New York: McGraw-Hill, 1967.

Helson, R. "Personality Characteristics and Developmental History of Creative College Women," *Genetic Psychology Monographs* 76 (1967): 205–256.

Phillips, T. L. *The Origins of Intellect: Piaget's Theory.* San Francisco: Freeman, 1969.

Radin, N. "Father-Child Interaction and the Intellectual Functioning of Four-year-old Boys," *Developmental Psychology* 6 (1972): 353–361.

Santrock, J. W. "Relation of Type and Onset of Father-absence to Cognitive Development," *Child Development* 43 (1972): 455–469.

Wallach, M. A., and Kogan, N. *Modes of Thinking in Young Children.* New York: Holt, Rinehart and Winston, 1965.

Chapter 11: Father, School, and Education

Biller, H. B. "Paternal Deprivation, Cognitive Functioning, and the Feminized Classroom." In *Child Personality and Psychopathology: Current Topics*, edited by A. Davids, pp. 11–52. New York: Wiley, 1974.

Blanchard, R. W., and Biller, H. B. "Father Availability and Academic Performance Among Third Grade Boys," *Developmental Psychology* 4 (1971): 301–305.

Bronfenbrenner, U. "The Psychological Costs of Quality and Equality in Education," *Child Development* 38 (1967): 909–925.

Fagot, B. I., and Patterson, G. R. "An In Vivo Analysis of Reinforcing Contingencies for Sex-Role Behaviors in the Pre-school Child," *Developmental Psychology* 1 (1969): 563–568.

Lee, P. C. "Male and Female Teachers in Elementary Schools: An Ecological Analysis," *Teachers College Record* 75 (1973): 79–98.

Lee, P. C., and Wolinsky, A. L. "Male Teachers of Young Children: A Preliminary Study," *Young Children* 28 (1973): 342–352.

Ostrovsky, E. S. *Children Without Men.* New York: Collier, 1962.

Preston, R. "Reading Achievement of German and American Children," *School and Society* 90 (1962): 350–354.

Sexton, P. C. *The Feminized Male.* New York: Random House, 1969.

Stein, A. H. "The Effects of Sex-Role Standards for Achievement and Sex-Role Preference on Three Determinants of Achievement Motivation," *Developmental Psychology* 4 (1971): 219–231.

Chapter 12: Father, Work, and the Child's Career Choice

Bardwick, J. M. *Psychology of Women: A Study of Biocultural Conflicts.* New York: Harper and Row, 1971.

Benson, L. *Fatherhood: A Sociological Perspective.* New York: Random House, 1968.

Biller, H. B. *Paternal Deprivation.* Lexington, Mass.: Lexington Books, D. C. Heath, 1974.

Brenton, M. *The American Male.* New York: Fawcett, 1970.

Crites, J. O. "Parental Identification in Relation to Vocational Interest Development," *Journal of Educational Psychology* 53 (1962): 262–270.

Douvan, E., and Adelson, T. *The Adolescent Experience.* New York: Wiley, 1966.

Erikson, E. H. *Identity: Youth and Crisis.* New York: Norton and Norton, 1968.

McCandless, B. R. *Adolescents: Behavior and Development.* Hindsdale, Ill.: Dryden, 1970.

Zytowski, D. G., ed. *Vocational Behavior.* New York: Holt, Rinehart and Winston, 1968.

Chapter 13: Divorced Fathers, Stepfathers, and Single Fathers

Bernard, J. *Remarriage: A Study of Marriage.* New York: Dryden Press, 1956.

Despert, J. L. *Children of Divorce.* Garden City, New York: Doubleday, 1953.

Egelson, J., and Frank, J. F. *Parents Without Partners.* New York: E. P. Dutton, 1961.

Gardner, R. *The Boys and Girls Book of Divorce.* New York: Science House, 1970.

Kirk, H. D. *Shared Fate.* New York: Free Press, 1964.

Klein, C. *The Single Parent Experience.* New York: Avon, 1973.

Raymond, L. *Adoption and After.* New York: Harper and Row, 1955.

Steinzor, B. *When Parents Divorce.* New York: Simon and Schuster, 1970.

Thompson, H. *The Successful Stepparent.* New York: Funk and Wagnalls, 1968.

Chapter 14: Fathers with Special Problems

Biller, H. B. "A Note on Father Absence and Masculine Development in Young, Lower-class Negro and White Boys," *Child Development* 39 (1968): 1003–1006.

Grier, W. H., and Cobbs, P. M. *Black Rage.* New York: Bantam, 1969.

Neugarten, B., ed. *Middle Age and Aging.* Chicago: The University of Chicago Press, 1968.

Parker, J. D. "Fathers of Children Conceived Out of Wedlock: Prepregnancy, High School, Psychological Test Results," *Developmental Psychology* 4 (1971): 215–218.

Pettigrew, T. F. *A Profile of The Negro American.* Princeton: Van Nostrand, 1964.

Rappoport, L. *Personality Development: The Chronology of Experience.* Glenview, Ill.: Scott, Foresman, 1972.

Sauber, M. "The Role of the Unmarried Father," *Welfare in Review* 4 (1966): 15–18.

Telford, C. W., and Sawrey, J. M. *The Exceptional Individual.* Englewood Cliffs, N.J.: Prentice-Hall, 1972.

Tuck, S. "Working with Black Fathers," *American Journal of Orthopsychiatry* 41 (1971): 465–472.

Chapter 15: Fathers with Problem Children

Biller, H. B., and Borstelmann, L. J. "Intellectual Level and Sex-Role Development in Mentally Retarded Children," *American Journal of Mental Deficiency* 70 (1965): 443–447.

Biller, H. B., and Davids, A. "Parent-Child Relations, Personality Development, and Psychopathology." In *Issues in Abnormal Child Psychology*, edited by A. Davids, pp. 48–77. Monterey, Calif.: Brooks/Cole, 1973.

Brutten, M.; Richardson, S. O.; and Mangal, C. *Something's Wrong with My Child.* New York: Harcourt, Brace, Jovanovich, 1973.

Cressey, D. R., and Ward, D. A. *Delinquency, Crime and Social Process.* New York: Harper and Row, 1969.

Davids, A., ed. *Issues in Abnormal Child Psychology.* Belmont, Calif.: Brooks/Cole, 1973.

Haley, J., and Hoffman, L. *Techniques of Family Therapy.* New York: Basic Books, 1967.

Kayton, R., and Biller, H. B. "Perception of Parental Sex-Role Behavior and Psychopathology in Adult Males," *Journal of Consulting and Clinical Psychology* 36 (1971): 235–237.

Kessler, J. W. *Psychopathology in Childhood.* Englewood Cliffs, N.J.: Prentice-Hall, 1966.

Koch, R., and Dobson, J. C. *The Mentally Retarded Child and His Family: A Multidisciplinary Handbook.* New York: Brunner-Mazel, 1971.

Spock. B. M., and Lerrigo, M. O. *Caring for Your Disabled Child.* New York: Macmillan, 1965.

Thomas, A.; Chess, S.; and Birch, H. G. *Temperament and Behavior Disorders in Early Childhood.* New York: New York University Press, 1968.

Chapter 16: Social Crisis and Social Fatherhood

Biller, H. B., and Meredith, D. L. "The Invisible American Father," *Sexual Behavior* 2 (1972):16–22.

Brenton, M. *The American Male.* New York: Fawcett, 1970.

Bronfenbrenner, U. *Two Worlds of Childhood: U.S. and U.S.S.R.* New York: Clarion, 1972.

LeMasters, E. E. *Parents in Modern America: A Sociological Analysis.* Homewood, Ill.: Dorsey, 1970.

Mitscherlich, A. *Society Without the Father.* New York: Harcourt, Brace, 1969.

Packard, V. *A Nation of Strangers.* New York: David McKay, 1973.

Toffler, A. *Future Shock.* New York: Bantam, 1971.

Winch, R. F. *The Modern Family.* New York: Holt, Rinehart and Winston, 1971.

Index